D0792422

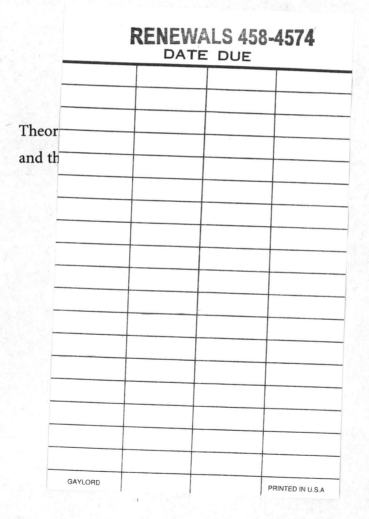

RENEWALS 458-4574
DATE DUE

GAYLORD   PRINTED IN U.S.A

Theor

and th

Theories of Dependent Foreign Policy and the Case of Ecuador in the 1980s

Jeanne A. K. Hey

OHIO UNIVERSITY CENTER FOR INTERNATIONAL STUDIES

MONOGRAPHS IN INTERNATIONAL STUDIES

LATIN AMERICAN SERIES NUMBER 23

ATHENS · 1995

Printed in the United States of America
All rights reserved
02 01 00 99 98 97 96 95   5 4 3 2 1

The books in the Center for International Studies Monograph Series
are printed on acid-free paper ∞

Library of Congress Cataloging-in-Publication Data
Hey, Jeanne A. K.
    Theories of dependent foreign policy and the case of Ecuador in
the 1980s / Jeanne A. K. Hey.
        p.   cm. — (Monographs in international studies. Latin
America series ; no. 23)
    Includes bibliographical references and index.
    ISBN 0-89680-184-5 (paper : alk. paper)
    1. Dependency. 2. Ecuador—Foreign economic relations.
I. Title. II. Series.
JX4011.H49 1995
327.866'009'048—dc20   95-13929
                                               CIP

For Thomas Christopher Hey Klak

Contents

List of Tables

Acknowledgements

Many individuals and institutions have supported me personally and professionally throughout this project. Travel funds for my first field research trip were made available through a grant from the Tinker Foundation. My second trip was largely financed by a Graduate Student Alumni Research Award from The Ohio State University. My field research in Ecuador was greatly facilitated by those who agreed to be interviewed and who helped me contact interviewees and access data. I thank Amparo Menéndez Carrión for providing me with research facilities at the Facultad Latino-americana de Ciencias Sociales (FLACSO) and Raúl Carrera for his entertaining companionship and engaging theoretical insights.

Margaret Hermann and Charles Hermann, working together and individually, provided me with invaluable assistance on this research. David Pion-Berlin was also an important contributor. Harold Molineu and Thomas Walker aided in guiding my revisions for final publication. This project would not have been completed, nor would I be where I am today, without the guidance and friendship of these and other scholars.

A circle of friends and colleagues at Miami University has been immeasurably influential in supporting me and my work. Of particular mention are Sheila Croucher, Patrick Haney, William Mandel, Michael Pagano and Douglas Shumavon. These are especially wise, gracious, and all-around wonderful people without whom my scholarship and emotional well-being would suffer greatly.

Rachel Anderson, Nicholas Paine, and Tiffany Petros were extremely helpful and genial assistants. They aided in preparing the final revisions and facilitated in completing what is usually the worst part of a large research project.

I thank all the members of my family (too numerous to mention!) for their constant love and support. I am especially grateful to my parents, Jeanne Cooper Hey and E. Berry Hey, Jr., for instilling in me the value of education and supporting me in the decisions I have made. As time passes, I am increasingly aware of how rare and valuable these parental qualities are.

My greatest thanks go to Thomas Klak for his constant intellectual and personal support. His contributions to this project and to my professional development are impossible to detail here, but are much appreciated and valued. He has been my companion during all stages of this project, including field research, brain storming sessions, writing and editing. This book is dedicated to him with love and thanks.

Theories of Dependent Foreign Policy
and the Case of Ecuador in the 1980s

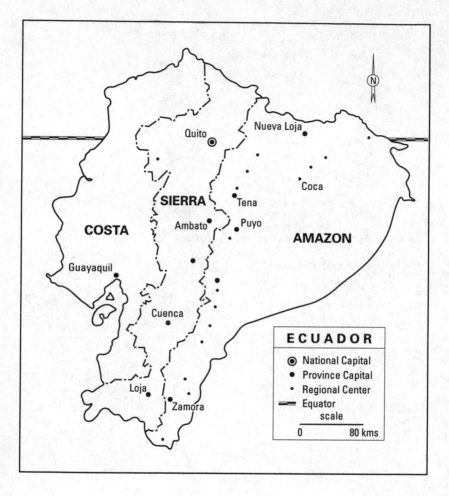

Figure 1. Informational Map of Ecuador

Introduction

Dependent Foreign Policy Theory

I. INTRODUCTION

WHAT IS the relationship between economic dependence and foreign policy? Recent research on this question has failed to identify reliable patterns of dependent foreign policy behavior. Most scholars agree that economic dependence influences foreign policy in some manner, but disagree on the nature and extent of that influence. The theoretical and empirical work treating dependent foreign policy has generated an ambiguous and often contradictory picture of how economically dependent states operate in the international arena. Numerous theories applied to a variety of countries deliver very different explanations of the process through which dependent leaders create foreign policy. In this monograph I attempt to simplify this theoretical complexity and to identify the most important forces at work in the dependent foreign policy making process.

A principal purpose of this monograph is to evaluate a series of leading dependent foreign policy theories. The research problem is the following: numerous competing theoretical approaches claim to explain dependent foreign policy. Research to date has failed to identify which approach or approaches prevail. The problem is compounded by the fact that many theories differ from each other substantially and anticipate contradictory results. For example, some theorists expect dependent states to generate foreign policies in alignment with core preferences, while others expect anti-core foreign policy behavior. Some theoretical approaches claim that domestic sources of foreign policy are relatively unimportant while others view internal factors as essential. This study seeks to identify the most potent theoretical approach (or combination of approaches) and to identify the conditions under which different explanatory factors will prevail.

II. COMPARATIVE CASE STUDY METHODOLOGY

The bulk of this work consists of a treatment of a series of examples, or case studies, of Ecuadoran foreign policy. This methodological choice was born from a frustration with the inability of quantitative approaches to produce valid claims about dependent foreign policy process as well as outcomes. The advantage of a case study approach is that it allows for, and indeed requires, an in-depth examination of the competing forces which generate foreign policy. The method also reveals a variety of complex patterns in Ecuador's foreign policy that heretofore have not been uncovered in most dependent foreign policy studies; these are outlined in the concluding chapter. The remainder of this chapter examines this methodological choice and introduces the six dependent foreign policy theories analyzed in this book.

A. Problems with quantitative approaches in dependent foreign policy

Most studies that attempt to generalize findings on dependent foreign policy apply statistical analyses to United Nations General Assembly (UNGA) voting data. The reliance on UNGA votes is quite understandable. The data set contains a large number of cases readily observable both longitudinally and across different countries and regions. The disadvantage of this method is, of course, that the analyst knows nothing of the foreign policy process or of the people behind the decisions. Most scholars have been willing to accept this deficiency in order to perform analyses with a large sample size and to achieve what are deemed generalizable results. They have been particularly willing to forgo information on the foreign policy process and policy-makers because they hypothesized that structural variables mattered more than subsystem factors in determining dependent foreign policy outcomes.

I disagree with using the UN voting approach as the sole or even primary manner to study dependent foreign policy. Three reasons substantiate my view. First, as is detailed below, studies that rely on UN voting have delivered very mediocre results. The vast majority have hypothesized that economic dependence leads to foreign policy alignment with the core. Numerous inquiries have failed to demonstrate a strong correlation between these two variables. Despite this deficiency, scholars continue to generate many UN voting-based studies (see, e.g., Kegley and Hook 1991). The staying power of this approach may be a function of the ease with which UN voting studies are completed. Paraphrasing Robert A. Dahl (1971:206), Arend Lijphart described a similar process in a branch of comparative politics: "One reason why so much attention has been given to the relationship between regime and socioeconomic level, in spite of the fact that this relationship is far from a perfect one, is simply that reasonably acceptable (if by no means satisfactory) 'hard' data are available from which to construct indicators" (Lijphart 1975:173). The inability of UN voting studies to produce reliable results suggests that the method is inadequate. The structural relationship between core and periphery is an insufficient basis on which to predict dependent foreign policy behavior. This begs researchers to go beyond correlations and to look inside the policy process and the dependent countries' political systems. A case study approach is at the very least an alternative method that should be explored for its explanatory power.

A second and related flaw of UN voting studies relates to validity. Quantitative analyses of dependent foreign policy make enormous assumptions about policy-makers' motivations and behavior. Even those UN voting-based studies that do identify a relationship between dependence and foreign policy behavior (e.g., Keohane 1966; Wittkopf 1973; Richardson 1978; Richardson and Kegley 1980) show only correlations. The causal mechanisms behind the correlations are largely derived without empirical examples. The demonstrated relationships may be spurious and have proven unreliable. Case studies should therefore be employed to check whether the foreign policy process described in quantitative studies but not tested by them is present (Russet 1970:428).

A third problem is that UN voting does not necessarily, or even probably, reflect a country's overall foreign policy. Most foreign policy actions occur outside of the United Nations. Recent foreign policy initiatives that would not have been captured by UN voting studies include the Arias Peace Plan, Argentina's decision to invade the Falklands (Malvinas), and the decisions by Israel, the Palestinians, and many Arab states to attend peace talks. Tomlin (1985) demonstrates that a state's foreign policy behavior within the UN may not even reflect the content of its behavior outside of the UN. A concern with foreign policy behavior in general demands an approach that examines initiatives and decisions occurring outside of the UN forum.

B. Case studies

These flaws and shortcomings of the quantitative methodology have led me to a case study approach. Specifically, I examine a series of like examples of dependent foreign policy. This approach does not specifically address differences between dependent and non-dependent cases. Rather, dependence is used as the contextual basis upon which cases are drawn. Dependence is treated not as a variable, but rather as a *situation* within which other phenomena, such as the foreign policy relationship between Ecuador and the US, assumes particular relevance (Duvall 1978:54). The situation, or context, of dependence determines the types of questions asked of each case and excludes certain types of variables at the outset (Ragin 1987:47).

Numerous methodologists and foreign policy scholars have advocated variations on this "similar case" approach. A recent "state of the discipline" article encourages empirical case study analysis to increase understanding of foreign policy behavior (Gerner 1992:9). George (1982:25) suggests that a focus on similar cases representing a unique, defined set of phenomena reduces the number of critical variables observed and helps to isolate their effects. Ragin (1987:47) observes that a well constructed comparative case study uses theory to identify the conceptually important defining parameters from which the cases are to be drawn. The case study analysis then tests hypotheses and draws conclusions which are relevant within those parameters. Eckstein (1975:113) discusses "crucial case studies" useful for theory testing. Crucial cases represent the phenomenon to be explained so closely that the theory being tested should definitely apply (Eckstein 1975:118). In other words, a theory's failure to explain crucial cases may be grounds for its dismissal. Lijphart (1975:159) also advocates a case study approach and specifically suggests augmenting single country studies with numerous intra-state observations. Examination of many cases with a single country facilitates conclusions because external variables are more easily controlled (Lijphart 1975:166-67).

Following from these suggestions I examine in detail twelve examples of Ecuador's foreign policy during the Osvaldo Hurtado (1981-84) and León Febres Cordero (1984-88) administrations. Ecuador during this period is a crucial case in that it was heavily dependent on the United States. Chapter 2 details the extent and nature of that dependence. Furthermore, the Reagan administration supervised US foreign policy throughout the entire period under study. This provides a general control for US interests and behavior. The Ecuadoran example also provides significant variation on a number of critical domestic variables such as leaders' preferences and opposition influence. This variation is necessary to test the theories presented in the next section.

Once I had deemed Ecuador in the 1980s an appropriate setting for a study of dependent foreign policy, specific policies needed to be isolated for study. I selected cases according to three criteria: First, cases should directly tap Ecuador's dependent relationship with the United States. Each case represents an issue relevant to both Ecuadorans and US policy-makers. This criterion leads to cases most likely to uncover a relationship between dependence and foreign policy if one indeed exists. In other words, this criterion assures crucial cases. Second, cases should represent similar issues under different administrations. For example, foreign policies dealing with foreign investment, revolutionary Nicaragua, and regional multilateralism are examined for *each* administration. This facilitates comparison across administrations. Third, cases should represent diplomatic as well as economic issue areas for each president. This final criterion was chosen in response to the many foreign policy analysts who claim that issue area is an important variable for distinguishing types of foreign policy behavior (see, e.g., Richardson 1976, 1978; Potter 1980; Richardson and Kegley 1980; Armstrong 1981; Ferris 1981, 1984b).

These guidelines provided me with a generous set of cases. From them I chose six for which I had collected the most useful data. These six general foreign policies (listed in table 1) contain a variety of sub-policies, or decisions points, which benefit from individual observation. For this reason, the concluding chapter is based on twelve different foreign policy acts rather than six. Together they illustrate a broad range of dependent foreign policy behaviors and will act as a solid base for comparative conclusions both about the different administrations' foreign policies and the foreign policy theories.

Table 1: Case Studies of Ecuador's Foreign Policy Examined

Osvaldo Hurtado	1. Ecuador's policy towards revolutionary Nicaragua.
	2. Ecuador's legislative reforms governing foreign investment in the petroleum industry.
	3. The Conferencia Económica Latinoamericana (CEL), a regional conference designed to alleviate Latin America's foreign debt.
León Febres Cordero	4. Ecuador's joining the Contadora Support Group and breaking relations with revolutionary Nicaragua.
	5. Operation Blazing Trails, a US military operation in Ecuador aiding in road construction.
	6. The Overseas Private Investment Corporation (OPIC) agreement Ecuador signed with the United States.

A final methodological point concerns the manner in which each case study is carried out. Alexander George (1982:27) suggests that "structured focused comparisons" contribute to theory building if the researcher asks a series of questions of a number of comparable cases. These questions aim to extract the theoretically important elements of each case. The questions are standardized to ensure that each case is treated equally and to facilitate comparison. Following George, I ask of each case whether particular criteria, or *defining conditions*, needed to confirm each theory are present. These defining conditions determine whether a case is a fair test of a theory. For example, as is discussed below, a defining condition of the domestic politics approach is that some domestic political group hold a position on the issue at hand. If no domestic political group cares about the foreign policy issue, then the case does not meet the defining condition and should not be treated as a proper test case for that theory. Once the defining conditions are met, I ask whether the policy outcome conformed with the theory's expectations. Returning to the same example, the theory of domestic politics will only explain a case if indeed the domestic political group's policy choices were implemented. Each case study chapter thus evolves as an investigation of the applicability of the different theories. Each case is then categorized according to the theory or theories that apply to it. The comparison of the cases presented in the concluding chapter, then, allows for theoretical conclusions to be drawn.

III. THEORIES AND DEFINING CONDITIONS

This section reviews six dominant theories of dependent foreign policy: compliance, consensus, counterdependence, realism, leader preferences, and domestic politics. The first three have been developed specifically to explain foreign policy of *dependent* states. The remainder are more general theories of foreign policy that also claim explanatory power for dependent countries.

A. Compliance

i. Theoretical grounding

Moon claims that "the conventional wisdom of international relations holds that the foreign policy behavior of weak states is largely determined by external forces" and that this view is "now thought so unexceptional that it no longer requires defense" (1985:297). Moon's statement reflects the notions born in political realism that characterize the compliance model of dependent foreign policy studies. This view argues that Third World states, lacking the economic and military resources that constitute power in the global system, *comply* with hegemonic powers' wishes because to do otherwise would invite economic or military sanctions. Third World foreign policies, then, reflect more the interests of other global powers than of their own national governments. As Richardson explains, "compliance is a sacrifice, wherein actors abandon their preferences as they conform to another's dissimilar foreign policy wishes" (1981:102). According to compliance, economic dependence affords the United States formidable power to determine the foreign policy of its Latin American dependencies such as Ecuador. Not only can the US force Ecuador to adopt policies the former prefers, it is also assumed that those policies oppose Ecuadoran preferences and national interests. In order to understand Ecuador's foreign policy, then, an examination of its dependent relationship with the US as well as an understanding of US policy preferences is needed.

A compliant foreign policy may respond to overt coercion by the core, or merely to implicit threats. The existence of an asymmetrical trade relationship may suffice to compel weaker states to produce pro-core foreign policies in hopes of attracting economic rewards and avoiding economic punishments (Armstrong 1981: 408). While the compliant view of dependent foreign policy behavior is strongly associated with the power politics characteristic of realist theory, it also relates to branches of dependency theory that see Latin Americans trapped in a global economy in which they are forced to adopt policies against their wills and national interests (Pion-Berlin 1986:330). Both realist and dependency theories rely on international variables to explain policy outcomes. Accordingly, compliance relies on the distribution of hemispheric power to account for Latin American foreign policy behavior.

Although criticism against it has recently intensified, compliance remains the prevailing explanation of dependent foreign policy behavior. Many empirical studies have tested its thesis—that dependent states develop foreign policies favorable to the core— and have recorded variable results. The vast majority have relied on UN voting data to demonstrate foreign policy agreement between periphery and core. Keohane recorded a high degree of UN voting agreement between Latin America and the US in the early 1960s, explaining that agreement as a function of the United States' unique ability as a superpower to use threats and promises to achieve foreign policy submission from its dependencies (Keohane 1966:18). Wittkopf (1973) produced similar results in a later study. In an ambitious examination of the foreign policies of US dependencies between 1950 and 1972, Richardson (1978) showed that dependencies voted with the US more often than non-dependencies, particularly on Cold War issues. Richardson argued that compliance was higher for Cold War votes because the US valued them highly and was therefore more likely to punish or reward dependencies' voting behavior on Cold War issues. Like Keohane and Wittkopf, Richardson found that Latin America's foreign policy agreement with the US was higher than that of US dependencies from other regions.

In the 1980s, tests of compliance began to yield troublesome results. As one review of this body of theory stated, "it appears the death knell is being sounded" for the bargaining model that expects compliance to result from asymmetrical economic relationships (DeRouen and Mintz 1991:44-45). Richardson and Kegley (1980) found that the ability of the United States to exact compliant behavior was in decline. Other studies that correlated economic dependence with foreign policy compliance by Rai (1980), Armstrong (1981), Ray (1981), and Menkhaus and Kegley (1988) all demonstrated very weak relationships. A critical test of compliance by Kegley and Hook (1991) examined the success of the Reagan administration's explicit policy linking US aid disbursements to foreign policy compliance as expressed by United Nations votes. Even when the US explicitly threatened to cut off aid, US dependencies failed to comply. Kegley and Hook explained the failed policy partly as a function of the Reagan administration's inability to implement the policy consistently. A perhaps more important explanation of the weaker states' failure to vote with the US is the fact that pro-US votes in the UN often did not conform with their national interests (Kegley and Hook 1991).

Despite the weakness of dependence-compliance findings, compliance remains a powerful approach to explaining dependent foreign policy behavior. The notion that weak states consider their economic vulnerability when implementing foreign policy is intuitively quite compelling. Certainly, many instances of compliance have been documented, both in studies relying on UN voting data as well as in individual case studies.[1] Also, the readily available data with which compliance studies are performed (UN voting data and state-level economic indicators), as well as the relative ease of their statistical manipulation, no doubt contributes to compliance studies' staying power.

Compliance theory's difficulty lies in its attempt to be a grand theory accounting for the majority of dependent foreign policy behavior. It is more likely that compliance emerges under particular conditions of dependence, around specific issue areas and by certain types of leaders or regimes. These questions are examined in the ensuing case studies. Case study examinations of compliance are particularly needed given that the vast majority of compliance tests have relied on UN votes. Compliance was confirmed if a dependent state voted in the same way as the US in the UN General Assembly. As is discussed above, this is a weak measure at best. The next section outlines a much more taxing set of criteria needed to identify compliance in an in-depth case study.

ii. Defining conditions

Principal among the defining elements of a compliant foreign policy is a *conflict of interests between the US (or any other Northern*

---

1. Menkhaus and Kegley (1988), for example, demonstrate that Somalia complies with its most important trading partner, Saudi Arabia. Also see Ferris (1984b), in which Mexico's compliant behavior in the economic realm is described.

actor such as the IMF, World Bank, or multinational corporation) and
Ecuador. The compliance model holds that the US is able to force a
dependent country to do what it otherwise would not (Moon 1983:
319-20). The majority of compliance-based studies (e.g., Keohane
1966; Wittkopf 1973; Richardson and Kegley 1980; Armstrong 1981)
are not concerned with the preferences of the foreign policy makers in the periphery. They nonetheless *assume* that dependent
states' interests run contrary to those of the core. In other words,
there is no need to consider the preferences of Ecuador's leaders
because it is known that they diverge from those of leaders in the
US. Ensuing case studies will reveal the danger in that assumption.
In many cases, Ecuadoran policy-makers' preferences conformed
with those of their US counterparts. Policy disagreement between
core and periphery should not be assumed, but documented.
Therefore, a clear outline of the policy preferences of actors within
Ecuador and the US is needed to indicate the degree to which interests conflict. Such information can be obtained from a variety of
sources: interviews, speeches, and the writings of leaders and other
policy formulators and analysts.

A second defining factor of a compliant foreign policy is *the
issue's salience to Ecuadoran leaders*. Richardson (1981:102) reminds
us that if the subject is unimportant to the weaker state, foreign
policy entails no sacrifice and thus is not an example of compliance. Measuring importance is difficult as it requires a judgment of
a government's priorities. The importance of an issue is indicated
by the frequency with which it emerges in the speeches and writings of Ecuadoran government officials. An issue that is repeatedly
addressed by a variety of government officials in key public fora
will be considered important. A second indicator of salience is the
degree of commitment an administration shows to the matter at
hand. Policy-makers will devote a significant amount of time and
energy to implementing a policy they consider salient.

Once a conflict of interest and salience are established, a policy
meets the defining conditions for compliance. In order for compliance to explain, it must then be determined that the policy conformed more with US policy preferences than with Ecuador's. This
will entail a judgment of the match between the policy and the
expressed interests of Ecuador and the US. Evidence of direct

pressure from the US in the policy formulation process would also help to confirm a compliant foreign policy. Such pressure could come in many forms: personal contacts, public pronouncements of US policy preferences, and threats to withhold economic benefits. However, evidence of such direct pressure is not a requisite for defining a compliant policy. The implicit threat of economic punishment may cause Ecuador to comply with US wishes. The US need not exercise its influence in any direct way (Armstrong 1981:408).

B. Consensus

i. Theoretical grounding

While dependency theorists are rarely concerned with foreign policy directly, an application of dependency theory to this area finds dependent foreign policy outcomes similar to those expected by political realists. Common versions of dependency theory hold that cooperation among periphery and core elites maintains an international economic system that benefits the core states at the expense of peripheral development (see, e.g., Caporaso 1978; Duvall 1978; Cardoso and Faletto 1979; Valenzuela and Valenzuela 1981:27; and Frank 1986). According to this view, Latin America's *comprador* class consists of an economic elite whose financial interests are inextricably tied to its country's relationship with foreign capital. This group lobbies for a pro-core foreign policy and the intensification of dependent ties in order to further its parochial interests (Richardson 1978:73; Ferguson 1987:155). Because this class usually dominates politics, dependency theorists generally expect that Latin American foreign policies will reflect the interests of the United States and the multinational corporations based there.

This interpretation holds that Latin American elites will develop a pro-core policy for two principal reasons. First, many are raised in an environment in which ties with the US economy are lauded. In many cases, Latin American elites are educated in the US and maintain business ties with their counterparts in the US and other parts of the industrialized West. Therefore, these Latin American elites will hold ideological views similar to economic leaders in the US and develop foreign policy accordingly. Second, many Latin American political leaders themselves maintain business ventures with Northern investors, or represent local businesspeople with these ties. A pro-US policy will maintain and improve the US-Latin American business environment and serve the specific financial interests of Latin American elites (Moon 1987:44; Biddle and Stephens 1989:414).

Bruce Moon (1983, 1985) applies a dependency framework to the study of foreign policy compliance. Moon finds that the compliance model inadequately captures the basis of policy alignment between the US and its dependencies. His studies of UN voting agreement between the US and its dependencies finds a consistency of foreign policy alignment over time for which bargaining processes cannot account. Moon argues that *consensus* among leaders in periphery and core leads to foreign policy alignment. A consensual relationship develops over time and is ingrained in the political and development philosophies among policy and corporate elites in both periphery and core. This is quite different from compliance, which explains any particular compliant behavior as a form of payment for a specific economically dependent relationship in an isolated period of time. Whereas Richardson and Kegley (1980) describe the foreign policy agreement process as antagonistic, Moon describes it as collaborative and mutually beneficial, at least for elites.

i. Defining conditions

The cooperation that would confirm consensus in a case of Ecuadoran foreign policy may be difficult to identify. The dependency notion relies on a long-term relationship in which obvious isolated acts of influence peddling may be missing. It also includes a history of economic relations between elites in both the US and Ecuador (Moon 1983:320). Finally, dependency theory claims that economic and political leaders in Ecuador will have "interests, values, and perceptions" more in common with elites in the US than with the majority of Ecuadoran people (Moon 1983:321). None of these indicators can be used as clear evidence for a foreign policy derived through consensus. A history of elite cooperation between

Ecuador and the US will be a constant in all of the foreign policy cases observed in this study. It can be argued that both President Hurtado and President Febres Cordero, although to different degrees, have more in common with elites in the US than with the masses in Ecuador. Therefore it is necessary to demonstrate that the cooperative and consensual elements are the determining and operative factors in a particular foreign policy case, rather than simply part of the context and background in which all Ecuadoran politics operate.

The defining condition for consensus is that *a clear coincidence of opinion between policy-makers in the US and in Ecuador* exists on the matter at hand. This will be discerned through methods similar to those described above—a review of policy-makers' speeches, writings, policy statements, and interviews. These sources must reflect a high degree of concordance on the general ideological approach to an issue as well as agreement on specific policy options preferred. If the policy involves negotiations between the US and Ecuador, these negotiations should occur in an environment which is more relaxed than tense, in which both sides are more accommodating than competitive. It is impossible to expect that there will be no conflicts of interest or points of contention in negotiations between two states. However, participants will consider these areas of conflict less significant than the general agreement, and will be willing to sacrifice a victory on such a point rather than see the negotiations collapse and the policy abandoned.

A second element, that the policy be *designed to provide some benefit to the economic and/or political elites in Ecuador*, would help to confirm consensus but is not necessary. Its emergence would indicate that a policy conforms strictly to dependency theory. However, a purely diplomatic policy, for example, may be born in ideological consensus, though it might not generate any tangible economic benefits for elites. A policy that does serve elite economic interests could also serve other sectors of Ecuadoran society. Indeed, it is likely that an economic policy, even if in reality serving elite interests, will be advertised as serving the national economic interest. Nor must the policy necessarily deliver those benefits to the elites. Many policies malfunction during implementation or simply fail to work as their designers intended. Also necessary is advocacy for the policy by the economic and/or political elites in Ecuador. Particular attention should be paid to policy statements and activities by Ecuador's Chambers of Production, the leaders of the capitalist class.

Core-periphery agreement and elite benefits set up the conditions for a consensus-based policy. In order for consensus to explain, the policy enacted must conform with core preferences.

C. Counterdependence

i. Theoretical grounding

Increasingly, foreign policy analysts focusing on Third World countries disagree with the most basic of political realists' and dependency theorists' generalizations. In many cases, economically dependent states not only fail to follow the core's lead, but in fact pursue foreign policies directly aimed at antagonizing or countering the interests of the hegemon (Ray 1981; Menkhaus and Kegley 1988; Biddle and Stephens 1989).

Counterdependence is one explanation of a dependent state's anti-core foreign policy. This theory explains that electorates and policy-makers in the Third World, frustrated by the economically negative and politically demeaning effects of a dependent relationship, advocate an anti-core foreign policy to counter the consequences of economic dependence (Richardson 1978:68). In perhaps the best elaboration of counterdependence, Biddle and Stephens (1989) explain that Jamaican Prime Minister Michael Manley's anti-US foreign policy in the 1970s was "a direct product of the negative and contradictory aspects of dependent development itself" (Biddle and Stephens 1989:412). Because of an economically dependent relationship, the US had been able to force Jamaica to adopt a development plan that brought uneven economic growth, increased poverty for the poorest Jamaicans, increased levels of unemployment, and resulted in an inequitable distribution of wealth. Frustrated with such conditions, popular sectors in 1972 elected Manley, a democratic socialist who implemented a foreign policy antagonistic to the Western powers and in favor of Third

World solidarity (Biddle and Stephens 1989:414-23). Dependence caused resentment among Jamaican voters and leaders, which generated a foreign policy designed to counteract that dependence.

A critical component of counterdependence, therefore, is affect. Hermann, Hermann, and Hutchins describe affect as "the actor's current sentiments as manifested in his/her behavior. In foreign policy affect becomes the discernible current feelings of a government toward another government or other external entity" (1982:208). Under counterdependence, the adverse economic consequences of dependence cause negative affect, which is expressed in foreign policy toward the core. A counterdependent policy may begin with a popular mandate, as in the Jamaican case (Biddle and Stephens 1989:419-21). A popular mandate is not a defining condition, however. Political elites may design a policy to overcome Ecuador's dependence on the US without necessarily responding to popular demands. As the majority of Ecuadoran people are disenfranchised from the political system, lack of popular mandate is more likely in Ecuador than in Jamaica.

ii. Defining conditions

A defining condition of the policy is that it must clearly be designed to *reduce economic or political dependence*. The logic through which the policy would achieve a reduction in dependence must be apparent, with a discernible relationship between Ecuador's dependent circumstances and the content of the policy. Examples include multilateral efforts designed to counteract the regional strength of the US, diversification of economic partners, and diplomatic initiatives aimed at asserting Ecuador's independence. It is probable that the leader will make clear publicly that the policy operates independently of and against the US. The United States and/or other core actors will probably resist the policy. Such resistance most likely will be consistent with the degree of threat posed by the Ecuadoran policy. If the counterdependent policy is a small measure posing little threat, we would not expect strong core opposition.

D. Realism

i. Theoretical grounding

Realists and neorealists view states as similar units that struggle to advance their "national interests" and to preserve and strengthen the state (Morgenthau and Thompson 1985:3-17; Waltz 1986a:110, 116; Dougherty and Pfaltzgraff 1990:81-127). Realism expects Ecuador to implement foreign policies in pursuit of its national interests, most often defined in economic and military terms, but also including prestige (Morgenthau and Thompson 1985:86-100). Even though some realist and neorealist authors have provided clues as to its definition, the term "national interest" is replete with definitional problems (Dougherty and Pfaltzgraff 1990:124-125).

A second fundamental concept is power, which has a dual purpose in realist theory. It is both a means and an end. States use power to pursue their national interests. However, power is also a national interest in itself, a goal to be pursued in international interaction (Morgenthau and Thompson 1985:5, 115-83). Morgenthau and Thompson's classic text, *Politics among Nations*, details many elements of power, such as geography, natural resources, industrial capacity, military capabilities, and quality of leadership (Morgenthau and Thompson 1985:127-79). It is the crucial role of national leaders and policy analysts to evaluate correctly a nation's power relative to its adversaries.

The ideas of national interest and power present particular difficulties when applied to the developing world (Dougherty and Pfaltzgraff 1990:124-25). Morgenthau's treatment of the national interest and national power focus almost exclusively on concepts and examples pertinent to the industrialized world. For a researcher interested in the foreign policy of dependent states, it provides very few useful insights. For example, Morgenthau explains that states, in their pursuit of increased power, seek three possible objectives: world empire, continental empire or local preponderance (Morgenthau and Thompson 1985:69-71). Clearly, the first two have little applicability to most of the developing world. The third, local preponderance, is perhaps a foreign policy goal of some Third World countries. However, in discussing local preponderance, Morgenthau cites historical examples such as the experiences of Bismarck, Hitler and Louis XIV (Morgenthau and Thompson 1985:71). The reader is left with little understanding of the conditions under which a state like Ecuador, suffering acute economic crisis, might seek regional status.

Similarly, the section in *Politics among Nations* which treats national power evaluation emphasizes the difficulty in determining the relative power of states with comparable military and economic capabilities (Morgenthau and Thompson 1985:170-83). While the reader learns of France's power over Germany in post World War I Europe, one is left with few tools to consider power's role in the relationship between modern day United States and its much weaker Latin American allies. Kenneth Waltz justifies the focus on great powers (1986b:92). He claims that a parsimonious realist theory relying on the global distribution of capabilities prohibits researchers from examining the multitude of small and relatively insignificant states. Waltz's claim certainly makes sense and may not pose a problem for international relations theorists. The focus on great powers nonetheless hinders realism's contribution to students of dependent foreign policy.

Despite the fact that realism rarely addresses weaker states, it is possible to operationalize national interest and power in a dependent context. Economic development has been identified as a primary national interest of Latin American states (Coleman and Quiros-Varela 1981:40; Ferris 1984a:275; Van Klaveren 1984:12). This was particularly true during the economic crisis of the 1980s and especially for Ecuador, which has remained poorer and less industrialized than nearly all of its neighbors. Policies of prestige also develop in dependent states, but rarely in pursuit of global or regional empire status. Instead, Latin American aspirations for prestige are generally limited to regional recognition in a particular issue area. Numerous Latin American leaders, such as Oscar Arias of Costa Rica, Belisario Betancur of Colombia, and Carlos Andrés Pérez of Venezuela, to name a few, have placed themselves in positions of regional diplomatic leadership which enhanced their countries' regional reputations. Related to the prestige notion is the more traditional definition of national interest as the maintenance of national territorial integrity. In fact, territorial concerns are quite immediate to Ecuadorans, who lost half of their national territory to Peru in a brief 1941 war. Ecuadoran leaders do not forget the potential of territorial loss and its impact on development and regional status.

The concept of power also differs for weak states. Whereas strong powers seek and use power to maintain global influence, weak states need power for less ambitious, but no less important, goals. As is discussed in the preceding paragraph, Ecuadoran leaders will likely seek regional recognition rather than the global dominance US leaders pursue. Leaders in both places must consider whether they have sufficient power to achieve their respective goals. Power for a dependent state is measured in the same way it is for a core state: whether it has sufficient resources to achieve policy success. Ecuador's necessary resources will be much more modest than those of the US, but may be equally difficult to acquire because of the former's economic weakness and dependence.

While realists and neorealists may not directly speak to weak states, the concepts they derive are nonetheless important to examine in dependent foreign policy theory. The central concepts of realism, national interest, and power, are defined in this study as they apply to dependent states. Ecuador is considered to pursue its national interest when it devises a policy aimed at enhancing national development or regional prestige. Power is indicated by Ecuador's ability to maintain the resources needed to pursue a particular foreign policy goal.

ii. Defining conditions

Evidence for a development enhancing policy may be difficult to identify as development is a multi-faceted concept which could be manifest in a number of ways. I identify a development-led policy as one which is specifically aimed at *improving Ecuador's economic performance or situation*. Such a policy will likely operate in the economic realm, but a diplomatic initiative intended to improve economic relations with another country, for example, could also be motivated by development concerns. The policy must also be accompanied by specific and repeated references to its development prospects. As in other cases, a development policy must contain a logical and traceable strategy that would improve Ecuador's development levels.

Because few Latin American states aspire to *global* power or prestige, we are likely to find evidence of *Ecuador's attempts to maintain and improve its status and prestige within Latin America and the Caribbean.* Repeated and specific references to Ecuador's desire to improve its regional status need to accompany this type of policy. The policy aims to influence the opinions or behavior of actors in the regional, rather than the domestic, sphere. The logic by which the policy improves regional prestige and power also needs to be evident. A likely realm within which prestige-enhancing policies are to be found is Ecuador's relations with Peru. Ecuador's loss to Peru not only deprived the former of a large mass of territory but dealt a severe blow to its regional prestige.

Does Ecuador have the resources needed to achieve the foreign policy goal at hand? This is the power-related defining condition of a realist policy. A primary criterion for determining the answer is whether or not the policy failed as a result of Ecuador's inability to follow through on the policy. If there is evidence that Ecuador had insufficient resources to see the policy through, the case will not conform with realism. Resources take many forms, including the economic funds needed to complete a development project, military resources needed to overcome an armed adversary, diplomatic commitment to a particular foreign policy goal or a host of other resources the country requires to implement a policy goal. In some cases, judging whether Ecuador had sufficient resources to implement a policy goal will be relatively simple. For example, in the case of a development project to which an administration commits funds, it is not difficult to determine whether those funds were available. However, in other cases, such as diplomatic initiatives, the evaluation of whether the country had sufficient diplomatic resources to see the policy through will be more subjective. Careful *investigation of actors' motives and commitment, based on interviews and writings, as well as other sources,* will reveal the degree to which an administration devoted itself to a policy.

E. Leader preferences

i. Theoretical grounding

Another body of foreign policy theory, one not confined to the study of *dependent* states, considers the role of individual leaders on foreign policy development and outcomes. Stated in general terms, theories focusing on *leader preferences* claim that an understanding of a state's leader (or other chief foreign policy-maker) will contribute greatly to explaining the country's foreign policy behavior (M.G. Hermann 1978; Hermann and Hermann 1989:365). This relationship is thought to be particularly relevant to Third World foreign policies. In his "Pre-Theories" essay, James Rosenau hypothesized that "idiosyncratic," or leadership, variables would prove most important for explaining less developed countries' foreign policy behavior (Rosenau 1990:165, 168). Numerous scholars have identified Latin American leaders as crucial elements in any explanation of the region's foreign policy. Because foreign policy decision-making is ordinarily concentrated at the top of government structures, they argue, leaders' personalities and styles become particularly important (Davis 1975:11-12; Lincoln 1981:7; Van Klaveren 1984:15).[2] In the language of Hermann and Hermann (1989), *predominant leaders*, those executives maintaining considerable control over the foreign policy-making process, occur frequently in Latin America.

Jensen (1982:14-16) and Holsti (1976:30) outline the conditions under which idiosyncratic variables are expected to prevail as explanations of foreign policy behavior. A summary reveals six situations in which leadership variables should be of particular importance. A leader's impact on foreign policy is expected to increase when

---

2. A recent study by Hagan (1989) does not formally address leader preferences as a source of foreign policy change, but indirectly contributes to this literature. Hagan demonstrates that changes in regime, even mild ones such as a change from one party to a similar party or intra-party leadership changes, contribute significantly to explaining shifts in foreign policy behavior as measured by UN voting. In many cases, these modest regime changes are little more than replacements of the people at the top of government structures. In essence, they represent *leadership* changes. Therefore, Hagan shows that changes in leaders lead in many instances to foreign policy behavior modifications.

1. his or her personal interest in foreign policy is high;
2. the degree of decision-making latitude afforded the leader is high;
3. foreign policy decisions occur at the higher echelons of government;
4. the foreign policy problem at hand is non-routine;
5. the foreign policy problem at hand is unclear to the decision-makers, requiring that the leader act without full information; and
6. long-term foreign policy planning is taking place.

This study will not specifically address whether leader preferences prevailed under these conditions. However, this list suggests that Ecuador will be an appropriate case with which to test leader preferences against other theories of dependent foreign policy. Foreign policy decision making in Ecuador is concentrated at the top of government. In fact, the most recent constitution gives the executive exclusive control over foreign policy. Similarly, Ecuadoran leaders have little choice but to be interested in foreign policy questions, as their country is so vulnerable to global economic circumstances. Also, as is described in chapter 2, the two leaders examined in this study, Osvaldo Hurtado and León Febres Cordero, differed greatly both in ideology and style. These differences allow for an examination of the degree to which leadership differences contribute to foreign policy behavior variation.

ii. Defining conditions
The first defining condition is that the leader must *demonstrate interest and concern in international affairs or in the particular foreign policy problem at hand*. This can be ascertained from a review of the executive's writings and other communications previous to his arrival to the presidency. Second, the leader must *demonstrate an active participation in the foreign policy process* under consideration. Was the policy designed largely in the executive office? Did the leader become personally involved in the policy rather than leaving it to other levels of the bureaucracy? Affirmative responses to these questions indicate that a predominant leader may be at work.

If the ultimate decision rests with the leader and the policy conforms with his preferences, the policy will be explained by leader preferences. This requires that the policy conform with the leader's ideology and foreign policy orientation. Again, evidence of the leader's views on the policy problem as learned from a review of his writings will provide the information necessary to compare the policy with his views. An insensitive leader will probably not meet significant opposition from his advisers. If he does, such opposition will not be heeded.

F. Domestic politics

i. Theoretical grounding

The final theoretical approach evaluated here concerns the role of domestic political actors in the foreign policy process. While many Latin American leaders are powerful, they must maintain legislative, electoral and other types of support to rule effectively and to remain in office. Accordingly, foreign policy is expected to act as a tool with which to gain domestic political favor. Foreign policy will therefore sometimes reflect the preferences of domestic political groups (Appleton 1975:56). Barry Ames (1987) explains public policy spending in Latin America as a process through which leaders distribute funds according to political aims. Leaders spend to satisfy the groups that will keep them in power. This study considers whether leaders act in this fashion in the foreign policy realm, where significant resources are rarely disbursed and about which few Latin American political groups have an intense interest (Cochrane 1978:463).

A theory of domestic politics necessarily implies that domestic *opposition* groups are able to influence foreign policy. If the only groups served were those that supported and agreed with the administration in power, there would be little need to look beyond the leader's preference to explain foreign policy. However, the notion of opposition is quite vague. Opponents range from those who philosophically oppose a government's choices but nonetheless support its right to govern to those seeking total policy change and even the ouster of the regime (Tuchman 1992:6-7). Charles Hermann (1987) and Joe Hagan (1987) argue that regime *vulnerability* and *fragmentation* are crucial in determining domestic political impact on foreign policy. Vulnerability is defined as "the likelihood that the current regime will be removed from political office" (Hagan 1987:346). Regime fragmentation increases with the degree to which the political leadership is fraught with divisions, such as competing personalities and political groups.[3]

Regarding vulnerability in Ecuador, Hurtado and Febres Cordero were fortunate that few groups sought their ouster. The military, the group best equipped to effect a coup, was committed to the new constitution. The generals demonstrated no interest in overthrowing either president, even when conflicts arose between the military and the executive branch. While some economic elites reportedly wanted to oust Hurtado, the military refused to participate (Corkill and Cubitt 1988:91). Most Ecuadoran political actors were pleased that the country had returned to democratic rule and remained committed to its maintenance. Vulnerability was therefore rather low. Fragmentation was more of a problem. Ecuadoran presidents are not assured of congressional majorities. Both Hurtado and Febres Cordero faced intense opposition from the Ecuadoran Congress on a number of issues, including foreign policy matters. Additional actors outside of government, such as the Chambers of Production, labor groups, and student organizations, also applied pressure. The degree to which foreign policy-makers responded to domestic political groups will be examined in the case study chapters.

ii. Defining conditions

The primary defining condition of domestic politics is that an *opposition group demonstrates a preference different from the leader's.* Once that has been established, domestic politics will explain if (1) there is an indication that the administration's preferences are not being implemented, and (2) there is evidence that domestic opponents' interests are being served. Reviews of domestic actors' policy positions, as indicated in public statements, press releases and other

---

3. A review of recent studies of domestic political influences on foreign policy is provided in Gerner (1992:7-9). It reveals a rather scattered set of studies focusing on elites, public opinion, and domestic political groups. It also demonstrates that, overwhelmingly, the majority of these studies have examined non-dependent states.

information sources will reveal preferences which can then be compared with the chosen policy. There should also be evidence that the executive clearly designed the policy with opposition interests in mind. The policy should therefore be accompanied by significant publicity aimed at making it clear that the regime is working in the opposition's interests. It is not necessary that the opposition express contentment over the policy. Ecuadoran politics are often too divisive to expect that an opponent would recognize a policy concession.

Falsification of this theory would require that the leader followed a policy aimed at satisfying the interests of his administration over that of domestic actors. A lack of interest or participation in the policy problem from domestic groups would also negate the domestic politics approach. Finally, a covert policy, or one around which the administration attempts to keep publicity at a minimum, would also indicate that domestic politics are not at work. Such secrecy would deny the administration the political points it wants to win from satisfying domestic opponents.

IV. SUMMARY

The theoretical diversity that political scientists have generated to explain dependent foreign policy is at once impressive and troubling. It is impressive in that the composite of these theories reflect the complexity of the phenomenon to be explained. There is little reason to expect that dependent foreign policy should be uni-dimensional, that is that it only responds to economic dependence. That a wide range of theories have developed to explain dependent foreign policy indicates its multi-faceted nature. This theoretical diversity is troubling in that the different approaches presented here often contradict each other. Their mere existence suggests that foreign policy analysts remain divided over even the essential elements of an adequate explanation of dependent foreign policy.

This study contributes to our understanding of which theories best explain dependent foreign policy. It systematically evaluates each of the six theories through their application to a set of crucial cases of Ecuadoran foreign policy. It is not expected that this analysis will provide conclusive evidence to dismiss any theory or to identify another as the definitive explanation of dependent foreign policy. Rather, it seeks to treat the theories methodically so that their claims may be evaluated and the conditions under which they apply may be specified. Before treating the case studies and theories, it is appropriate to review Ecuador's foreign policy history as well as its economic dependence and political circumstances during the 1980s. These are the subjects of the next chapter.

2   Ecuador in the 1980s

Cases for Dependent Foreign Policy Theory

I. INTRODUCTION

ECUADOR IN the 1980s provides an ideal setting for the study of dependent foreign policy. The two regimes examined here, the Osvaldo Hurtado administration (1981-84) and the León Febres Cordero administration (1984-88), held very distinct ideological views on foreign policy. Also, Ecuador relied heavily on the United States during this period and therefore represents an ideal example of a dependent state.

This chapter supplies much of the contextual information required to make the case studies fully accessible to the reader and demonstrates Ecuador's aptness as the subject of a dependent foreign policy study. It begins with a review of Ecuador's foreign policy history and traditions. It continues with an examination of various indicators of Ecuadoran dependence and a review of the core actors that influenced foreign policy decision-making in Quito. The chapter concludes with a comprehensive treatment of Presidents Hurtado and Febres Cordero, their administrations, the political and economic circumstances characterizing their terms, and their foreign policy activities.

II. ECUADORAN FOREIGN POLICY

In addition to its appeal as an ideally dependent state, Ecuador is also an attractive object of study because foreign policy scholars have paid it little attention. A number of factors account for this inattention. There is a sense in the literature on Latin American politics that Ecuador is an uninteresting or unimportant case. Many edited volumes, for example, eschew chapters on Ecuador in favor of in-depth studies of Argentina, Brazil, Chile, Peru, Colombia, Venezuela and Mexico (see, e.g., Ferris and Lincoln 1981; Lincoln and Ferris 1984; ECLAC 1985; Canak 1989b; and Stallings and Kaufman 1989). Former President Osvaldo Hurtado claims that Ecuador has been overlooked because of its small size, its relatively unimportant strategic location, and the absence of severe political problems in its history (Hurtado 1990a). Far from being unworthy as an object of study, Ecuador is a representative Latin American country in that it exhibits the political and economic characteristics common to the region, such as revolutionary movements, military dictatorships, and a large foreign debt. However, it has avoided the excesses of severe political repression and economic collapse that might generate more interest in Ecuador independent of the rest of Latin America (Corkill and Cubitt 1988:1).

Hurtado also blames Ecuadoran foreign policy leaders for a lack of vision that has kept the country from gaining foreign policy renown. Ecuadorans are quite "provincial" and "contrary to what is foreign," Hurtado stated in an interview, referring to the deep-seated regional disputes within the country (Hurtado 1990a).[1] Journalist and former aide to Hurtado, Hernán Pérez, echoed these sentiments, remarking that the country's regional rivalries prevent Ecuadorans from developing a sense of national interest that would drive foreign policy. He added that members of the diplomatic corps enjoy "playing the diplomatic games," which include lofty statements in defense of human rights and against aggression in international fora. However, these same people are reluctant to implement bold policy that would earn Ecuador a reputation as an international or regional leader (Pérez 1990).

An important scholar of Ecuadoran politics, John Martz, similarly conveys a sense that the country's foreign policy is not a theoretically engaging subject. Martz calls for the use of "traditional

---

1. All translations from interview transcripts in Spanish are the author's.

analytic lenses" to study Ecuador's foreign policy, claiming that the small country "may be understood without elaborate displays of intellectualized model-building and conceptual systematization" (J.D. Martz 1990:1-2). While Ecuador's small size and accessible policy-making community undoubtedly make it easier to study than a larger country such as Brazil, it does not necessarily follow that Ecuador's foreign policy processes are less complex or more traditional. In fact, this monograph reveals a wide variety of foreign policy behaviors and processes operating during a short period of Ecuador's recent history.

Most of the studies that do examine Ecuador's foreign policy have perpetuated the notion that the country is an unimportant foreign policy-maker or case with which to study dependent foreign policy. Overwhelmingly, books and articles on the subject focus on three aspects of Ecuadoran foreign relations: the territorial dispute with Peru, the fishing zone dispute with the United States, and Ecuador's adherence to a set of foreign policy principles (see, e.g., Terry 1972; M.J.R. Martz 1975; Lecaro Bustamante 1988; Carrión Mena 1989; El Ecuador y los Problemas Internacionales 1989; J.D. Martz 1990). These themes have dominated both the content and analysis of Ecuadoran foreign policy.

The content and scope of Ecuador's foreign policy have varied with national leadership changes. One Foreign Ministry official recently complained that Ecuador too often advanced a "governmental policy" when what it needed was "state policy" that remained consistent across time (Urrejola Dittborn 1991). Despite these fluctuations, which too often go unnoticed by researchers, all Ecuadoran leaders have had to address Ecuador's territorial dispute with neighboring Peru. The conflict over approximately two hundred thousand square kilometers of the Amazon basin dates to the colonial era. During most of the first half of this century, Peru maintained effective control over the land, although Ecuador had de jure sovereignty. In 1941, Peru invaded the territory. Ecuador's military, no match for the Peruvians, quickly capitulated. In 1942, under threats of military force, the Ecuadoran Congress ratified the Rio Protocol, ceding half of Ecuador's national territory to Peru. Governments in Quito have since called the Protocol unjust and invalid and have reasserted Ecuadoran sovereignty over the area (M.J.R. Martz 1975:383-86). Ecuador has never maintained sufficient military superiority to challenge Peru on the battlefield and has instead employed diplomatic channels to contest Peru's control over the territory. Armed border clashes in 1981 rekindled national furor over the matter (J.D. Martz 1987:267). The dispute with Peru is perhaps the single issue that unites Ecuadorans of all classes and from all geographic regions (Terry 1972:54-55). Accordingly, politicians have exploited the conflict to gain popularity and to divert attention from severe domestic problems.

A second theme of Ecuador's foreign policy concerns its claim to sole rights to fishing and subsoil exploitation within two hundred miles of its shores. Since the 1945 unilateral Truman Proclamations on the Continental Shelf and Fisheries, the United States has claimed the right to fish the area. Ecuador began seizing and fining US tuna boats in 1951 and most administrations have insisted on continuing the practice as long as US boats enter Ecuadoran territory (M.J.R. Martz 1975; J.D. Martz 1987; MRE 1980:17). The US government pays the fines for captured boats, leaving little incentive for US tuna fishermen to abide by Ecuadoran law (J.D. Martz 1990:12-14). The "tuna wars" have periodically made US-Ecuador relations quite tense, though both parties appear content to continue with the status quo.

A third theme that commonly appears in studies of Ecuador's foreign policy is its traditional adherence to a set of foreign policy principles. These guiding principles of Foreign Ministry conduct include non-intervention in foreign states' affairs, equality of states, the rule of law, pacific settlement of international disputes, non-recognition of territorial conquest, self-determination of peoples, promotion of representative democracy, Latin American integration, human rights, and the fostering of international development (Terry 1972:137; Lecaro Bustamante 1988). Foreign Ministry bureaucrats remain particularly committed to these standards, and leaders often cite Ecuador's adherence to these principles when explaining a particular foreign policy decision. Nonetheless, Ecuador's loyalty to them has varied with changes at the presidential level.

An understanding and appreciation of these foreign policy themes is important. References to them emerge throughout the present study. However, the overemphasis on these topics in the literature has led to an absence of systematic examinations of the domestic and international political machinations behind Ecuador's foreign policy. It has also generated the impression that Ecuador's foreign policy is much more limited in scope that it actually is. This study focuses not on these themes but instead examines a series of individual case studies from a variety of issue areas. This demonstrates that Ecuadoran foreign policy is not only empirically rich and diverse, but also provides excellent cases with which to examine foreign policy theory.

III. ECUADOR'S ECONOMIC DEPENDENCE ON THE UNITED STATES

A prominent Guayaquil banker and former minister of finance recently said that "Ecuador isn't 100 percent dependent on the US, only 99.5 percent" (Aspiazu 1991). While the banker's assessment is somewhat exaggerated, it reflects Ecuadorans' understanding of the severity and consequences of their country's reliance on the United States. That dependence was perhaps most acutely experienced in Ecuador's economic policy during the 1980s. Austerity measures aimed at reducing Ecuador's debt meant severe economic sacrifices for most Ecuadorans, particularly the working classes (J.D. Martz 1987:321; Acosta 1990a:15, 25). While the relationship between economic dependence and Ecuador's economic policy and performance is rather direct, the impact of dependence on foreign policy is less clear.

A sophisticated debate concerning which measures of dependence are appropriate for the study of foreign policy currently flourishes in the literature (Richardson 1978, 1981; Richardson and Kegley 1980; Ray 1981; Menkhaus and Kegley 1988). Scholars agree that dependence must be measured with both absolute and relative indicators. In other words, a dependent country must share a significant volume of economic activity with the more powerful country. In addition, it should be demonstrated that the dependent country relies on the core state to a much greater extent than it relies on any other state. If a state's dependence is diffused among a number of trading partners, for example, that state's political vulnerability to any single partner will be diminished. If, however, the state's trade behavior overwhelmingly favors one partner, vulnerability will increase and the state will be an appropriate subject for a dependent foreign policy study. By all measures, Ecuador during the 1980s was extremely dependent economically on the United States. This section reveals Ecuador's dependence in both absolute and relative terms on the dimensions most commonly cited in the literature as critical to a dependent relationship: trade, aid and foreign investment (Richardson 1978, 1981; Richardson and Kegley 1980:195; Armstrong 1981:401-3). Owing to its enormous influence over Ecuador's economic performance and vulnerability during the 1980s, the country's foreign debt is also reviewed (Cypher 1989; Guillén R. 1989).

A. Trade

Ecuador during the 1980s was in many ways the classic example of a weak country, dependent on trade and therefore vulnerable to the uncertainties of the international market. First, its import substitution experiment never experienced the success of other Latin American states, particularly in the Southern Cone. An extremely truncated internal market combined with a highly skewed distribution of wealth has limited Ecuador's ability to develop markets for local industries (Schodt 1987b:108; Conaghan 1988:10-11). The discovery of oil exporting opportunities in the 1960s directed the few resources that had been devoted to internal industrialization to the development of the petroleum trade. The national bourgeoisie, mostly wealthy exporters and landowners, did not join in the state's industrial development projects in the 1970s. The government thus developed many state enterprises which were strongly opposed by the private sector (Corkill and Cubitt 1988:29-30). The result has been that Ecuador generates little income from many unproductive, state-run industries and continues to rely on export of primary products.

Second, Ecuador's exchange rate exhibited a precipitous decline throughout the Hurtado and Febres Cordero years (see table 2). In 1982, as part of an emergency economic recovery program, Osvaldo Hurtado devalued the sucre for the first time in ten years. The sucre has continued to fall since that time, to more than one thousand sucres to the dollar in 1991. The devaluations were seen as necessary by Ecuador's creditors and some of its financial planners, particularly in the Febres Cordero administration. Devaluations increased the volume of exports necessary for foreign exchange, but weakened Ecuador's ability to import goods, services and technology.

Table 2: *Average Annual Exchange Rates*
(sucres : US dollar), 1972-1988

1972-1981	25.00
1982	30.03
1983	44.12
1984	62.54
1985	69.56
1986	122.78
1987	170.46
1988	495.00

Source: Aráuz 1990:110.

Third, Ecuador's trade profile represents a classic core-periphery relationship. Most exports are primary products that are often low in demand and susceptible to significant fluctuations on the world market. Between 1982 and 1987, a full 89 percent of all exports were primary products (Banco Central 1989a:114). Throughout the period under examination, crude petroleum was by far Ecuador's most important export, followed by bananas, shrimp, coffee, and cacao (Banco Central, 1990b). These goods are also more vulnerable to natural and other disasters than are finished goods. For example, floods in late 1982 and early 1983 decreased agricultural output by nearly one third (Corkill and Cubitt 1988:52). An earthquake in 1987 demolished much of the Trans-Ecuador pipeline, causing the cessation of petroleum exports for six months. Ecuadoran imports, on the other hand, have been concentrated in the areas of higher-priced consumer goods and equipment and technology for agriculture and industry (Schodt 1987b:109; Banco Central 1989a:132).

This primary product-export/high technology-import trade structure made Ecuador financially vulnerable, particularly during the 1980s, when the country needed foreign exchange to pay creditors. The fact that Ecuador's trade is highly concentrated with the US makes it all the more dependent. Table 3 depicts trade with the US as a proportion of Ecuador's total trade throughout the Hurtado and Febres Cordero administrations. Ecuador's export dependence was particularly intense, peaking in 1984 when nearly 66 percent of all Ecuador's exports were sent to the United States. The percentage of imports that originated in the US remained at a relatively constant, but significantly high, level throughout the period.

Table 3: Trade with the US, 1981-1988

Year	Total value of all exports	Exports to the United States	Percentage of total	Total value of all imports	Imports from the United States	Percentage of total
1981	2168	768	35.42	1694	611	36.07
1982	2237	946	42.29	2159	833	38.58
1983	2226	1163	52.25	1311	487	37.15
1984	2620	1726	65.88	1396	544	38.97
1985	2905	1695	57.11	1767	620	35.09
1986	2186	1333	60.99	1810	547	30.22
1987	1928	1056	54.77	2158	559	25.90
1988	2193	1006	45.87	1714	568	33.14

Source: Banco Central (1989a:121, 124, 149, 152; 1990a).
Note: Figures except for percentages are in millions of US dollars.

The US was by far Ecuador's most important trading partner in both exports and imports. Table 4 provides figures that allow for a comparison of the influence of Ecuador's trading partners. Together, tables 3 and 4 demonstrate the predominance of the US in both Ecuadoran exports and imports. In 1985, for example, the US accounted for 57.11 percent of all Ecuador's exports. That same year, all of Latin America, the Caribbean and the entire European continent received only 10.44 percent of Ecuadoran exports. Table 4 also demonstrates the decline in exports to Latin America throughout the 1980s. Exports within the region accounted for a high of 31.57 percent of Ecuador's total exports in 1982. By 1985, that figure had dropped to a mere 10.44 percent. That Latin American states all suffered economic crises during the decade and were forced to reduce imports account for much of this decline. At the same time, the United States increased its imports from Ecuador, offsetting some of the negative effects of the decline in regional exports, but intensifying Ecuador's reliance on the US as a trading partner. Ecuador's import dependence on the United States during this period was less intense than in exports. Nonetheless, a comparison of the figures in tables 3 and 4 reveals that the United States remained the most important single source of imports during the period under study. Only by 1987 had all of Europe and all of Latin America and the Caribbean each surpassed the United States as importers to Ecuador.

Table 4: Trade with Latin America and Europe, 1981-1987

Year	Percentage of total exports to Latin America and the Cariibbean	Percentage of total exports to Europe[a]	Percentage of total imports from Latin America and the Caribbean	Percentage of total imports from Europe[a]
1981	22.51	0.07	22.82	21.55
1982	31.57	0.04	17.89	22.96
1983	26.47	0.04	17.94	28.46
1984	11.40	0.04	23.97	22.52
1985	10.44	0.06	24.06	23.54
1986	11.57	0.10	18.99	29.14
1987	22.29	0.09	26.51	26.43

Source: Banco Central (1989a:121, 124, 149, 152)
[a] Includes members of the European Community, the European Free Trade Association, the Council on Mutual Economic Assistance, and other countries on the European continent.

It is appropriate at this point to pay particular attention to Ecuador's most important export since the 1970s, petroleum. Table

5 reports Ecuador's increasing reliance on oil as a source of export revenues. By mid-decade, nearly 70 percent of all exports were crude or petroleum derivatives. Table 5 reveals a significant drop in petroleum as a proportion of total exports. This should not be misinterpreted as the result of attempts to diversify exports. Rather the drop is due to a considerable decline in world prices in 1986 and the cessation of oil exports after the 1987 earthquake.

Table 5: Petroleum exports, 1981-1988

Year	Total value of all exports	Value of crude exports	Percentage of total	Value of derivative exports	Percentage of total
1981	2,168	1,175	54.20	167	7.68
1982	2,237	1,390	62.13	136	6.08
1983	2,226	1,552	69.71	93	4.18
1984	2,620	1,678	64.04	157	5.97
1985	2,905	1,825	62.82	102	3.51
1986	2,166	912	42.13	70	3.24
1987	1,928	875	39.74	101	4.56

Source: Aráuz (1990:100)
Note: Figures are in millions of US dollars.

It is difficult to fathom the extent of petroleum's impact, both positive and negative, on the Ecuadoran economy. Petroleum revenues were responsible for enormous economic growth rates, averaging over 11 percent a year in the early 1970s. The state received the bulk of oil profits, permitting it to finance development projects without having to tax heavily the private sector (Schodt 1987b:105, 107). Nevertheless, economic growth financed by oil revenues in the 1970s fostered a "bonanza mentality that has led to wild spending, speculation, and great waste" (Levy and Mills 1983:7). As a result, Ecuador is as indebted as many of its non-oil exporting neighbors. Also, petroleum experienced wide price fluctuations and was vulnerable to natural disaster throughout the 1980s. So, while at times oil has provided Ecuador with unprecedented windfalls, it has also been a very unreliable source of income. This has posed particular difficulties for Ecuador's state budget. During the Hurtado years, an average 43.44 percent of each year's budget was financed by petroleum revenues. During the Febres Cordero years, the figure was 44.28 percent and would have been much higher but for low oil revenues in 1986 and 1987 (Aráuz 1990:95).

Ecuador's petroleum, ironically, only served to increase the country's dependence in the 1980s. Not only were Ecuadorans dependent on income from a volatile source, the fact that exports are highly concentrated in the US market increased Ecuador's dependence on the US. By the mid-1980s, Ecuador was exporting well over half of its crude to the US (SALA 1989:536). The US has also been Ecuador's primary customer for oil derivative products (Banco Central 1989b:72). Hence, the US is the most important buyer for Ecuador's most important export commodity (*El Comercio* 1983c). As will be discussed below, Ecuador's oil industry also depended on the US for vital investment to finance further petroleum exploration and extraction.

B. Foreign aid

Ecuador also relies heavily on foreign aid transfers from the US government to finance development projects and, more recently, economic survival. Table 6 provides figures on US economic and military assistance throughout the Hurtado and Febres Cordero years. US aid grew throughout the period, reaching nearly $65 million in 1986. Table 6 also indicates that aid increased significantly when the pro-Reagan Febres Cordero came to power. A 60 percent increase in US bilateral aid occurred in 1985, Febres Cordero's first full year in office.

Added to these figures are US contributions to Ecuador through multilateral institutions such as the World Bank, the Inter-American Development Bank, and the United Nations. Ecuador relies even more heavily on these types of multilateral assistance than it does on strict bilateral US aid (table 6). However, Ecuadoran reliance on multilateral assistance should not be construed as a significant diversification of its economic dependence. The US is the principal provider of funds to most of these institutions, and thus has considerable power over aid decisions. As table 6 indicates, multilateral aid to Ecuador increased by nearly 150 percent in 1985. A 65 percent increase followed in 1986. Table 6 further reveals Ecuador's increasing dependence on foreign aid. Combined aid from the United States and international institutions accounted for a quite significant 7.4 percent of the state budget in 1981. By 1987, that figure had reached 36.5 percent. These figures point to the acute crisis of economic dependence Ecuador experienced throughout the 1980s. That more than one third of its state budget derived from foreign assistance, most of it from the United States, means that Ecuadoran economic survival was directly linked to the US government's willingness to continue that assistance.

Table 6: Aid as a Proportion of Ecuador's State Budget, 1981-1987

Year	Economic aid	Military aid	Total US bilateral aid[a] (a)	Total multilateral aid[b] (b)	Total aid (a+b) as percentage of state budget
1981	18.5	4.3	25.5	94.6	7.4
1982	22.9	5.0	27.9	444.0	29.9
1983	26.6	4.6	31.2	209.1	17.4
1984	28.9	6.7	37.1	117.8	9.7
1985	51.9	6.7	58.6	287.8	12.6
1986	60.4	4.5	64.9	473.7	34.5
1987	45.6	4.5	52.0	464.2	36.5

Source: Calculated from SALA (1989:761, 770) and Aráuz (1990:95, 110).
Note: Figures are in millions of US dollars.
[a] Includes grants and loans administered by USAID, Peace Corps, other US agencies, and loans administered by the US Export-Import Bank.
[b] Includes all loans and grants from the World Bank, International Financial Corporation, International Development Association, Inter-American Development Bank, United Nations Development Program and other United Nations agencies.

C. Foreign investment

During the 1980s, curtailed credit and a weak economy combined for a dramatic decline in domestic investment in Ecuadoran industry and agriculture. Whereas gross domestic investment between 1965 and 1980 had averaged 9.5 percent of Ecuador's annual growth rate, that figure plummeted to -3.2 percent between 1980 and 1989 (World Bank 1991:218). Ecuador looked to foreign investors, principally in the United States, to compensate for the decline in local investment, but was largely disappointed. Ecuador during much of the 1980s, with the possible exception of its petroleum industry, was not an attractive investment market. Its population, approximately eight million in 1982, offered a small market (Schodt 1987b:2). Andean Pact restrictions on foreign investment, which included clauses requiring national participation and eventual ownership in all foreign enterprises, inhibited investment. Furthermore, many investors from the industrialized countries were themselves suffering from a global recession that curtailed their ability to invest in risky foreign enterprises.

Despite these obstacles, direct foreign investment remained an important source of income for Ecuador in the 1980s. The US had accounted for much of the investment revenues that flowed into Ecuador during the oil-boom years in the 1970s (Corkill and Cubitt 1988:31). Between 1982 and 1987, US direct foreign investment in all industries averaged $368.58 million per year. Combined direct foreign investment from all countries accounted for 8.3 percent of Ecuador's GNP in 1985 (SALA 1989:794, 799). The US has far surpassed other states as the primary source of Ecuador's foreign investment. In 1988, the US accounted for 32.4 percent of all direct foreign investment. All members of the European Community accounted for only 20.7 percent the same year (EIU 1988:41).

Foreign investment has been particularly crucial in the petroleum industry. A Texaco-Gulf consortium played a critical role in exploring for and exporting crude throughout the early 1970s, the earliest and most prosperous days of Ecuador's brief oil export history (Aráuz 1990:74). Between 1973 and 1989, only two of the seventeen oil blocs explored and exploited were managed solely by the Ecuadoran Petroleum Company, CEPE. Ten of those investments involved direct participation by US petroleum companies (Banco Central 1990a:67-68). Considering the vital importance of oil revenues to Ecuador's economic well-being (table 5), the impact of US investment in this area increased Ecuador's dependence all the more. Both Presidents Hurtado and Febres Cordero sought to increase foreign participation in the petroleum industry. Such a policy was expected from the pro-foreign investment Febres Cordero. However, that Hurtado, an economic nationalist, implemented this policy indicates the severity of the economic crisis and the importance of foreign investment to its resolution.

D. Debt

Ecuador's debt during the 1980s soared into unimaginable, and unpayable, amounts. The process of indebtedness followed the route common throughout the hemisphere. Considered a good credit risk in the 1970s, Ecuador's military government borrowed heavily from willing Western banks. A collapse in oil prices, a contraction of demand for Ecuador's exports, and increases in interest rates swelled Ecuador's debt burden throughout the 1980s (table 7). Service of the debt consistently deprived Ecuadorans of nearly one-third of export revenues (table 7). Economic policy throughout the decade aimed to manage the debt through a series of austerity measures and renegotiation packages.

Ecuador's debt profile is of particular importance. In 1987, 15.1 percent of the total foreign debt was owed to foreign governments, 19.91 percent was owed to international organizations, and 60.58 percent was owed to private banks, mostly in the US (*Statistical Abstract of the United States* 1990:860). Like most of Latin America, Ecuador owes the vast majority of its debt to private commercial banks. This is in contrast to Africa, for example, where only 29.1 percent of the foreign debt is owed to commercial banks (Bradshaw and Wahl 1991:252). Private commercial loans carry higher and more variable interest rates than do most loans from governments or multilateral institutions. Furthermore, a commercial bank "typically does not provide funds for projects that enhance physical quality of life. Instead, commercial loans are allocated to business enterprises that emphasize profit and economic expansion" (Bradshaw and Wahl 1991:254).

Table 7: Ecuador's Foreign Debt, 1981-1987

Year	Total debt	Debt service ratio[a]
1981	5,868	23
1982	6,633	30
1983	7,381	27
1984	7,596	31
1985	8,111	27
1986	9,076	31
1987	10,284	31

Source: Corkill and Cubitt (1988:79) and Aráuz (1990:111).
Note: Figures are in millions of US dollars.
[a] Debt payments as percentage of exports.

E. Summary

Ecuadoran economic dependence on the United States through-out the Hurtado and Febres Cordero administrations remained consistent and severe. Ecuador relied heavily on the US in critical areas of economic vulnerability such as trade and debt. Ecuador's oil trade, by far its most important source of export funds, was concentrated in US markets. The US was also the primary provider of crucial aid and investment funds throughout this period. Policy-makers in Quito necessarily considered the US reaction to political and economic decisions they made. A trade embargo or other sanction by the US would have intensified an already severe economic crisis. The historically positive relations between the US and Ecuador made such drastic measures unlikely. In times of financial crisis, however, Ecuador could little afford even slight punitive measures against its economy. This economic vulnerability must be considered during any analysis of Ecuador's external behavior, whether it emanate from the pro-Febres Cordero administration or the more nationalist administration of Osvaldo Hurtado.

IV. ECONOMIC POWER CENTERS

This section reviews the interests and activities of the US government, and the IMF and its associate institution, the World Bank.

All were major players in Latin American finance and politics during the 1980s. The discussion reveals that Ecuador presented few threats to US strategic interests. Hence, the US and its allies pursued a primarily economic policy towards Ecuador and many of its neighbors. That policy sought to maintain and strengthen a free market economic orientation throughout the region. Such a policy served the interests of the US government and particularly corporations with investment and banking activities in Ecuador. However, austerity imposed economic hardship on much of the Ecuadoran population.

A. The United States

The role of the United States in Ecuador during both the Hurtado and Febres Cordero administrations was quite consistent. Both presidents ruled during the Reagan years in the US (1981-88). President Reagan's tenure in the White House corresponded to the worst years of economic crisis Latin America had experienced since the 1930s. The region's increased economic weakness and vulnerability enhanced the potential influence of the United States. The Reagan administration's strict adherence to a neo-liberal economic program for the region allowed the Latin Americans little maneuvering room in economic planning.

What were the Reagan administration's goals for Latin America, and for Ecuador in particular? Facing a decline in US regional and global hegemony that many Reagan supporters attributed to Jimmy Carter's failed foreign policy, the Reagan administration sought to reestablish and maintain political and economic influence over Latin America (Insulza 1983; Lagos and Plaza 1985:68-69; De S.C. Barros 1985:37). The administration's most obvious and highly publicized regional interest was strategic: to keep communist and socialist forces from spreading throughout Latin America. This goal was most prominently pursued in Central America, where massive amounts of military and economic aid, covert operations, and propaganda programs aimed to limit the influence of the Nicaraguan government and prevent insurgent groups from coming to power in El Salvador and Guatemala. Illegal drug cultivation and trafficking was a second issue of increasing concern to Washington throughout the 1980s. The US sponsored a series of programs, most notably in Bolivia, Colombia, Mexico, and Peru, aimed at curbing the supply of drugs to the US (Carrera 1990:95). Less publicized were US objectives in South America, particularly in Ecuador, where leftist rebel threats and drug cultivation were relatively meager.[2]

The United States' primary interest in Ecuador during the Hurtado and Febres Cordero administrations was to steer Ecuador and other Latin American states towards a free market economic model (Lagos and Plaza 1985:70; White 1988; L. Carrión 1991; Carrión Mena 1991). This policy served US national interests in the short-term and long-term. In the short-term, free market-based economies in Latin America meant open channels and immediate opportunities for US corporations involved in international trade and investment. Open economies provided access for US corporations to markets, raw materials, and cheap labor (Lagos and Plaza 1985:76). The free market model was also considered efficient and the most likely to generate foreign exchange needed to service external debts (Acosta 1990a:18). In the long term, US hegemony is served by the existence of a liberal international, or at least hemispheric, order in which the United States has disproportional control over markets, productivity, and sources of capital and technology (Gilpin 1987:72-76; Molineu 1990:107).

The United States' expectation that Latin American states would follow free market guidelines in economic policy manifested itself significantly in two important areas: US prescriptions for Latin American development and the management of the debt. The Reagan administration promoted development in the region largely through encouraging private capital investment (Molineu 1990:98). Two US government agencies fostered this type of development scheme. The Overseas Private Investment Corporation (OPIC) insured private investments in Third World countries against nationalization, drastic currency devaluations, and revolu-

---

2. The drug issue has increased in importance between the US and Ecuador since the late 1980s. The Febres Cordero administration signed agreements with the US government promising to police drug cultivation, processing, and trafficking activities in Ecuador (MRE 1985:35; EIU 1985b:6). The Borja administration (1988-92) also cooperated with the US on the drug question (Carrera 1990:93-102). Nonetheless, the amount and type of US resources committed to the drug war in Ecuador pale next to those devoted to other drug exporting countries.

tion. The Export-Import Bank assisted US exporters by providing credit to Latin American states so they could purchase US exports. Both of these agencies advanced free market prescriptions in Latin America while simultaneously serving the particular interests of US investors and trading companies. Similarly, much of US economic assistance to Latin America arrived with the condition that it be used to buy US-produced goods and services (Molineu 1990:98-101). This strategy, combined with Ecuador's enhanced economic vulnerability during the 1980s, intensified Ecuadoran dependence on the United States in trade.

Washington's approach to the region's debt also had a decidedly neo-liberal economic flavor. The Reagan administration encouraged each debtor to manage its problems individually with creditors. This strategy avoided treating the debt as a regional problem in need of a political solution that might favor a large-scale write-off of Latin America's debt (Stallings 1987:314; Molineu 1990:107). One exception to this policy was the 1985 Baker Plan, named for the US treasury secretary who developed it. While the plan called on private banks and multilateral lending institutions to disburse new loans to the region's debt-ridden countries, it also required those debtors to adopt strict free-market economic policies (Acosta 1990b:318-19). The Baker Plan thus enticed Ecuador with short-term funds to stave off a liquidity crisis, while serving US interests in the long-run through the adoption of free market reforms. During his 1985 visit to Ecuador, Secretary of State George Shultz emphasized his host's need to open its trade barriers and institute other structural adjustments (MRE 1985:11). Such reforms are difficult to refuse when tied to the disbursements of new loans.

B. The IMF and World Bank

During the 1980s, when overt US political and economic pressure on Latin America was readily met with cries of "imperialism," the Reagan administration was fortunate that it rarely had to intervene directly to force economic reforms in Latin America. Nor did US corporations have to exert overt pressure to achieve favorable investment climates. The International Monetary Fund (IMF) and the World Bank[3] assumed the role of Latin America's economic police during the 1980s. The recession and debt crisis experienced by Ecuador and most other Latin American countries substantially increased the leverage of the multilateral lenders. In order to qualify for IMF and World Bank low-interest loans, the lender had to agree to an economic austerity package. Austerity typically included reductions in consumption (particularly imports), cuts in government spending, wage freezes, currency devaluations, reduction and elimination of government subsidies, increases in exports, denationalization of industry, and the provision of foreign investment incentives (Canak 1989a:19; Biersteker 1990:484-85; Bradshaw and Wahl 1991:245).

IMF influence extended far beyond the conditioning of its own loans. The institution's stamp of approval emerged as the symbol of a country's willingness to play by the rules of a liberal international economy. As such, IMF approval was necessary not only for IMF disbursements, but also for crucial debt renegotiation agreements with private banks. Both the IMF and World Bank became the central global agents for coordinating the renegotiation and collection of Latin America's debt owed to multilateral and bilateral public bodies as well as to private creditors (Bradshaw and Wahl 1991:254). Similarly, foreign investors were more likely to finance projects in IMF-endorsed countries (Canak 1989a:220-22; L. Carrión 1991; Carrión Mena 1991). If a country agreed to IMF austerity, it was rewarded with the emergency cash, as well as some longer-term investments. Otherwise the debtor would risk default and isolation from the international financial community.

In this way the IMF and World Bank contributed significantly to US economic interests in the hemisphere. US government loans, both direct and those disbursed through multilateral institutions, were protected by IMF policies. Private creditors and investors in the US were also served by the IMF/World Bank policies of ensur-

---

3. Traditionally the IMF has attended to its members' short-term liquidity crises while the World Bank has assumed financing of long-term development projects. During the 1980s, however, and under the direction of the US government, the World Bank took on much of the responsibility for ensuring that Third World debtors instituted the "proper" economic programs. The policy recommendations of the two have essentially been the same since the early 1980s (Canak 1989a:21; Biersteker 1990:483).

ing free-market policies in Latin America. With these institutions pressuring Latin American economies, the US government per se did not have to act as the regional bully. The US role in the liberalization of Latin American economies during the 1980s should not be underestimated, however. The US controls 19.29 percent, the largest of any member, of IMF votes. The second largest contributor to the Fund is the United Kingdom, which controls only 6.69 percent of IMF votes (Bradshaw and Wahl 1991:255).

Former executive adviser on international affairs to Rodrigo Borja, Francisco Carrión Mena, described US influence over Ecuador through the IMF and similar institutions. The United States, he said,

> does not have to send soldiers here. Instead the United States [achieves certain economic policies] through mechanisms of international credit. It is not always visible, but the United States would like to condition loans to Ecuador on the requirement that [the recipient] implements this or that measure. The United States doesn't have to do this. Rather, the IMF simply conditions [the loan], saying "Fine, in order to arrive at an agreement for the next renegotiation of the debt, you have to agree to certain conditionalities." The IMF requires certain policies in order to obtain credit. (Carrión Mena 1991)

Foreign Ministry official Leonardo Carrión echoed similar sentiments. When asked why Presidents Hurtado and Febres Cordero pursued similar debt policies despite their ideological differences, Carrión responded:

> you must look at the influence of the United States government over the decisions of the IMF. The IMF is largely controlled by the United States. And the United States attempts to get [Ecuador's] economies to have a certain type of opening, a type of structure that allows foreign investments. The Carter era had pressures about human rights. During the Reagan era the pressure was about the liberalization of the economy. There were almost orders from the Government of the United States. [It said to us,] "You [Ecuador] liberalize your economy, and if you don't do it, you will have nothing [in terms of new loans]." (Carrión 1991)

V. PRESIDENTS HURTADO AND FEBRES CORDERO

This final section introduces Presidents Osvaldo Hurtado and León Febres Cordero, reviewing their personal and political histories as well as the political dynamics that characterized their administrations. Each leader's foreign policy style and content is also presented, revealing extremely disparate personalities and ideologies.

A. Osvaldo Hurtado

1. Political background

Unlike most of Ecuador's leading politicians, Osvaldo Hurtado is not a native of either of Ecuador's major urban centers, Quito and Guayaquil. Born and raised in the provincial capital of Riobamba, and educated as a lawyer in Quito's Catholic University, Hurtado dedicated his young adulthood to organizing and later leading Ecuador's Christian Democratic party, Democracia Popular (DP). The party's platform commits itself to "the fundamental objective of serving the political expression of popular organizations in the countryside and cities" and cites four basic doctrinal principles: humanism, community socialism, democracy and Latin American nationalism (TSE 1989:91). The party supports redistributive economic and social policies and generally opposes the interests of large scale industrialists and land-owners.

Despite its attraction to popular interests, DP has never enjoyed great popular appeal. Always considered a party of the *sierra* (highlands), DP has failed to gain backing in Ecuador's heavily populated coastal zone. During the late 1970s, when an end to Ecuador's military rule was being negotiated, Hurtado participated in the framing of the political parties law. He was known as a scholar and a teacher in Quito's Catholic University—an important resource for Ecuador's return to constitutional government but hardly a well-known politician himself. As one observer of Ecuadoran politics put it, Hurtado was "very academic, very analytic, well dressed, extremely capable and intelligent. He had genuine social concerns. But as a politician he was cold. [Unlike other politicians], he didn't give big speeches in the city squares" (Carrión Mena 1991).

Hurtado entered the political scene during Ecuador's most recent transition to constitutional rule. His economic and political savvy was attractive to Jaime Roldós, the 1979 presidential candidate who handpicked Hurtado as a running mate. Roldós himself had been an unlikely presidential contender. The outgoing military triumvirate had placed a clause in the electoral laws forbidding the candidacy of the country's leading populist and would-be president, Assad Bucaram. Bucaram chose Roldós, husband of his niece and a loyalist of Bucaram's Concentración de Fuerzas Populares Party (CFP), to be the party's candidate. Representing the coast and the highlands respectively, Roldós and Hurtado campaigned with a platform for reform in all areas of economic and social policy. Their election in April of 1979, won with 68 percent of the national vote, demonstrated a clear mandate for change. Roldós was only 38 years old, his running mate was a mere 39 (Levy and Mills 1983:5; Conaghan 1987:148; Corkill and Cubitt 1988:44-45).

The new constitution called for the vice president to head the National Development Council. In this capacity, Hurtado directed economic and social policy for the administration. Comfortable in a policy planning role, Hurtado dedicated his efforts to implementing a social reform package in a hostile political and economic environment. Politically, an unfriendly congress confronted the administration. When Roldós refused to act as a proxy president for Bucaram, the elder politician organized a strong opposition Congress against the young executive. Although Roldós had been elected with a substantial majority in Congress, all hopes for a productive executive-legislative pact were dashed when the conflict within the CFP made almost impossible the passage of legislation. Roldós's energy was directed more toward vetoing bills than towards implementing his promised reforms (Conaghan 1987:148-49; Menéndez Carrión 1988:128). Economically, Hurtado realized that Ecuador was living its last days of credit access and that indebtedness would soon become the most critical economic issue facing the poor country. By January 1981, economic straits were forcing consideration of austerity measures (Schodt 1987b:143). Implementation of reform promises was further complicated by an armed border clash with Peru in early 1981. Then, in May of 1981, as the administration's popularity was waning, Jaime Roldós was killed in an air crash. The country's shock at the death of their president was matched only by their astonishment that a relatively unknown university professor was now their leader.

2. The Hurtado Presidency

Hurtado assumed command of Ecuador as it was entering its most severe economic crisis in the post-war period. Opposition from Congress, business leaders, and organized labor made governing almost impossible. Ecuador's business elites remained Hurtado's most vehement critics, accusing him of extreme leftism in political and economic policy. His successor, León Febres Cordero, claimed that "next to Osvaldo Hurtado, Mao Tse Tung is a child" (Febres Cordero 1991). One of Febres Cordero's economic advisers called Hurtado "half Indian," implying that he is uncultured and stupid (Juez 1991). Febres Cordero's foreign minister asserted that Hurtado "hates the private sector. He hates businessmen. He hates everyone who is capable of taking a risk and of generating wealth" (Terán Terán 1991). The most common accusations are that Hurtado acted in the interests of an oversized and inefficient state bureaucracy and debilitated free enterprise (J.D. Martz 1987:254, 377; Emanuel 1991; Pallares Sevilla 1991). The immediate animosity Hurtado received from the business community made impossible the national unity needed to support difficult economic policies (Hurtado 1990b:133). Rumors that economic elites were urging military leaders to overthrow Hurtado circulated frequently. Hurtado claimed in an interview with the press that there "wasn't a cocktail party" in which business leaders did not urge the armed forces to overthrow the government (SENDIP 1984a:240). The recency of a bourgeois-supported military dictatorship made fears of a coup very real (Conaghan 1988:126-27).

The criticism was largely unwarranted. Hurtado was certainly no more a "statist" than had been the military leaders of the preceding decade (J.D. Martz 1987:377; Conaghan 1988:124). For example, he strongly sought foreign investment, particularly in the oil industry. His economic and social platform guaranteed opportunities for industrialization and a respect for private property (Mills 1984:92).

Hurtado's economic program was quite similar to that of his right-wing successor, Febres Cordero (Levy and Mills 1983). Most important, in 1983 Hurtado instituted a highly controversial economic policy which overwhelmingly benefitted the business community. The policy was called *sucretización* and called for the state to assume responsibility for the private sector debt, most of which was owed in dollars. Private sector debtors paid off their loans to the state in sucres, not in dollars, thereby freeing them from the tremendous financial burden incurred when the sucre devalued against the dollar. The *sucretización* gave a large subsidy for private sector debtors and is generally considered a policy coup for private business (Acosta 1990a:25, 1990b:306-8; Aspiazu 1991; Macías Chávez 1991; Emanuel 1991; Pallares Sevilla 1991).

Why did the business community lash out so fervently against Hurtado? Two changes that occurred in elites' operating atmosphere contributed to their hatred for Hurtado. First, the young president excluded economic elites from his policy-making circles (Schodt 1987b:145-46, 1989:177; Conaghan 1988:52, 127; Hurtado 1990b:131). Business leaders were eager to return to a constitutional democracy led by men who, if not members of their own ranks, at least were open to industrial leaders' influence. When Roldós and his successor failed to act as economic elites had hoped, the latter were severely disappointed (Conaghan 1987:147). Hurtado maintained a rather closed circle of policy-makers, and maintained more open channels for labor leaders than he did for economic elites. As Hurtado put it, the business leaders "knew they couldn't pick up the phone and give me orders in a country where the government traditionally ruled in consultation with the Chambers [of Production]" (quoted in Conaghan 1988:127). Second, Hurtado's government coincided with the beginning of Ecuador's economic crisis and the austerity policies that accompanied it. Industrialists who had become accustomed to unreserved credit access and high profit returns during the 1970s found in the 1980s that sound economic policy invariably carried economic costs. The Hurtado administration bore the heaviest political brunt of the elites' adjustment process.

3. Foreign policy

In foreign policy, Hurtado was low-key but consistent. Roldós had made foreign policy a high-profile element of his administration. He sponsored a regional conference on human rights, which earned him a favorable reputation in Latin American diplomatic circles. Roldós had strongly favored regional integrative efforts and publicly opposed US policy in Central America. Hurtado maintained Roldós's foreign policy principles, but pursued them in a less conspicuous manner. Diplomatically, Hurtado favored open relations with all states. In Roldós's first year in office, Ecuador had arranged to establish relations with fifteen states, including the People's Republic of China, Cuba, Vietnam, and Albania (MRE 1980:27). Hurtado completed that effort and oversaw Ecuador's incorporation into the Non-Aligned Movement in September of 1981 (MRE 1983:77; Hurtado 1990c:356). Initially, he strongly supported the Andean Pact, which his development plan had targeted as a primary source of markets for Ecuador's exports (Levy and Mills 1983:18). However, Hurtado left the presidency rather disgusted with the Pact's performance and its members' failure to comply with the regulations (Hurtado 1990b:152-53). His commitment to the principles of non-intervention, peaceful resolution of conflicts, human rights, and national sovereignty was constant, but not highly publicized.

Among his most courageous foreign policy actions was an attempt to reconcile Ecuador's border conflict with Peru. Early in his term, Hurtado called for a "national consensus" to resolve the border problem (J.D. Martz 1987:326; Hurtado 1990c:355-56). Given that Ecuador's recovery of lost territory was a practical impossibility, Hurtado was essentially asking Ecuadorans to accept the status quo and to put the Peruvian question behind them. Political opponents such as Febres Cordero used the opportunity to disparage Hurtado, calling him a traitor "to our most sacred principles." Even members of Hurtado's own Foreign Ministry, who had spent years cultivating the image of Peru as an enemy, balked at the suggestion that the border conflict be resolved (Pérez 1990). "Evidently," Hurtado reflected later, "conditions in the country were not favorable for the success of my initiative" (Hurtado 1990b:154-57).

Accordingly, he abandoned attempts to work out the conflict with Peru.

Hurtado appeared somewhat more comfortable dealing with economic foreign policy matters, which he considered to be in the most desperate straits. He consistently warned domestic and international audiences of the looming economic crisis. In speeches, he frequently referred to inequities between North and South, calling for more fair trade practices to favor Third World development. His 1983 UN General Assembly speech was dedicated almost exclusively to the need for a global response to Latin America's economic plight (MRE 1984:95). He emphasized the debt problem, and organized the first major Latin American conference on that theme in January of 1984 (see chapter 5).

Hurtado's relations with the United States were quiet but sound. In reference to this relationship, Hurtado claimed in his memoirs that both the "confrontation and subordination" that characterize US-Latin American relations are extreme, and that he preferred a relationship based on mutual respect and consideration (Hurtado 1990b:153). He did not provoke Washington on the critical questions surrounding US policy in Central America at the time. In international fora, his administration criticized specific elements of US activities in the region, such as mining Nicaraguan harbors and the arming of the *contras*. However, Hurtado praised the Kissinger Commission, a team of investigators led by Henry Kissinger, whose report on the region was seen by many as a justification for continued US intervention in Central America (MRE 1984:115). Hurtado's Foreign Ministry was critical of the Reagan administration's bilateral approach to its relations with Latin America, stating that multilateral efforts were preferable for regional development. US secretary of state George Shultz personally telephoned Hurtado and counseled him against establishing diplomatic relations with Cuba. According to Hurtado, he responded by telling Shultz that the US policy to isolate Cuba was inappropriate and that Latin American economic instability was a greater threat to US interests than was revolutionary Cuba. Hurtado proceeded to institute diplomatic ties between Quito and Havana (Hurtado 1990b:153). Nonetheless, the Foreign Ministry made clear in its annual report that maintenance of Ecuador's positive relations with the United States should be prioritized given that the US was Ecuador's principal trading partner (MRE 1982:113-14). Much of Hurtado's 1983 visit to the US was spent attracting investors and trading partners to Ecuador (MRE 1983:139). Good relations between the two countries was further aided by Washington's support for Ecuador's fledgling constitutional government. The Reagan administration publicly denounced military governments and was pleased to see non-revolutionary, democratically elected governments operating within the hemisphere (J.D. Martz 1987:329-30; Conaghan 1988:127).

Overall, Hurtado's foreign policy was pragmatic, not extraordinary in its successes or limitations. As his time in office was characterized by domestic political and economic crisis, Hurtado had little time to devote to international affairs. When asked by Venezuelan president Carlos Andrés Pérez why he didn't seek a more active international presence, Hurtado responded, "because I live overwhelmed with domestic problems" (Hurtado 1990b:149). He maintained a low-profile foreign policy dedicated to advancing Third World economic and political interests while always making sure not to incur the wrath of Ecuador's greatest trading partner, the United States. As his term came to an end in August of 1984, Hurtado could express pride in having maintained a consistent foreign policy in a such a challenging domestic political environment.

B. León Febres Cordero

1. Political background

León Febres Cordero represents the model of a Latin American right-wing industrialist and politician. A self-made millionaire, he was a natural champion of free enterprise (Corkill and Cubitt 1988:77). His training as an engineer in New Jersey gave his education authenticity in the eyes of many Latin American elites, who consider Ecuadoran education inferior to that of the US (Emanuel 1991). He managed the empire of Ecuadoran export magnate Luis Noboa, an experience that provided him with crucial connections to the domestic industrial community. Before becoming the Social Christian party's successful presidential candidate, he presided over

Guayaquil's Chamber of Industry, the strongest of the country's Chambers of Production.

A detractor described him as a man who "doesn't discuss what he thinks [to be correct] and doesn't consider others' opinions. What he thinks *is*" (Salvador 1991). A supporter characterized him as "impulsive but brilliant" (Juez 1991). In total contrast to his academic predecessor, Febres Cordero was outspoken and in many ways conformed to the prototype of a macho Latino. In all policy areas, he was an ardent advocate of free market principles and an equally strong opponent of anything he considered linked to international communism (J.D. Martz 1990:23).

Febres Cordero won his political fame as an opponent first of the military regimes of the 1970s and then of the Roldós/Hurtado administrations. He led the attack against the military's state-led development model (Conaghan 1988:88; Conaghan, Malloy, and Abugattas 1990:12). He was relentless in his attacks against Hurtado. "I was the principal opponent to Hurtado in the Congress," he stated accurately and proudly. "I was personally responsible for many impeachments" (Febres Cordero 1991). Strongly endorsed by the business community both in Guayaquil and Quito, Febres Cordero narrowly won 1984's run-off election with his eventual successor, Rodrigo Borja (Menéndez Carrión 1988:129).

2. The Febres Cordero Presidency

Like his predecessor, Febres Cordero faced dismal economic conditions which made difficult the implementation of campaign promises aimed, somewhat paradoxically, at popular and elite groups alike. Elected with only 51.9 percent of the vote, Febres Cordero did not have a strong popular mandate. His defeat of Borja was attributed mostly to coastal voters' loyalty to local candidates and to general frustration with the Hurtado administration's economic performance (Schodt 1989:182). An opposition Congress also confronted him throughout most of his term. Immediately after Febres Cordero's presidential victory, opposition parties that had won the vast majority of congressional seats organized into the Bloque Progresista (Progressive Bloc) to oppose executive policies (Conaghan 1987:151). During his first year, only sixteen of seventy-one congressional delegates could be counted on to support his policies. In October of 1985, Febres Cordero organized a small majority which allowed him to pass legislation postponing until June congressional elections scheduled for January. Febres Cordero claimed the postponement was necessary to allow citizens with expired voting cards to renew their voting eligibility. Most saw it as a move designed to stack the Congress with pro-administration delegates (Zuckerman 1986:487; J.D. Martz 1986:B110). Febres Cordero's predecessor, Osvaldo Hurtado, called the legislation "the most shocking fraud in the history of Ecuador" (EIU 1986:5). At the same time, Febres Cordero called a national plebiscite that asked whether independents could run for office, "confirming in this way their equality as citizens before the law" (Menéndez Carrión 1988:132). This was an attempt to reverse the constitutional requirement that candidates belong to a political party. Febres Cordero wanted a larger pro-administration bloc in Congress without having to negotiate with small parties and their "opportunistic leaders" (J.D. Martz 1986:B110; Schodt 1987a:B107). Seventy percent of voters opposed the plebiscite. Despite the delay, Febres Cordero also experienced a net loss of supporters in Congress (Schodt 1987a:B109). The electoral outcome marked the end of his congressional majority and the beginning of his decline in popularity.

In June 1986, a clear opposition majority ruled Congress. There was some hope that both the executive and legislative branches would reduce their mutual hostilities and cooperate in the interest of Ecuador's beleaguered economy. However, immediately after the new Congress' inauguration, Febres Cordero announced a final set of economic reforms designed to complete his free-market model for Ecuador. Congress, reconsolidated into the opposition Bloque Progresista, declared war. Febres Cordero's opponents set themselves to the task of impeaching members of the executive cabinet. Principal among these attempts were the impeachments of Finance Minister Alberto Dahik and Interior Minister Luis Robles Plaza. Charges against Dahik centered on the constitutionality of his economic policy. The hearings lasted nearly a month, during which the minister was hospitalized twice for nervous breakdowns (Schodt 1987a:B110-B11). Congress charged Robles with human rights abuses, accusing him of ordering illegal searches and arrests and failing to prevent torture, disappearances and murder of political prisoners (EIU 1987:3). As he responded to other impeachments, Febres Cordero overruled the action against Robles and maintained him in the cabinet (EIU 1988:3). Febres Cordero's attitude towards congressional action against him was indicative of his governing style during the last two years of his administration. He increasingly relied on authoritarian tactics to pass his policy proposals. He ignored congressional resolutions and enacted many economic policies by decree (Menéndez Carrión 1988:132; Schodt 1989:172).

3. Foreign policy

In foreign policy, Febres Cordero had little tolerance for the niceties of most diplomatic meetings. In his Foreign Ministry's first annual report, the foreign minister announced that the administration would follow a "pragmatic" foreign policy. He added that the president had put into place a "political style which consists of doing what he says and saying what he thinks" (MRE 1985:7-8). When asked to describe his views on foreign policy, Febres Cordero responded that foreign policy "has a primordial end—to better the standard of living of the people that one governs by means of cultural, political, diplomatic, and [commercial] exchange" (Febres Cordero 1991). In short, Febres Cordero had a no-frills approach to foreign policy. He spent little time exhorting the virtues of Ecuador's traditional foreign policy principles of non-intervention and peaceful conflict resolution. Instead he focused his international efforts on serving Ecuador's interests as he defined them. As such, in most cases his foreign policy greatly reflected his personal preferences.

In the diplomatic arena, Febres Cordero was skeptical of regional integrative and other multilateral efforts. He involved himself minimally in the Non-Aligned Movement and spoke little about popular issues in the region such as the New International Economic Order, human rights, apartheid, and regional debt initiatives. He minimized Ecuador's participation in and adherence to the Organization of Petroleum Exporting Countries (OPEC) and the Andean Pact, many times threatening to withdraw from the organizations (J.D. Martz 1990:24; Carrión Mena 1991; Morejón Pazmiño 1991:1; G. Salgado 1991:2). His argument against OPEC was that it failed to provide Ecuador with the preferential quotas it deserved as a modest producer whose exports were too small to affect global prices. Febres Cordero argued that he had a fundamental right to satisfy Ecuador's needs for export income before considering the collective needs of OPEC members. During the 1986 OPEC crisis, in which global oil prices plummeted and members threatened to violate production quotas, Febres Cordero criticized Arab OPEC members for their involvement in terrorism (Acosta 1990b:324). The Andean Pact was the target of strong Febres Cordero administration efforts to modify its restrictions on foreign investment (MRE 1987:71). Early in his administration, Febres Cordero blatantly violated the Pact's regulations. There were rumors that Febres Cordero would pull out of the Non-Aligned Movement. Ecuador remained a member but refused to accept many of the resolutions adopted in the Movement's 1986 meeting in Harare, Zimbabwe. Instead, Ecuador produced its own declaration outlining its disagreement with other members (MRE 1987:48).

During his first years in office, Febres Cordero shared economic policy making with three US-educated technocrats: Alberto Dahik, Carlos Julio Emanuel, and Francisco Swett. The team aimed to depoliticize economic policy-making, a process supported by the new constitution. Febres Cordero, knowledgeable about economics, acted as a mediator between his economic team and the industrialists he represented politically (Conaghan 1988:42; Conaghan, Malloy, and Abugattas 1990:12, 19, 23). Internationally, Febres Cordero aimed to build a strong relationship with foreign investors and creditors. He maintained a positive image with the international banking and business community until his last year in office, when his economic policy crumbled due to cabinet departures and overspending in tough financial times. On debt policy, Febres Cordero maintained an open and constructive relationship with private creditors and international lending institutions. He rejected a multilateral approach to solving Latin America's debt crisis and pursued instead a close relationship with Ecuador's biggest creditor, the United States (MRE 1987:18).

Febres Cordero shunned multilateralism in all foreign policy areas, focusing instead on bilateral relations. His relationship with the US was the "fundamental keystone" to his foreign policy (J.D. Martz 1990:25). As Ecuador's greatest source of trade revenues, credit, and investment funds, the US naturally attracted much of Febres Cordero's attention. However, Ecuador's relationship with the US during the Febres Cordero years went beyond that of the rest of Latin America, which also found itself intensely dependent on the US. Febres Cordero's ideological compatibility with Ronald Reagan made for a relationship that was bound not only by the necessities of economics, but by doctrinal convictions as well. As president-elect, Febres Cordero visited Washington for talks with President Reagan and Secretary of State Shultz, and New York for negotiations with potential investors (Corkill and Cubitt 1988;2; J.D. Martz 1990:23). During Reagan's 1986 visit to Quito, he called Febres Cordero a "model debtor" and "an articulate champion of free enterprise" (Zuckerman 1986:484; J.D. Martz 1990:24). The Reagan administration was particularly pleased when Febres Cordero announced early in his administration that he would support the US war on terrorism and drug trafficking (EIU 1986:5). Febres Cordero was rewarded for his strong pro-US position. The Reagan administration pressured private and public creditors to treat Ecuador leniently. Ecuador was targeted as among the first recipients of Baker Plan funds (EIU 1986:6; Zuckerman 1986:484; Corkill and Cubitt 1988:77; Acosta 1990b:321).

Febres Cordero left office with public opinion against him. During his last year, facing an opposition Congress and caring little for the economic conditions his successor would inherit, he spent wildly on popular development programs aimed at improving his national reputation (Conaghan 1989:139). Candidates from his Social Christian party nonetheless came in third in the January 1988 presidential elections, preventing them from participating in the run-off election (EIU 1988:3). He has publicly argued with the vast majority of his administration and his friendship endures with only very few. He remains outspoken on political events and a visible right-wing force in Ecuador. He currently is the mayor of Guayaquil.

VI. CONCLUSION

The extent of Ecuadoran dependence and the variability between the foreign policy orientations of Hurtado and Febres Cordero create an ideal setting within which to study the effects of dependence on foreign policy. Both leaders faced dependence, a fragile political system, and severely deteriorated economic conditions. Yet, as will be shown in the remaining chapters, they frequently developed very different foreign policies.

Each of the following case study chapters examines in detail an individual example of Ecuadoran foreign policy. Subsequent to the story of each case is an application of the six dependent foreign policy theories outlined in chapter 1. The conclusion (chapter 9) synthesizes the theoretical findings of the six case study chapters.

3   Hurtado's Policy Towards
Revolutionary Nicaragua

I. INTRODUCTION

CENTRAL AMERICA became a major foreign policy issue for
Latin America in the 1980s. The principal issue at stake involved,
somewhat ironically, not the behavior of the Central American governments themselves, but that of the United States. Washington's
intervention in Central America during the early 1980s quickly
became the most contentious political and security issue facing the
region. This was most pronounced in Nicaragua, where in addition
to a US-sponsored economic embargo, the Reagan administration
financed the *contras* to fight against the Sandinista revolutionary
government. The US differed with the majority of Latin American
governments, which were willing to grant the Sandinistas the right
to rule Nicaragua uninhibited by US military and economic
warfare. The most visible opponents of US interventionism in the
early to mid-1980s were represented by the Contadora Group.
Contadora, comprised of Colombia, Mexico, Venezuela, and
Panama, organized in early 1983 to seek peace in Central America.
Contadora clearly opposed US policy in Nicaragua (Bagley and
Tokatlian 1987; Moreno 1991:17; Hey and Kuzma 1993). Hence, an
additional foreign policy problem facing Latin American leaders
was whether to support the Contadora effort and oppose US policy by doing so.
     President Osvaldo Hurtado's response to these issues as manifest
in his policy towards Nicaragua is the subject of this chapter.

Hurtado came to power in the wake of the death of President Jaime Roldós, a strong supporter of the Sandinistas. Hurtado's own party opposed "imperialist" foreign policies such as that implemented by the United States towards Latin America throughout modern history (Hurtado 1990c:38-39). Accordingly, the Hurtado administration publicly and repeatedly criticized US interventionism in Nicaragua. However, a second theme of Hurtado's Nicaragua policy also emerged. Despite the anti-imperialist elements of his rhetoric, Hurtado failed to support Nicaragua. Privately, Hurtado was critical of the Sandinistas. The administration's Nicaragua policy was thus marked by its consistent adherence to principles of non-intervention and self-determination, but also by its failure to support Nicaragua strongly in its battle against the United States.

This case contains many elements of a useful test of dependent foreign policy theory. Nicaragua in the early 1980s was salient to US and Latin American leaders alike. It therefore generates the likelihood for confrontation between the two. The question of US intervention addresses directly many of Latin American leaders' concerns about security, sovereignty and foreign policy independence. Finally, it is important to remember that throughout the Hurtado administration, Ecuador suffered from extreme economic weakness and dependence that must be considered when examining foreign policy choices involving issues critical to US security concerns.

II. HURTADO'S BELIEFS

Osvaldo Hurtado's political views before he arrived to the vice presidency are reflected in the pronouncements of Ecuador's Christian Democratic party he founded and led. Within the hemisphere, Christian Democrats had a strong reputation for global and regional diplomatic activity in favor of Latin American solutions. In Ecuador, Hurtado maintained the theme of strong Latin American unity in face of domination and even imperialism from the United States. The Christian Democrats' 1971 party platform for which he was primarily responsible identified four clear foreign policy principles. First, it called for a foreign policy that was "independent and open to all peoples of the world," that would release Ecuador from its "international dependence." Second, it advocated regional and subregional integrative measures. Third, it called for Ecuador's foreign policies and activities to align with "the Third World, whose interests and problems are related to our own." Finally, the platform rejected "the policies of imperialist blocs, great powers' spheres of influence," and the global tendency to marginalize international organizations (Hurtado 1990c:38-39). The author of this document, Hurtado, left no doubt as to his proclivities in international affairs. He would advance a pro-Third World and Latin American foreign policy designed to minimize superpower dominance in the global system. One would expect that President Hurtado, once in office, would not only tolerate revolutionary Nicaragua within the hemisphere, but take its side against the US-backed *contras*.

In 1979 Hurtado became vice president to Jaime Roldós, a strong and vocal opponent of US intervention in Nicaragua. Roldós had made "hands off Nicaragua" a foreign policy theme, visiting Nicaragua to offer its government moral and financial support even before he took office (L. Carrión 1990). At his inauguration, Roldós spoke of Nicaragua's "heroism" (J.D. Martz 1987:248; Villacís 1991:1). The Roldós administration provided small amounts of development aid to Nicaragua as part of the Latin American Economic System's (known by its Spanish acronym, SELA) Committee of Action and Help for Nicaragua project (MRE 1981:42). With President Roldós highly interested in and committed to foreign affairs, Vice President Hurtado intervened little in foreign policy, occupying himself principally with the management of the nation's economy. No public discrepancies arose between them. Hurtado stated in one 1979 interview that he "agreed completely with all of [Roldós's] points of view on the economic and political situation of the country" (Hurtado 1990c:227).

III. THE HURTADO POLICY TOWARDS NICARAGUA

When Hurtado assumed the presidency with a commitment to continue the political agenda of Jaime Roldós, most observers expected that he would maintain a strong pro-Nicaragua position.

Instead, Hurtado scaled back Ecuador's support for Nicaragua both at home and in international fora. John Martz characterized the Hurtado policy: "while there were occasional diplomatic niceties and predictable banalities in praise of peace and the good intentions of the Contadora Group, he avoided the rhetorical commitments which had been common for his predecessor" (J.D. Martz 1987:329-30).

Hurtado's policy towards Nicaragua was consistent, if low-key. In every forum in which reference to US policy in Nicaragua was called for, Hurtado and his representatives reiterated Ecuador's adherence to the principles of self-determination of peoples and non-intervention in the affairs of sovereign states (MRE 1981:42, 1983:91, 154; Lecaro Bustamante 1988:298-307; Valencia Rodriguez 1989b:114-15). These statements implicitly criticize US Central American policy. Similarly, Hurtado rejected the Reagan administration's portrayal of the Central American conflicts as East-West, rather than North-South, issues (*El Comercio* 1984a). In the United Nations, the Organization of American States and in Ecuador's annual Foreign Ministry reports the administration's policy on the conflict between the United States and Nicaragua is without exception in reference to these general principles. Occasionally, the administration advanced a more specific policy position, but it was always in strict adherence to non-intervention and self-determination. For example, administration representatives stated that the conflicts in Nicaragua and in Central America in general were born not in ideological differences but in socioeconomic inequalities (Lecaro Bustamante 1988:301). Outsiders such as the United States, the Soviet Union, and Cuba were therefore encouraged to distance themselves from the conflict (MRE 1983:155). The administration also refused to choose sides in the Nicaraguan war, claiming that such an act would violate non-intervention. It did, however, provide strong verbal support for the Contadora Group in its attempts to mediate a peaceful solution to the wars in Central America (MRE 1983:154-55).

Individual foreign policy actions towards Nicaragua were very few. The development aid Ecuador had provided Nicaragua through the SELA project was never mentioned in Hurtado's Foreign Ministry reports. Hurtado did not travel to Nicaragua, but met with Nicaraguan president Daniel Ortega on two occasions, once at a UN General Assembly meeting in New York and again when Ortega stopped in Ecuador on his way to an inauguration in Argentina. In both cases, the Foreign Ministry reported that Hurtado reiterated Ecuador's commitment to peaceful resolution and to international law (MRE 1984:148-49). The meetings produced no formal agreements. The strongest public support Hurtado provided Nicaragua was in endorsing a document entitled "Declaration of Problems of America" in July 1983. The document, signed by numerous regional leaders in Caracas, formalized their support for Contadora (Lecaro Bustamante 1988:303). While it was perhaps a generous gesture towards peace in Central America, the declaration carried no financial or diplomatic responsibilities.

Ecuador under the Hurtado administration could be counted on to support non-intervention and self-determination. However, it did not advance the kind of pro-Sandinista positions that Nicaragua, suffering an economic embargo and a *contra* war sponsored by the US, desired from its Latin American neighbors. President Roldós and the Contadora members had provided that kind of support. It is important to point out that Hurtado had the opportunity to radicalize his position. He could have continued the Roldós policy, as he had promised to do shortly after the president died (Hurtado 1990c:277). He could have joined Contadora, or at least supported it more fervently. He could have publicized Nicaragua's plight and called for strong measures in international fora such as the UN, the OAS, and the Non-Aligned Movement. These apparently low-cost measures would have maintained Jaime Roldós's policy and conformed with Hurtado's foreign policy views as expressed before he became president. Instead, Hurtado chose a policy of inaction. His failure to bolster the Sandinistas is as significant as an actively pro-Nicaragua policy would have been.

IV. EXAMINATION OF THE DECISION

Why did Hurtado pursue a dual policy? His failure to support the Sandinistas is most puzzling. This section examines why Hurtado did not develop a more forceful policy. It considers factors at the international, domestic, and personal level that influenced Hurtado's decision to curtail his activities in Nicaragua.

A. International pressures

Compliance theory would explain Hurtado's failure to pursue a more forceful policy towards Nicaragua as a reaction to US pressure to deradicalize his policy. The Reagan administration was fully committed to its campaign against the Sandinistas (Hey and Kuzma 1993). The *contra* war and the economic embargo, at a minimum, aimed to keep the Nicaraguan government financially strapped, unable to export its ideology and unpopular with its people. Many have argued that these measures were indeed designed to force the ouster of the Sandinistas (see, e.g., Molineu 1990:204). Given the Reagan administration's dedication to its policy against Nicaragua, it is reasonable to expect that Washington would pressure its regional allies to support, or at least to refrain from opposing, the US policy in Central America. Did the Reagan administration directly or indirectly threaten Hurtado with sanctions or diplomatic isolation to keep him from supporting Nicaragua?

"I wouldn't dare say what [compliance theory] suggests. There was absolutely never any direct pressure," stated Luis Narváez, a principal Foreign Ministry aid to President Hurtado on regional diplomatic affairs (Narváez 1991). This rejection of the notion that Washington influenced Ecuador's behavior towards Nicaragua is echoed by other managers of Ecuador's relations with Nicaragua (L. Carrión 1990; Pérez 1990; Terán Terán 1991). President Hurtado remembers no Reagan administration attempts to influence Ecuador's behavior towards Nicaragua. According to Hurtado, President Reagan mentioned the Nicaraguan question during Hurtado's 1983 visit to the White House. Hurtado reminded the US executive of Ecuador's commitment to non-intervention and the matter was dropped. Hurtado also denies that Ecuador's economic vulnerability to the United States was a factor in determining the strength of his Nicaragua policy (Hurtado 1991). There is no evidence that the Reagan administration linked Hurtado's policy towards Nicaragua to US economic or diplomatic relations with Ecuador.

It is intriguing that the United States did not pressure Ecuador and other regional allies more to support its anti-Nicaragua campaign. The US was certainly in a position to assert its will in the region. In the mid-1980s, most of Latin America was suffering an economic crisis characterized by debt owed to US banks. Had the US chosen to condition economic assistance or debt renegotiation on Latin Americans' policy towards Central America, Latin American leaders could have been forced to choose between economic survival and solidarity with neighboring Nicaragua.

Two factors account for the Reagan administration's failure to pressure Ecuador to support US Central American policy. First, the United States, while committed to the military and economic battle against the Sandinistas, maintained the pretense that diplomatic channels were the most appropriate manner to resolve disputes in the region. Although US negotiations with Nicaragua were "characterized by uncertain terms, shifting conditions, ideological rhetoric, and charges of bad faith and deceit," the Reagan administration never relented in its self-portrayal as committed to diplomacy (Molineu 1990:210). Direct pressure on Latin America to isolate Nicaragua would have undermined this image. This was particularly true given the Reagan administration's support of numerous newly democratic regimes in Latin America, including Ecuador's (J.D. Martz 1987:329-30; Conaghan 1988:127; Molineu 1990:159). The Reagan administration clearly believed that the existence of the Sandinista government threatened US interests enough to warrant direct intervention in Nicaragua's affairs. However, Ecuador presented no similar threats that could justify interference in Hurtado's diplomatic decisions.

Second, and more importantly, the US did not need Latin American support for its policies in Nicaragua. Washington approached the conflicts in Central America in a primarily bilateral manner. The Reagan administration considered regional integrative efforts at peace such as the Contadora Group and Costa Rican President Arias's Peace Plan more as interventionist nuisances than as viable options for regional conflict resolution (Bagley and Tokatlian 1987:47; Lewis 1987; Moreno 1991:17; Hey and Kuzma 1993). Had the administration considered regional support for its

Central American policies crucial, it would have treated Contadora members, for example, quite differently. Contadora advanced a decidedly pro-Sandinista peace package (Bagley and Tokatlian 1987:47; Moreno 1991:17; Hey and Kuzma 1993). The Reagan administration did not utilize its leverage over the Contadora states, all of which suffered from weak and dependent economies in the mid-1980s, to force a softening of either Contadora's rhetoric or the content of its peace proposals. Instead, the US rhetorically supported both Contadora and the Arias Peace Plan when it was politically expedient to do so. At the same time it maintained support for the *contras* and the economic embargo against Nicaragua despite their clear violation of both Latin American peace proposals. This behavior reveals the Reagan administration's calculation that Latin American support was not sufficiently important to US policy success in Central America to warrant intervention in Latin American states' foreign policies.

If the threats posed by Contadora and Arias were not strong enough to draw US action against them, Ecuador's bilateral policy towards Nicaragua certainly did not warrant a reaction from Washington. Edgar Terán, Ecuador's foreign minister under the Febres Cordero administration, reflected on the US failure to consider Latin America an important partner in its strategic policy. "Geopolitically, Latin America doesn't interest [the United States] practically at all. Latin America is not a great danger" (Terán Terán 1991). Terán's statement captures the essence of the Reagan administration's attitude towards Latin America's participation in Central American conflicts. It did not matter what Latin American governments did or felt about US policy in Nicaragua. It was therefore unnecessary to influence Latin American opinions on the matter.

B. Domestic pressures

Domestic political actors made few attempts to influence Hurtado's Nicaragua policy. The debate on the Nicaraguan revolution and the US policy response to it has been more muted in Ecuador than in the United States. Since Ecuador was not a principal actor in the conflict, few domestic groups had an interest in influencing the Hurtado administration's policy (Pérez 1990). Upon assuming office, Hurtado conveyed no intentions to radicalize Ecuador's policy towards Nicaragua beyond that pursued by Jaime Roldós. Domestic actors, perceiving little threat or opportunity in Hurtado's Nicaragua policy, essentially allowed Hurtado to deal with the issue as he chose.

The primary forum for discussion of Nicaragua was Ecuador's universities, principally the Central University in Quito. Student and faculty groups frequently denounced US intervention in Central America, but did not overtly criticize Hurtado for not supporting Nicaragua more strongly. University organizations are typically ineffective in modifying government foreign policy behavior. However, had this been a case in which student and faculty groups been able to exert influence, they would have pressured Hurtado to *intensify* his opposition to US policy, rather than to subdue it. Hurtado's mild policy towards Nicaragua is evidence of the university groups' weakness as foreign policy actors. Congress essentially ignored the issue. That Hurtado's approach to Nicaragua did not violate Ecuador's foreign policy traditions or endanger the country's diplomatic reputation was sufficient reason to permit the executive branch to assume full responsibility for the policy. Similarly, labor groups and the Chambers of Production were too occupied with matters of economy to intervene in a policy question that did not directly affect their interests (Pallares Sevilla 1991).

A potential source of influence was the military, the support of which Hurtado needed to maintain his fragile control over government (J.D. Martz 1987:303). It could be argued that the military, just recently returned to its barracks, would want Hurtado to abstain from a pro-Sandinista policy so as not to stir revolutionary fervor at home. This logic fails to apply to the Ecuadoran case. The military governments that ruled from 1972 to 1976 themselves advanced a revolutionary, redistributive domestic economic program and a pro-Third World, anti-imperialist foreign policy (Hurtado 1980:258; Conaghan 1988:9; Corkill and Cubitt 1988:25; Schodt 1987b:121). Also, no revolutionary threat existed in Ecuador to warrant concern about Ecuador's diplomatic position vis-à-vis Nicaragua.

The most important domestic influence on Hurtado's policy towards Nicaragua was not an actor but an economic and political situation. The weak economy forced Hurtado to implement unpopular austerity programs. Politically, the government was fragile. Roldós's death had not only been a national shock, it created a political vacuum. Congress feuded over the appointment of a vice president. Some called for Hurtado's resignation, accusing him of plotting to kill Roldós. Even though the military supported Hurtado, his Democracia Popular party was almost without representation in Congress. Hurtado thus had to struggle to pass every piece of legislation. Additionally, the young president was forced to contend with national fury over the border war with Peru, which had caused numerous Ecuadoran casualties in early 1981. Similarly, the floods that destroyed much of 1983's agricultural exports dealt a harsh blow to an export-based economy already suffering from low oil prices and depletion of international reserves. The tremendously difficult domestic political and economic challenges Hurtado faced made it difficult for him to advance an active and controversial foreign policy towards Nicaragua, especially early in his tenure (L. Carrión 1991; Carrión Mena 1991; Terán Terán 1991).

C. Hurtado's views on Nicaragua

Even at the end of his administration, however, Hurtado did not radicalize his Nicaragua policy. This suggests that domestic constraints played only a minor role in restraining his behavior towards Managua. President Hurtado's own views on Nicaragua provide a fuller explanation. President Hurtado demonstrated a firm commitment to non-intervention and self-determination early in his political career. These beliefs are manifest in his denunciation of US interventionism. The principles on which this part of the policy is based are firmly established in Ecuador's foreign policy traditions and remain standards of conduct guiding Foreign Ministry behavior (Lecaro Bustamante 1988). Hurtado understandably allowed his Foreign Ministry bureaucrats to manage the public component of the policy, as their principles matched his own in regard to US interventionism.

What accounts, then, for the second part of the policy? Why did Hurtado not support Nicaragua more strongly? Hurtado's views towards revolutionary Nicaragua and US policy towards it provide some answers. Before arriving in government, Hurtado had advocated a pro-Third World and anti-imperialist foreign policy. He had not, however, specifically expounded on Nicaragua since the 1979 revolution. One manner by which to gauge Hurtado's views towards US intervention in Nicaragua is to observe his attitude towards the larger question of Central American conflicts and US participation in them. Most Latin American leaders in opposition to US funding of the Nicaraguan *contras* also contested US policy in El Salvador. Contadora members and many individual Latin American leaders opposed US intervention in both Central American countries, as well as in Guatemala and Honduras, calling for a demilitarization of the conflicts and a strict adherence to non-intervention (Purcell 1987:113; McNeil 1988:191). A consistent policy called for withdrawal of US participation in all of Central America, not just Nicaragua.

Hurtado's policy towards El Salvador was not particularly anti-imperialist. He supported neither the Salvadoran government nor the FMLN (the Salvadoran insurgency group), blaming both sides for a failure to reach a negotiated settlement. The Hurtado administration did advocate non-intervention in El Salvador, but was careful to condemn the United States, the Soviet Union, and Cuba for internationalizing the conflict (MRE 1984:142). Hurtado advanced a similarly equivocal position in a 1983 speech in Caracas in which he blamed the breakdown of talks between US and FMLN officials on "the intransigence of the guerrillas, the Salvadoran government and the representatives of the United States" (MRE 1984:115).

Hurtado's policy on El Salvador, or lack thereof, can be explained in part by his lofty position in the International Christian Democratic Party. Hurtado had not only founded Ecuador's branch of the Christian Democrats, but had maintained a strong presence in the party's regional and global debates. The western hemisphere's branch of the party, the Christian Democrats of America, elected Hurtado as their president in 1985, just over one year after he left national government (*El Comercio* 1985g). In the 1980s, among the world's most famous Christian Democratic presidents was José Napoleón Duarte of El Salvador. The Reagan administration had identified Duarte as the best hope for US policy success in El Salvador for two reasons. First, as a political moderate, Duarte was attractive to the international community. Reagan's support for Duarte would draw less criticism than would support for a more right-wing leader, such as Roberto D'Aubisson. Second, Duarte would work with the United States and allow the Reagan administration to continue its preferred policies in El Salvador (Molineu 1990:220-21). If Hurtado had wanted to act as a strong opponent to US policy in El Salvador, he would have had to criticize his fellow party member Duarte as well. Hurtado's strong party affiliation worked to minimize his antagonism towards the Duarte-Reagan alliance (L. Carrión 1991). This limitation may also have acted to constrain his policy towards Nicaragua. The lack of consistency between a policy that failed to criticize US intervention in El Salvador and one that strongly opposed similar intervention in Nicaragua may have invited criticism from domestic and international observers. Hurtado instead advanced low-profile policies in both countries, policies that allowed him to maintain favor among the world's Christian Democrats and avoid accusations of inconsistency in his Central American policy.

A second way to assess Hurtado's personal views toward Nicaragua is to observe his opinion towards the Contadora Group. One would have expected Osvaldo Hurtado, a clear proponent of regional solutions and organizations, to support strongly the group's activities and even to seek membership in Contadora. However, when asked directly about his feelings on Contadora, Hurtado revealed that he was less enthusiastic about the group than one would have expected. In a 1991 interview, Hurtado explained that he did not join Contadora because he was not invited, but concedes that he could have lobbied for and achieved Ecuadoran membership in the Group. He did not do so for two reasons: "First because Contadora was already filled with a large number of countries. Why add another? . . . I am not a politician who has to be present in every scene, especially in those to which I have not been invited. If there is an initiative underway, I don't like to complicate things. [Second], Ecuador has not traditionally been very involved in Central American politics" (Hurtado 1991).

Hurtado's grounds for not involving himself or Ecuador in Contadora appear reasonable. But they are weak explanations for his behavior. First, Contadora hardly comprised "a large number of countries." Only four members, Colombia, Mexico, Panama, and Venezuela, participated. Furthermore, Hurtado had demonstrated throughout his administration an eagerness to take part in multilateral associations much larger than Contadora. His avoidance of Contadora cannot so easily be accounted for by the fact that others were already taking care of the Central American situation and that he did not want to "complicate things."

Second, his observation that Ecuador had not acted as a principal actor in Central American politics is true but irrelevant. Neither Hurtado nor his predecessor and running mate Jaime Roldós heavily relied on tradition in foreign policy. Before Roldós, Ecuador's relations with Nicaragua had been "episodic," and subject to the whims of individual leaders in both countries (Ontaneda 1990). Roldós had broken with Ecuador's relatively isolationist diplomatic history to promote a pro-Sandinista and pro-human rights foreign policy. Hurtado had also broken with tradition in attempting to resolve the border conflict with Peru and joining the Non-Aligned Movement. Hurtado was more of an internationalist than most of Ecuador's former presidents. Ecuador's diplomatic convention had not kept him from pursuing the foreign policies of his choice before. If Hurtado were to follow any foreign policy tradition in Nicaragua, it should have been that established by Jaime Roldós, whose foreign policy Hurtado promised to continue. Hurtado's recognition that Ecuador had not customarily acted in Central America is a convenient justification, but not an explanation for his failure to pursue a strong policy in Nicaragua.

A better explanation for Hurtado's mild policy is found in the president's personal sentiments about the Sandinistas in Nicaragua. While Hurtado is committed to Third World nationalism, he is not a revolutionary. This critical difference put him at odds with the Sandinistas. He did not travel to Nicaragua, despite his promise to uphold Roldós's foreign policy. Hurtado felt that the Nicaraguan government's domestic and international agendas were too radical. These sentiments are evident in Hurtado's own description of his meetings with Ortega:

> Yes, I met with Ortega various times and had long conversations with him. I insistently asked him to hold elections. I told him that it was absolutely necessary that he have elections in Nicaragua. [But] he insisted on delaying. He never accepted me. I insisted many times. The other thing I told Ortega was that he would be smart to develop an effectively non-aligned foreign policy, because his alignment with the Soviet Union and with Cuba created a conflict in the region and particularly with the US. I told him that my hypothesis was that the US would not try to overthrow Ortega if he would establish a regime that was effectively non-aligned and not dependent on the USSR and one that held free elections. "You [Sandinistas] say that you are popular," I told him. "Why don't you hold elections?" He delayed. [He said the delays were due to] the war, and that they had to consolidate the revolutionary process. (Hurtado 1991)

A number of revealing and intriguing indicators of Hurtado's views towards Sandinista Nicaragua are found in this quote. First, Hurtado was clearly suspicious of the Nicaraguan government. He questioned the Sandinistas' commitment to revolutionary democracy. The last sentence in his quote was stated with particular incredulity, as if Ortega's reference to the war and the consolidation of the revolutionary process were insufficient excuses for a failure to hold elections. Hurtado's disbelief in the Nicaraguan government's dedication to democratic reform made him unlikely to support that government in its battle with the United States.

Second, Hurtado's quote reveals a clear antagonism between the Nicaraguan and Ecuadoran presidents. Despite his oft-repeated commitment to non-intervention in the internal affairs of other states, Hurtado apparently felt quite comfortable pressuring Ortega for reform in domestic as well as foreign policy. The Nicaraguan leader responded with justifications for not holding elections, which incidentally were held in November 1984, three months after Hurtado left office. Many other Latin American leaders, such as

Contadora members, were willing to allow the Sandinistas a few years to consolidate the revolution before elections were held (Molineu 1990:199). Dismantling the bureaucracy established during decades of Somoza dictatorship coupled with the implementation of the progressive social reforms were sufficiently massive tasks to justify a delay in elections. Hurtado disagreed, believing that Nicaragua was moving towards Soviet-aligned totalitarianism. Hurtado's concern manifested itself in a reserved foreign policy towards Nicaragua.

Finally, Hurtado's quote demonstrates his sympathies with the Reagan administration's policy towards Nicaragua. Hurtado's comments to Ortega that the US would stop its intervention if Nicaragua pursued a non-aligned foreign policy and democratic processes at home are very generous to the Reagan administration. Many critics of Washington's policy in Nicaragua argued that the Reagan administration was motivated not by a desire for democracy and independence in foreign policy in Nicaragua, but by an ambition to destroy Nicaragua's experiment with socialist development (see, e.g., Chomsky 1985:128-37). In contrast, Hurtado believed that so long as Nicaragua did not represent a security threat, as indicated by its alignment with the Soviet Union, the US would leave the Sandinistas alone. Keeping Hurtado's understanding of Washington's motives in mind, it is plain why he did not develop a more strongly anti-US policy towards Nicaragua. Hurtado opposed Washington's methods in Nicaragua, principally the interventionist aspect of US policy. He repeatedly stated his disagreement with the United States' military approach to Nicaragua. However, Hurtado agreed with many of the Reagan administration's goals for Nicaragua. These views explain why the Ecuadoran president did not advance a policy more strongly supportive of the Sandinistas in their battle against the Reagan administration.

D. Summary

This section has examined the international, domestic, and personal factors influencing the Hurtado administration's policy towards revolutionary Nicaragua. International factors played a small role. The US government did not pressure Ecuador to refrain from a pro-Nicaragua foreign policy as might have been expected. The Reagan administration did not need Ecuador's support for its policies in Central America. In addition, policy-makers in Washington wanted to maintain the image that dialogue and non-interference were important principles of US regional diplomatic behavior. Hurtado also received little pressure from domestic political actors on his Nicaragua policy. Student associations demanding support for revolutionary Nicaragua were placated by Hurtado's commitment to principles of non-intervention and self-determination. Other domestic groups showed little or no interest in Hurtado's Nicaragua policy, which was considerably less radical than that of his predecessor, Jaime Roldós. More important domestic factors included the tremendous economic and political difficulties Hurtado faced in governing Ecuador. Hurtado assumed control in the country's recent post-transition period, characterized by war with Peru and severe economic crisis. The president had little time or energy to devote to a strong Central American policy.

The strongest determinants of Hurtado's mild policy towards Nicaragua are found in the president's own views towards the Sandinista government and the motivation behind the Reagan administration's Nicaragua policy. Hurtado's distrust for Daniel Ortega's commitment to democratization and foreign policy non-alignment led the former to curb his support for the Nicaraguan revolution. Similarly, Hurtado displayed a moderate position towards US policy, believing that the Reagan administration was motivated principally by security concerns in the region, and not by a desire to destroy Nicaragua's revolutionary experiment. These sympathies with Washington and antagonism towards Managua account for the content of Hurtado's policy towards Sandinista Nicaragua.

V. THEORETICAL APPLICATION

This section applies six theories of foreign policy to the two-fold policy the Hurtado administration developed towards Nicaragua. The first and most visible component was Ecuador's oft-repeated dedication to the principles of non-intervention and self-determination. This commitment implied Ecuador's rejection of the US government's policy of military intervention in Central America in general, and of the arming of the *contras* specifically. Second, Hurtado's policy towards Nicaragua was mild, and much less supportive of the Sandinistas than many had anticipated from the Christian Democrat president. Hurtado's rejection of the Reagan administration's policy did not entail embracing the Nicaraguan government's management of domestic or international affairs. As such, the Hurtado administration failed to provide Nicaragua the type of support it received from the Contadora members and from other states within the region and around the globe.

A. Compliance

This case appears to contain all the defining conditions of compliance. Ecuador was weak, dependent, and vulnerable to US pressure. The Reagan administration placed a high priority on its Nicaragua policy. One would anticipate that the US government would pressure Ecuador and other Latin American states to support Washington's policy towards Nicaragua. The evidence, however, demonstrates that compliance does not apply.

Hurtado's rejection of Reagan administration tactics in Nicaragua clearly does not conform to compliance's policy output criterion that Ecuador develop a pro-US policy. Ecuador's repeated insistence that the principles of non-intervention and self-determination be respected in Central America was not in accordance with US preferences, and as such does not exhibit the primary defining characteristic of a compliant foreign policy. Hurtado's failure to support the Sandinistas is a more likely candidate for compliance. To what degree was his administration's inaction in this area a reaction to US pressure or fear of reprisals? This is difficult to answer, as US preferences on this matter are somewhat ambiguous. Certainly, the Reagan administration would have preferred Latin American leaders not support the Sandinistas. Reagan suggested this to Hurtado during their White House meeting. Furthermore, in domestic and international fora Reagan and his aides made very clear their antagonism towards the Sandinistas. What is difficult to judge is how strongly US policy-makers felt about Latin American acquiescence on this issue. The record in the Ecuadoran case suggests that the US did not advance a significant effort aimed at exacting Hurtado's compliance. Furthermore, the element of Hurtado's policy that the US would have appreciated, Hurtado's pressure on Daniel Ortega to democratize and pursue a non-aligned foreign policy, was not publicized either at home or abroad. Hurtado kept quiet the most pro-US ingredient of his behavior towards Nicaragua. A compliant policy is most effective when its pro-US impact is known on an international scale. In the international arena, Hurtado strictly adhered to non-intervention and self-determination, behavior widely perceived as antagonistic to US policy in Central America.

Other necessary elements of compliance theory do not exist in this case. No obvious conflict of interest existed between the Hurtado and Reagan administrations. While the two clearly argued over the methods, their objectives for Nicaragua were similar. Hurtado's failure to support the Sandinistas is more a product of his disapproval of the Nicaraguan government than of pressure from the United States.

Indeed, there is no evidence that the US government pressured Hurtado towards any particular type of policy. Hurtado certainly knew that Nicaragua was highly salient to the Reagan administration, and that Ecuador was economically vulnerable to potential US pressure. President Reagan, however, did not push the issue when he met with Hurtado. Furthermore, US economic activities in Ecuador did not change as a result of Hurtado's Central American policy. Other countries in the region continued to oppose the US on this issue without suffering economic backlash. This was particularly true of Mexico, a leader of the Contadora Group and a primary recipient of US emergency financial assistance (Hey and Kuzma 1993). The US government understood that it could pursue its own Nicaragua policy regardless of Latin American support, and apparently concluded that intervention in regional foreign policies would be more costly than necessary.

Finally, compliance requires that the issue be salient to the

Ecuadoran administration. Otherwise, submission to US preferences entails no sacrifice. Nicaragua, as well as Central America in
general, was not highly salient to the Hurtado administration. A
marked decrease in the emphasis of Ecuadoran foreign policy
towards the region appeared with Hurtado's rise to power. While
other regional actors such as Contadora and later, President Oscar
Arias of Costa Rica, played a highly visible role in Central American
conflict resolution, Ecuador under Hurtado was most notable for
its lack of activity.

B. Consensus

It has been determined that Hurtado's rejection of US intervention was not consistent with US preferences. To that extent, the primary criterion of the consensus model is also absent in this
component of the policy. But consensus does ring true to the extent
that Hurtado's failure to oppose US policy was the result of agreement between Hurtado and Reagan that the Sandinistas were undemocratic and aligned with the Soviets. Hurtado was sympathetic to
the substance, if not the methods, of US policy.

The Reagan administration's commitment to opposing the
Sandinistas far outweighed that of the Hurtado administration. It
is important to remember that Hurtado's antagonism towards the
Sandinistas was a relatively minor and unpublicized component of
his policy. Hurtado's suspicions about Daniel Ortega were mild
compared to Reagan's. The Reagan administration repeatedly con-
demned Nicaragua for its ties with the communist world, its military shipments to rebels in El Salvador,[1] its Soviet-aided military
buildup, and its move towards totalitarianism (Kenworthy 1985;
Walker 1985:159-62; Molineu 1990:195-204). These charges, claimed
the Reagan administration, justified Washington's harsh reaction.
The extreme threat Nicaragua posed to hemispheric security and

---

1. This claim was particularly difficult to prove. Despite repeated allegations, beginning in February 1981, that Nicaragua sent Salvadoran rebels weapons, the Reagan
administration was never able to verify its claims. Not until November 1989, when
President Bush was in office, did the government of El Salvador find a weapons shipment
it was able to trace to Nicaragua. After years of unsubstantiated accusations against the
Sandinistas, many remain skeptical of the origin of the 1989 find (Walker 1985:160-61;
Molineu 1990:195-96).

democracy merited the Sandinistas' ouster through economic and military warfare. The intensity of these sentiments emanating from Washington far exceeded President Hurtado's. While Hurtado worried about the Sandinistas' democratization and foreign policy alignment, he did not accuse Nicaragua of shipping arms to the Salvadoran rebels, instituting a "totalitarian" state, or assembling a pro-Soviet militia. Despite these significantly different points of view, Hurtado made clear his agreement with President Reagan on two important counts. First, he felt that US policy motivations were essentially innocuous, aimed only at preserving US security and not designed to oust the Sandinistas from a position of power within the hemisphere. Second, Hurtado concurred with Reagan on the Sandinista government's threats to democracy in Nicaragua and Central America. Hurtado's insistence that Nicaragua hold free elections was very similar to concurrent White House demands. Both presidents advanced, though to varying degrees, notions of democracy and anti-communism for Nicaragua. Finally, Hurtado also demonstrated a sincere dislike for Daniel Ortega, a sentiment shared by President Reagan and his key foreign policy advisers, such as Jeane Kirkpatrick and Alexander Haig. The Reagan administration considered Ortega the leader of the "Marxist Sandinista takeover" in Nicaragua (Kenworthy 1985; Molineu 1990:195).

Consensus can account for Hurtado's failure to support the Sandinistas. Leaders in Ecuador and the US agreed that the Sandinistas threatened democracy in the hemisphere and thus did not deserve support. One relatively minor expectation of consensus, that the policy be aimed to benefit elites in Ecuador, does not emerge. Recall that domestic business leaders disassociated themselves wholly from Hurtado's Central America policy. However, given that this was a purely diplomatic policy, the lack of impact on domestic economic elites is not unusual and does not negate the applicability of the consensus model to this case.

C. Counterdependence

Hurtado's repeated insistence that the US respect non-intervention and self-determination is counterdependent. A review of the development of Hurtado's commitment to these principles finds that he advocated them at an early stage in his political career. Recall that in the early 1970s, Hurtado developed his party's foreign policy platform to include a rupture with "international dependence," alignment with the Third World and a rejection of the interventionism of "imperialist blocs" (Hurtado 1990c:38-39). These clearly counterdependent tenets partially survived and reappeared in a diluted form in Hurtado's Nicaragua policy. Hurtado's opposition to US interventionism in Nicaragua is consistent with his beliefs that superpower imperialism kept the Third World from experiencing true sovereignty. The policy is counterdependent in that Hurtado's opposition to US interventionism in Nicaragua would not have developed in the absence of a general condition of dependence. Furthermore, the US opposition expected of a counterdependent policy was present, but not strong.

In contrast, counterdependence cannot account for Hurtado's failure to support the Sandinistas. If Hurtado had been motivated wholly by a desire to counteract the dependence of Ecuador and the rest of Latin America on the US, he would have developed a more strongly pro-Nicaragua position. The Sandinistas' revolution, development model, and foreign policy were all extremely counterdependent in their rejection of the historical arrangement between Nicaragua and the United States. That arrangement, according to the Sandinistas, kept the majority of Nicaragua's people impoverished. A government program that broke with that tradition, counterdependence, was necessary for true development. For Hurtado's policy to conform with counterdependence, it would have allied more strongly with this Sandinista position. Instead, Hurtado conspicuously rejected providing the Sandinistas with the public international support they wanted and even chastised their leader in private.

D. Realism

Realist theory is a poor predictor of both components of Hurtado's foreign policy towards Nicaragua, though they meet the criterion that Ecuador maintain the necessary resources to implement the policy. Both components required only minimal diplomatic resources, as the possible consequences of these actions involved few risks. The resources needed to reject US interventionism were little more than diplomatic pronouncements which carried no threat for the US. The failure to support the Sandinistas essentially meant that no resources were expended.

However, these cases fail to pass the other tests of realism. First, Hurtado did not seek regional status with this policy. Had he joined Contadora, or been more fervent in his opposition to US policy, Hurtado may have gained recognition as a regional leader on the Nicaraguan problem. Instead, Hurtado advanced a very low-key policy, noted by its lack of ambition, that reinforced regional opinions about Ecuador as a non-active regional diplomatic actor. He might have gained regional prominence had he chosen to admonish Ortega publicly. Rather than pursuing such recognition, the Ecuadoran president kept his anti-Sandinista views very quiet.

Did Hurtado's policy advance Ecuador's development, as realism would also expect? There is nothing to suggest that Hurtado's criticism of either US interventionism or Nicaraguan domestic policy had anything to do with promoting Ecuador's development. It could be argued that Hurtado restricted his anti-US rhetoric so as to assure the maintenance of US development aid. In a 1991 interview, Hurtado absolutely rejected this suggestion (Hurtado 1991). Furthermore, and as mentioned above, other states advanced policies that were much more antagonistic to the US and were not punished economically. This was purely a diplomatic policy for which realist theory cannot account.

E. Leader preferences

Was Hurtado's Nicaragua policy consistent with his own preferences? Most of the evidence suggests that it was. One indicator of leader preferences is the qualitative change in Ecuador's Nicaragua policy that accompanies a change in leadership. During the Roldós administration, Ecuador was among the region's most vocal proponents of Nicaragua. Once Hurtado came to office, Ecuador's participation in matters related to Nicaragua decreased substantially. Similarly, the force behind the anti-US rhetoric weakened. This shift demonstrates that policy was directed from the executive office.

While it is difficult to say that Hurtado was actively involved in a policy noted for its inactivity, Ecuador's Nicaragua policy during the Hurtado years conformed to the president's own views on the subject. Leader preferences most wholly accounts for the dual nature of Ecuador's policy in Nicaragua. First, Ecuador denounced US interventionism and adhered strictly to policies of non-intervention and self-determination. Hurtado had developed and advocated these positions since the early days of his political career. Second, Hurtado failed to support Sandinista Nicaragua and pressured Daniel Ortega to modify his domestic and international behavior. This component of the policy is consistent with Hurtado's skepticism towards Nicaragua's domestic and foreign policy.

F. Domestic politics

Domestic politics explains neither of the components of Hurtado's policy towards Nicaragua. Domestic opposition on this issue was very limited. The most vehement political opinions within Ecuador came from the university groups promoting a pro-Nicaragua position. These student groups were not a relevant opposition group that Hurtado had to fear. Accordingly, Hurtado did not respond. There is no evidence that Hurtado's policies towards Nicaragua reflected any group's preferences over his own.

VI. CONCLUSION

The difficulty this case presents is in Hurtado's apparently contradictory policy in Nicaragua. Ecuador under his leadership adhered steadfastly to the principles of non-intervention and self-determination, a position which required Ecuadoran foreign policy to reject US intervention in Nicaragua. On the other hand, Hurtado did not proceed to include what many may have anticipated to be a corollary of an anti-interventionist foreign policy—active support for Nicaragua in the consolidation of its revolution and its battle with the United States. That Hurtado included the first component but not the second in his policy provides a challenge for existing foreign policy approaches.

Table 8: Hurtado's Nicaragua Policy

	Compliance	Consensus	Counter-dependence	Realism	Leader preferences	Domestic politics
Rejection of US intervention	no	no	yes	no	yes	no
Failure to support Sandinistas	no	yes	no	no	yes	no

Table 8 depicts the general applicability of the six foreign policy theories to Hurtado's policies in Nicaragua. It reveals that both leader preferences and counterdependence account for the anti-US component of the policy. Leader preferences combines with consensus to explain Hurtado's failure to support the Sandinistas. Recalling the discussion of these theories in section V, leader preferences explains the entire policy most fully. Osvaldo Hurtado's views on US interventionism and Sandinista practices accorded fully with the positions his country advanced on those issues. Counterdependence provides insight into the motivations behind Hurtado's anti-interventionist posture towards the US, while consensus best explains the motivation behind the anti-Sandinista position. As is true in other cases examined in this study, counterdependence and consensus co-occur with leader preferences to provide a full account of a policy.

That Hurtado pursued both pro-US and anti-US policies demonstrates the complexity of his views. While he is generally considered a counterdependent leader, particularly when contrasted with his successor, Febres Cordero, Hurtado is not a *revolutionary* leader. His counterdependent tendencies are not strong enough to sway him from a commitment to anti-communism and democracy. Hurtado adhered to these sentiments even when they guided him towards a policy that aligned with US preferences. Of course, his concomitant policy of denouncing US interventionism in Central America allowed him to maintain a public image of counterdependence.

Hurtado's simultaneous pursuit of a counterdependent and consensual policy also reveals the Ecuadoran president's foreign policy flexibility in this area. By pursuing a dual policy, Hurtado put himself in the position of potentially offending all of his critics and pleasing none. The United States was no doubt displeased by Ecuador's constant denunciation of its tactics in Nicaragua. Similarly, by failing to advocate the Sandinistas, Hurtado jeopardized his popularity with leftist groups in Ecuador. Hurtado in actuality received few complaints and was able to proceed with the dual policy as he saw fit. This appears to be a function of the low salience of Ecuador's Nicaragua policy for most of the international and domestic actors interested in this area. Ecuador's behavior towards Nicaragua, so long as it did not become too extreme in either ideological direction, was of little consequence to political actors in the US and Ecuador. In this sense, the dual policy actually shielded Hurtado from criticism. The Reagan administration was willing to withstand some criticism from Ecuador's Foreign Ministry because Ecuador did not advance a strong pro-Sandinista policy. Domestic leftists were placated by frequent denunciations of US tactics in Nicaragua, even if Hurtado did not fully support Nicaragua. Because neither set of potential opponents perceived Hurtado's policy as too extreme, he was able to pursue a policy conforming with his own preferences.

Perhaps most interesting is compliance's failure to account for Ecuador's behavior in this case. Despite the Reagan administration's strong commitment to its Nicaragua policy as well as Ecuador's economic dependence, the US applied little pressure on Ecuador to advance an anti-Sandinista foreign policy. Also, the mere threat of economic retaliation did not discourage Hurtado from consistently opposing US military and economic actions in Nicaragua. While this case appeared to be an ideal candidate for compliance, it emerged as an example of leader preferences, in many ways the opposite of compliance.

Also of interest is the failure of realist and domestic politics theories to account for this initiative. Realism's deficiency in this case is two-fold. Recall that realist theory when applied to Latin America expects leaders to pursue either regional or global visibility and power, or to advance development. By the first set of criteria, realism predicted Hurtado's behavior in the wrong direction. Rather than aligning himself with the Contadora Group, which gained considerable hemispheric prestige through its efforts for peace in Central America, Hurtado pursued a decidedly low-key policy that failed to win him any regional recognition. On the second criterion, realism's failure to explain Hurtado's behavior is born in the fact that the policy problem at hand had little to do with Ecuadoran development. Ecuadoran development would have been little, if at all, affected by Hurtado's decisions towards Nicaragua. This case illustrates the limitations of realism's expectations that Latin American states will pursue pro-development policies. It cannot account for diplomatic questions that may carry no foreseeable development consequences. For this reason, realism also expects states to implement policies designed to further regional status and influence. However, on this point, realism clearly failed.

That domestic political actors had little influence in determining Hurtado's Nicaragua policy is primarily a function of their lack of interest on this question. With so many critical economic and social questions facing domestic interest groups at home, few were concerned with an issue that had little direct impact on their interests. The failure of groups such as the Chambers of Production, the military, labor, and Congress to intervene in Hurtado's policy was also the product of their respect for his authority over foreign policy, as well as an impression that his actions would have little consequence on the domestic scene. Former president Roldós had implemented a quite radical policy towards Sandinista Nicaragua, a policy few domestic actors perceived as threatening. The one group strongly committed to this case, university associations, had little influence in the executive office.

4   Foreign Investment Reform
in Petroleum Policy

I. INTRODUCTION

IN AUGUST 1982, Osvaldo Hurtado signed into law two bills that opened Ecuador's oil industry to increased foreign investment. Hurtado had been convinced since he was vice president that current exploration rates would not produce sufficient oil revenues for the decade ahead (J.D. Martz 1987:336). By the time he reached the presidency, the economic crisis was fully evident even to the most reluctant observers. Hurtado worked diligently to achieve congressional approval of his reform package. The laws' passage was facilitated by a nation-wide consensus that the existing petroleum investment laws required reform. It was nonetheless difficult to work out a compromise between an executive eager to reform the legislation and a Congress wary of losing Ecuadoran autonomy over the oil industry.

This case appears to be an ideal example of a compliant foreign policy. Hurtado changed his views and adopted a pro-core position after his country entered an economic crisis. As is discussed below, however, the link between Ecuadoran dependence and Hurtado's policy is quite difficult to discern. Hurtado appears to have reacted less in response to dependence per se than to the economic crisis in general. US investors did not receive preferential treatment in Ecuador's reforms. Nonetheless, Ecuador did implement a policy that accorded with the Reagan administration's general policy prescriptions for Latin America. This outcome suggests that US power over Ecuador is less direct than is often assumed, but that the US may benefit from policies developed in Latin America under crisis.

II. THE NEED FOR REFORM

In 1972, Ecuador experienced sweeping changes in both its political and economic orientation. President José Velasco Ibarra was ousted from his fifth and final presidency in a military coup. The new leader, General Guillermo Rodríguez Lara, instituted a military dictatorship characterized by a strongly nationalistic economic policy. During the same year, Ecuador entered the affluent ranks of global petroleum exporters. The military government assumed control of the oil industry. While the state-led petroleum policy worked during the oil boom of the 1970s, by the 1980s nearly all sectors of Ecuador's society agreed it had to be changed.

Rodríguez Lara appointed a highly nationalistic minister of Natural Resources, former navy captain Gustavo Jarrín Ampudía.[1] Under Jarrín's guidance, Ecuador joined OPEC in 1973, just before oil prices soared and most of the organization's members placed an embargo on sales to the West. Jarrín instantly assumed leadership within OPEC, exercising a role far out of proportion with Ecuador's petroleum production (Ecuador is OPEC's second smallest producer). Jarrín was elected president of OPEC in 1974, only a year after his country had joined the organization and in spite of the fact that OPEC's Arab members were far more powerful. Although neither Ecuador nor Venezuela, the only other Latin American OPEC member, participated in the embargo, both countries were sanctioned by the US Congress in 1974. OPEC members were excluded from the Generalized System of Preferences, the 1968 agreement by which GATT member states could provide preferential treatment to Third World exporters. The sanctions were lifted during the Carter administration, but the image of Ecuador as a country hostile to

---

1. Except where otherwise noted, information on actors' beliefs and behaviors, as well as the political maneuverings that led to the policy outcome are found in John D. Martz (1987:346-55).

foreign interests remained for some time (MRE 1980:21; Schodt 1987b:116-19).

On the domestic front, Rodríguez Lara incorporated oil revenues into his designs for economic growth. He made state investment the cornerstone of his nationalist economic program and chose petroleum, both for its huge income-generating potential and because it was a nascent enterprise, as the leading state industry (Schodt 1987b:116). The Ecuadoran State Petroleum Company (Corporación Estatal Petrolera Ecuatoriana, CEPE) was activated in 1972 to manage exploration and extraction of petroleum reserves. CEPE's revenues financed impressive economic growth throughout the rest of the decade.

The military government's plans necessarily clashed with the expectations of foreign oil companies, which had explored Ecuador's oil potential since the turn of the century. After years of costly and mostly disappointing drilling, Texaco-Gulf discovered a large field of high-quality crude in Ecuador's Oriente region in 1967 (Schodt 1987b:104). The Rodríguez Lara administration took power just as oil exports were to begin and immediately set to the task of maintaining national control over production and profits. Under Jarrín's guidance, the government instituted laws which required foreign firms to renegotiate contracts signed under the previous administration. Many smaller firms abandoned their activities in Ecuador rather than deal with the new government. Exploration activities all but ceased during the early 1970s while the contracts were renegotiated in terms more suitable to the new government (Schodt 1987b:118-19). Jarrín's main objective was for CEPE to acquire a greater percentage of the foreign firms' holdings in the country. Under his leadership, Ecuador obtained a 25 percent share of Texaco-Gulf, which controlled the most valuable oil fields. Once that was achieved, Jarrín set his sights on obtaining a 51 percent share of all foreign holdings in Ecuador, a move that was considered too bold by both foreign and domestic private interests.

His appointment as president of OPEC and his formal proposal for the 51 percent share marked the pinnacle of Jarrín's career in Ecuador's oil industry. Five months after he was elected leader of OPEC, Jarrín was ousted from his ministerial post in Ecuador.

Pressure from national and international actors and circumstances led to his downfall. The national private sector worried that Jarrín's policies would scare away foreign investors in the petroleum sector. The Chambers of Production, the organized and powerful interest group serving Ecuador's private sector, also feared that capital flight would expand to other parts of the economy and lobbied for Jarrín's removal (Schodt 1987b:119). Internationally, Ecuador lost bargaining power vis-à-vis foreign oil investors as world oil production increased during 1974. The US government was also displeased with Jarrín's nationalist posture within Ecuador and on an international scale. Rumors circulated within the Ecuadoran leadership that the US would cut off military aid unless Jarrín were removed (Schodt 1987b:119; J.D. Martz 1990:16).

The military government's oil policy moderated somewhat after Jarrín's dismissal. Nonetheless, Rodríguez Lara and the military triumvirate that succeeded him in 1976 maintained laws that promoted CEPE's participation in oil production. Ecuador's reputation as unfriendly to foreign investors resulted in Gulf's exodus from the country. Gulf managers demanded that CEPE purchase the company's operations in Ecuador, arguing that the government's policies made it impossible to earn "a reasonable profit on its large unrecovered capital investment" (quoted in Schodt 1987b:120). Ecuador's international image and investment policies caused a decline in foreign investment in the oil industry, leaving much of the responsibility for petroleum exploration and production to CEPE (J.D. Martz 1987:104-5, 124, 202). Costly exploratory drilling and significant industry inefficiency left CEPE in financial straits by the end of the 1970s.

Ecuador entered the new decade in a precarious economic and political position. The Roldós/Hurtado team assumed command not only of a fragile constitutional democracy, but of a crumbling economy as well. Heavy debts and an extreme reliance on oil exports intensified the country's vulnerability to international economic conditions. Furthermore, Ecuador could not rely on OPEC's strength to keep oil prices high. OPEC in the early 1980s was fragmented, its members unable to agree on the distribution of production or prices (*El Comercio* 1982e). Despite Jarrín's moment of glory in OPEC, Ecuador remained a tiny producer, clearly unable to influence the international market or buyers' behavior. Reductions in prices and the volume of Ecuador's oil exports led to a severe decrease in oil income. Oil revenues during the first five months of 1982 were $100 million below what they had been for the same period in 1981 (*El Comercio* 1982e). Other Third World oil producers were also suffering effects of the global recession. The tremendous costs of oil production could not be sustained by poor states with little cash and large debts. Many, particularly in Africa, turned to foreign investors to exploit their oil fields (OGJ 1982b). Third World petroleum exporters who might have acted as OPEC partners to Ecuador in more stable times now became competitors in a buyers' market. Additionally, CEPE could not afford to assume the risk involved in the exploratory drilling. Without further exploration, Ecuador could not continue to export at rates required to meet its debt payments and to finance development. Reserves from already tapped wells were expected to dry up as sources of export crude by the mid-1980s (Corkill and Cubitt 1988:52; Salvador 1991).

These conditions generated a national consensus that the laws restricting foreign investment in Ecuador's petroleum industry had to be changed (J.D. Martz 1987:348). As an editorial in Quito's leading daily, *El Comercio*, put it, "lacking the financial and technological resources, as in the case of Ecuador, the most basic advice is to avoid risky investment and to invite foreign capital" (quoted in J.D. Martz 1987:345). Vice President Hurtado was among the Roldós administration's strongest advocates for the legislative reform. Under his guidance, the administration developed legislation that modified both the tax code for oil profits and the rules by which risk contracts for oil exploration and exploitation would be awarded. President Roldós was less enthusiastic about the reforms, and managed to send the proposed legislation to Congress only one month before his death in May 1981. Once in office, Hurtado placed a high priority on the passage of the proposals. The oil bonanza, during which Ecuador could afford a highly nationalistic policy on foreign investment, was over. The country was severely indebted, running out of known oil reserves, and unable to finance further exploration on its own. It was left to the young president to attract foreign investment to his country's most precious industry.

III. VIEWS ON THE LEGISLATION

The broad national and international agreement on Ecuador's need to attract foreign investment did not translate into a similar consensus on the specific measures and changes to be enacted. Any reform proposal was seen by some as insufficiently strong to attract investment and by others as an affront to Ecuador's sovereignty. This section considers that diversity of opinion, examining the pertinent national and international actors' views on the proposals for greater incentives to foreign investment in Ecuador's petroleum industry. Details on how discrepancies were worked out in the legislation are discussed in section IV of this chapter.

A. The Executive

Osvaldo Hurtado's views on foreign investment in the oil industry changed over time. During the 1970s, Hurtado's political and economic ideology adhered to nationalist principles in foreign and economic policy. Before arriving in elected political office, he had consistently advocated a nationalist approach to foreign investment policy. In a 1977 speech, he applauded the military junta's policies that "guard national sovereignty, [and] protect our natural resources." He specified that "natural resources are the property of the Nation and should be exploited by the State, if it is capable of doing so" (Hurtado 1990c:141). He further blamed Gulf for taking advantage of CEPE, a reference to Gulf's request for nationalization with lofty compensation. In his highly regarded text on Ecuadoran politics, *Political Power in Ecuador*, Hurtado decried the neocolonial ties that keep Ecuador dependent on and vulnerable to multinational corporations (Hurtado 1980:281). These indicators of Hurtado's views towards foreign investment, particularly in Ecuador's precious petroleum industry, lead one to expect that the president would have promoted restrictions on foreign investment and a strengthening of CEPE.

However, the responsibility of national political office and the severity of the Ecuadoran economic crisis tempered his nationalist aspirations. During the campaign, Hurtado authored the Roldós/Hurtado ticket's 21 Point Program for economic reform.

The new vice president, who became director of the National Development Council and the principal economic spokesperson for the administration, personally presented the program to the public in a televised address shortly after the election (Schodt 1987b:138). The 21 Points Program was a critical stage in Hurtado's conversion. The plan called for broad economic and social reforms designed to generate a more equitable distribution of wealth. Accordingly, it advocated increased spending in areas of education and agrarian reform. Realizing that success of the program required new funds, Vice President Hurtado sought to generate foreign exchange through increased exports, particularly of petroleum (J.D. Martz 1987:271; Schodt 1987b:136-39). As a result, the national development plan, touted as a highly nationalistic program, contained some distinctly non-nationalistic measures for increasing foreign investment in oil exploration and exploitation. The ambiguity in Hurtado's proposals for the oil industry was apparent. On one hand, the administration called for funds to finance new well drilling by CEPE, still referred to as "the principal instrument for the State to defend its sovereignty over its national resources" (J.D. Martz 1987:271). On the other hand, it also called for $300 million in new investments to the oil industry, many of which were anticipated to derive from private foreign companies. Hurtado's strong endorsement of this approach signalled a distinct change in his attitude towards multinational corporations, which he had before identified as the instruments of neocolonial domination.

As vice president, Hurtado had attempted to maintain a balance between advocating socially progressive reforms and liberalizing the economy in order to attract foreign funds and bring down budget deficits. As president, the policy ambiguity this approach produced all but disappeared. In his first presidential address, Hurtado made a strong case for national financial belt tightening (J.D. Martz 1987:303-4). Regular implementation of austerity packages followed. He almost instantly intensified pressure on Congress to pass legislative reforms aimed at increasing foreign investment in the petroleum industry. As he explained later, "I supported that law totally, completely" (Hurtado 1991).

A strong mandate from the president was necessary to pass the investment legislation. Hurtado relied on technocratic advisers and emphasized professionalism within his administration (J.D. Martz 1987:380). The president's strategy to obtain legislative reform in Congress was straightforward and centered on two tactics. First, Hurtado widely publicized figures on the depleting petroleum reserves in existing wells, claiming that Ecuador would soon be an importer of oil if new exploration were not forthcoming. Second, the administration lobbied Congress heavily, but in a non-confrontational manner. Hurtado called on his closest and most prestigious advisers, the ministers of Finance, Jaime Morillo Batlle, and Natural Resources, Eduardo Ortega, to pressure Congress to address the legislation favorably and quickly (*El Comercio* 1982c; Hurtado 1991). Together with his willingness to accept some changes in his proposed legislation (see below), this strategy awarded Hurtado a suitable petroleum policy reform package.

Hurtado's transformation from foreign investment critic to supporter parallelled a drastic downturn in Ecuador's economic conditions. The Osvaldo Hurtado who had advocated state control over Ecuador's oil industry during the boom years of the 1970s could hardly have imagined an economic crisis of the proportions he faced in the 1980s. A purely nationalistic position towards oil investment was no longer feasible if he wanted to keep the country financially afloat. Such a policy would have meant a sharp reduction in Ecuador's export revenues. This, in turn, could have led to a default on Ecuador's foreign debt and economic isolation within the hemisphere. Hurtado chose to risk Ecuadoran control over the oil industry in order to avoid these economic disasters. While critics on the left (e.g., Acosta 1990a, 1990b) accuse Hurtado of abandoning his principles, he is best seen as a pragmatic leader, committed to Ecuador's economic development but willing to adjust his methods to the situation at hand.

A final point that helps to explain Hurtado's commitment to increasing foreign participation in the oil industry concerns the policy's domestic appeal. The easing of restrictions on foreign investment paled in comparison to many other harsh austerity measures he implemented. Currency devaluations, subsidy cuts, and restrictions on imports had a direct impact on the lives of many Ecuadorans and therefore elicited much stronger opposition than did legislation aimed at increasing foreign investment. For example, in October 1982 Hurtado implemented the first full austerity package. Opposition was so intense, he explained, that he had to wait until Congress was out of session to announce the measures (Hurtado 1991). In a 1984 interview, Hurtado explained that "when I was going to make the decisions of October 1982, all my collaborators from the political sector asked me not to do it, because they believed that it would produce the fall of the government" (quoted in J.D. Martz 1987:331). That changes in oil investment laws were comparably mild and received widespread support from many sectors of Ecuadoran society (see below) meant that Hurtado had some political maneuverability to pursue them. Whereas he waited nearly a year and one-half to implement austerity measures, he called for oil investment reform immediately after his inauguration. The domestic political climate favored those reforms much more than it did the austerity packages.

B. The Legislature

Nearly all members of Congress agreed that Ecuador needed to increase foreign investment in the petroleum industry. Prospects for executive-legislative cooperation were marred by the eruption of a political crisis between the two branches in the summer of 1982, the period during which the petroleum legislation was debated. Hurtado's minister of Natural Resources, Eduardo Ortega Gómez, was impeached and ousted by Congress. The interpellation was led by two men who were ordinarily political adversaries: the Democratic Left's (ID) Hugo Caicedo and the Social Christians' León Febres Cordero. The former's complaints centered on a drilling contract signed under Ortega's direction between Ecuador and the Mexican-based Pemargo Corporation the previous year. Caicedo criticized the terms of the contract as overly favorable to Pemargo. He claimed that Ortega had violated Ecuador's national autonomy and had broken numerous laws designed to defend the country's interests in oil contracting. Ortega refused to resign when the charges were made public, deciding instead to subject himself to congressional questioning and a possible ouster. Congressional right-wing leader Febres Cordero unexpectedly joined the attack against Ortega months after Caicedo publicized his charges. "The Right, scenting a political kill, had belatedly added to ID charges wholly unrelated complaints over the handling of electricity rates," which were also the Ministry of Natural Resource's responsibility (J.D. Martz 1987:343). Ortega was unable to defend himself against a coalition of left and right forces in Congress, and was forced to leave office in September 1982 (J.D. Martz 1987:342-45).

The scandal occurred simultaneously with the administration's lobbying efforts for legislative reform on foreign investment. Ortega, the subject of the congressional investigation, was one of Hurtado's principal lobbyists. Few Congress members attempted to exploit the Ortega controversy to sabotage Hurtado's quest for legislative reform. Nonetheless, the Ortega censure revealed the fragility of Hurtado's support in Congress. Throughout the summer of 1982, a pro-government coalition dominated Congress. However, the two most important parties in that coalition, Izquierda Democrática (ID) and Concentración de Fuerzas Populares (CFP), quickly abandoned the president on the Ortega issue. Only two members, his own DP and the Roldosista party, voted against Ortega's ouster (El Comercio 1982j). Congress' willingness to pass legislation that conformed with Hurtado's policy preferences was more a product of substantive agreement than of political loyalty to the president. Fortunately for Hurtado, Ortega's ouster occurred after the signing of the reform legislation. In the end, however, it muted national celebration over achieving the reforms (J.D. Martz 1987:356).

That Congress passed the legislation in the wake of the Ortega censure demonstrates its commitment to the reforms. The reform's popularity also pushed Congress to support it. Hugo Caicedo, chair of the Economic, Agrarian, Industrial, and Commercial Committee in the Congress, took the lead in testing public opinion on petroleum legislation. Shortly after Roldós developed the reform proposals, Caicedo distributed a survey to 180 individuals and institutions. Respondents included representatives from the petroleum industry, political groups, labor unions, the Chambers of Production, universities, and government economic and development agencies. The response overwhelmingly favored reform. Ninety-three percent felt that current reserves were insufficient to meet growing economic demands. Eighty-four percent agreed that Ecuador could not afford to finance the needed exploration. Ninety-two percent believed that investors would respect Ecuador's sovereignty, while 85 percent were comfortable that new laws would prove constitutional (J.D. Martz 1987:347-48). These responses provided Caicedo and the left in Congress with an incentive and justification for supporting the administration in its campaign for reform legislation.

Congress' right-wing members, particularly Febres Cordero and his adherents, had favored changes in the investment legislation for years (J.D. Martz 1987:367-68, 381; Pallares Sevilla 1991). The right, ordinarily Hurtado's most vehement critics, acted as his allies on the investment reform issue. Hurtado's main concern was whether the left, particularly ID, would support him. Under Caicedo's leadership, ID agreed that it was vital to attract additional foreign investment to the petroleum industry, but warned that legislation must protect Ecuadoran sovereignty and the state's control over production and investment. As is discussed in section IV below, the legislative amendments that ID proposed did not alter the essential elements of the reforms, namely incentives to foreign investors. President Hurtado was willing to compromise with ID because such a compromise did not entail a substantial change in the new laws (J.D. Martz 1987:351-52).

C. Business leaders in Ecuador

The issue of foreign investment unites Ecuador's private sector leaders (Pallares Sevilla 1991). While the Chambers of Production on the coast and in the highlands regularly disagree on specific policy matters, they remain totally committed to advancing legislation attracting investors from the industrialized countries to Ecuador. This agreement is born in the almost universal adherence among Ecuador's business leaders to a free market ideology which rejects restrictions on foreign investment. Therefore, the campaign for increased foreign investment was a rare example of a policy in which Hurtado received support from Ecuador's business elites. Conservative *El Comercio* columnist Santiago Jervis echoed the sentiments of the business class when he wrote, the "taboo which says that it is patriotic to isolate ourselves and that the flow of transnational capital and technology is an imperialistic act per se, is disappearing so that now even the most extreme preachers in this respect have lost credibility in face of the fact that Communist powers like the Soviet Union and China have not hesitated to resort to this type of organization in order to develop their resources" (Jervis 1982).

Shortly before Congress' vote on the proposed legislation, Quito's Chamber of Commerce released a report criticizing the existing investment laws as "mercantilist" and oppressive to foreign oil interests (*El Comercio* 1982i). The capital's Chamber of Industry similarly released statements favoring the passage of reform legislation. The Chamber stressed that Ecuador would soon become an importer of oil if new exploration were not begun soon. Claiming that Ecuador had suffered "the grave consequences of policies of questionable nationalism," a reference to the military government's petroleum program, the industrialists specifically proposed that twenty exploration plots, ten in the Amazon region and ten off Guayaquil's coast, be opened to foreign investment (CIP 1982:18).

Even Febres Cordero, the right's strongest representative in Congress, did not oppose the executive on this issue. Although they certainly claimed that Hurtado could have done more to promote foreign investment, critics in Congress muted their protests to facilitate swift passage of the bill. Today, business leaders remember Hurtado's initiative in reforming petroleum investment legislation as one of the few things he did right. However, they are quick to remind anyone who will listen that the investment itself did not arrive until Hurtado was out of office (Pallares Sevilla 1991; Terán Terán 1991).

D. Popular groups

The strongest opposition to the opening of Ecuadoran oil fields to increased foreign investment came from the weakest political actors. However, even the anticipated opposition from university, peasant, and labor groups was moderate. Popular groups had focused their protests during the Hurtado years on economic austerity policies. Widespread strikes accompanied most currency devaluations, price hikes, and other measures aimed at tightening Ecuador's financial belt. As popular organizations concentrated their efforts on these immediate threats to their standard of living, unrest as a reaction to investment policy in the petroleum industry was mild (J.D. Martz 1987:280). Foreign investment was too distant an issue to merit this group's sustained attention and commitment, at least during the early 1980s. As a result, no popular mobilization occurred with regard to the proposed legislation (J.D. Martz 1987:368). A few leftists in academic and political circles claimed that Hurtado sold out to multinational corporate interests. These messages did not reflect the national mood and carried little weight in government.

E. The United States government

The US government played no visible role in the petroleum legislation reform process. Hurtado remembers the reform as an entirely national operation, free of interference from international entities (Hurtado 1991). The lack of participation by the US is somewhat surprising for two interrelated reasons. First, US oil companies, particularly Texaco, are principal investors in Ecuador's oil industry. One would expect Washington to exert pressure in their interests. Second, the US government had a history of intervening, at least indirectly, on the oil companies' behalf. In 1974, the US had pressured General Rodríguez Lara's administration to fire natural resources minister Gustavo Jarrín when his policies became too nationalistic and were perceived as intolerant of US investment.

The conditions that had precipitated US intervention in Ecuadoran oil policy in 1974 were not present in 1982. Multinational opportunities in Ecuadoran petroleum fields were improving, not disappearing as was feared during the military years. Ecuador in 1982 was moving away from its nationalist stance. It was politically preferable for the US to allow Ecuador to develop a more pro-investment stance on its own, rather than as a result of US pressure. This was particularly true given that in 1982 a democratically-elected government supported by Washington ruled Ecuador. The combination of electoral democracy and pro-foreign investment policies in Ecuador provided the US government with a public relations bonanza that would have been damaged by evidence of US intervention in Ecuador's domestic affairs. Furthermore, OPEC's decline and falling oil prices were sending Third World oil producers from all parts of the world to Western investors. Direct intervention on those investors' behalf was never needed less.

F. Foreign oil companies

The US also had reason to believe that the potential investors could take care of themselves. As the global supply of oil increased, world petroleum prices decreased and OPEC fell into disarray (J.D. Martz 1987:357). This situation improved the bargaining power of private foreign oil companies within Ecuador and other oil-producing states (OGJ 1982b; Schodt 1987b:120; J.D. Martz 1987:381). This was evidenced by the fact that Hurtado, an economic nationalist, so strongly sought increases in foreign investment for Ecuador's most important industry. Their increased leverage diminished the need for their direct participation in the reform campaign. Falling oil prices and an ineffective OPEC created a need within Ecuador to pursue foreign investment. There was no need for overt pressure on Ecuadoran political officials. "For the multinationals, pressures or overt conflict with the government were superfluous. The realities of the situation were apparent for all to see" (J.D. Martz 1987:381). Other factors also contributed to foreign oil companies' less than fervent pursuit of favorable investment terms in Ecuador. The country remained a tiny producer and a small contributor to any investor's overall profits. This was clear in Gulf's willingness to leave the country when the investment climate became somewhat inhospitable. Furthermore, the multinational firms that remained interested in Ecuador in the 1980s were less concerned with the details of profit levels than with access to future reserves. As political uncertainties in the Middle East intensified, multinational oil companies sought to gain holdings in alternative sources of petroleum such as Ecuador. That the Ecuadoran government allowed them to explore and produce oil was more important than the technicalities of profit levels agreed to in the legislation.

IV. GENERATING THE LAW

President Hurtado was fortunate to have so little dissent on the general principles of increased foreign investment in the oil industry. Generating a bill that Congress would agree to sign was nonetheless difficult (J.D. Martz 1987:348). Representatives of the executive and legislative branches worked to achieve a compromise piece of legislation that would attract foreign investment while not sacrificing all of Ecuador's autonomy over its oil production. Congressional responses and criticism of the administration's proposals were led by ID's Hugo Caicedo, an oil policy nationalist and the same congressional leader who led Eduardo Ortega's impeachment. With the right wing content that this type of legislation was being advanced, Hurtado concentrated on pleasing the left-wing congressional majority.

One month before Roldós's death, the administration advanced two bills. They were sent to the Economic, Agrarian, Industrial, and Commercial Committee, chaired by Hugo Caicedo, for review and modification. A major frustration for the Hurtado administration was the bills' delay in committee. The Committee had failed to respond to the bills a full fourteen months after they had been introduced (*El Comercio* 1982a). Administration pressure and the country's deteriorating oil export performance combined to focus the Committee's attention on oil investment reforms during June and July of 1982.

The first bill considered a revised tax scale on foreign profits. The proposed tax scale was applied to the volume of reserves discovered by foreign enterprises. With the tax scale tied to the amount of reserves expected, profits would be taxed at a rate fixed before drilling began. Caicedo and his supporters responded that reserves were difficult to predict, adding that it would be safer to tax the amount of crude actually produced. Caicedo worried that CEPE, which participated jointly in all production ventures, would absorb a loss if reserves had been overestimated. More important was the possibility of underestimating the amount of reserves. It was possible that the company would produce much more crude than at first anticipated, but would be taxed at a rate commensurate with the initial reserves predictions (*El Comercio* 1982c).

The second bill proposed changes to the types of contracts foreign firms would sign. The executive proposed a system by which CEPE could contract for a foreign firm's services, with the risk assumed by the latter. Payment terms were to be negotiated in individual contracts. In the event of a find, foreign firms would be reimbursed for expenses and paid for services. The bill called for the multinationals to decide whether payment would be in cash or in kind. The administration also proposed that exploration blocs (of 200,000 hectares in the Oriente and 400,000 offshore) be rented out for four-year terms, with a two-year extension option. No single firm would be awarded more than two blocs, and only one in the Oriente. Hurtado envisioned that CEPE would sign these exploration agreements with both private and public petroleum corporations. If no petroleum were found, the property would revert to Ecuador.

Members of the Committee again judged that the terms were too favorable to the foreign firms and would leave Ecuador unnecessarily vulnerable. They considered the option of payment in cash or in kind as needlessly generous. Caicedo clashed strongly with Natural Resources Minister Ortega over the manner in which contracts would be awarded. The congressional leader pushed for a legislative role in the awarding of contracts. Furthermore, Caicedo disagreed with the informality of the awards process. He proposed a formal call for bids on the exploration blocs, arguing that a competitive process would more likely prove favorable to Ecuador (*El Comercio* 1982c).

Throughout June and July of 1982, administration and congressional leaders designed legislation acceptable to both. In early June, the Committee announced its modifications to the bills and sent them to the full Congress for debate. The full Congress approved the majority of the Committee's version of the bills, but sent them back for further review, requesting modifications favoring the administration's objectives (*El Comercio* 1982d). In mid-July, the Economic, Agrarian, Industrial, and Commercial Committee had revisions ready for a second debate in the full Congress (*El Comercio* 1982f). President Hurtado sent a personal representative, René Sánchez, to advocate the bills' passage (*El Comercio* 1982h). By the end of the month, the Congress had approved the legislation and sent it to the executive office.

On 6 August 1982, Hurtado signed two bills that encouraged foreign investment and incorporated nearly all of Congress' demands. In both cases, terms in the new laws were more precise than they had been in the administration's proposals. It was agreed that the tax scale would apply not to the volume of reserves, but to the amount of crude produced. Foreign firms would pay income tax at the same level as other firms, to a maximum of 44 percent. Additional taxes were imposed if production exceeded thirty thousand barrels per day (*El Comercio* 1982g). On exploration contracts, foreign firms contracted for service were allowed to be reimbursed for their expenses in crude. However, CEPE was given the choice of paying for services in cash or in kind. A streamlined system of bidding was implemented that increased competition but also avoided the delays often associated with a formal bidding process. Bids were reviewed by a committee made up of the ministers of natural resources and industry and trade, and Ecuador's inspector general. CEPE's general manager acted as secretary (OGJ 1982c). Furthermore, firms that rented exploration blocs were not allowed to transfer their rights to other companies without CEPE approval.

With the exception of a legislative role in the contracts awarding process, the resultant legislation incorporated all of Congress' wishes. The laws improved the terms under which foreign firms could operate in Ecuador's oil industry, but nonetheless left the state with "considerable authority" (J.D. Martz 1987:352). While the administration had allowed numerous revisions to its initial drafts, the essence of its proposals remained unchanged. The new laws were sufficiently attractive to foreign investors to please the administration, but also adequately protective of CEPE's control over the industry to satisfy more leftist members of Congress. Because Congress, particularly the ID party, agreed with the proposals' general principles, it did not propose modifications which would undermine the objectives of the laws. Hurtado's greatest frustration with Caicedo's participation in the reforms was aimed less at the legislator's substantive critiques than at the delays his involvement entailed (Hurtado 1991).

V. CONSEQUENCES

The Hurtado administration experienced virtually no deleterious effects as a result of the new legislation. The few members of the left in Ecuador who opposed the policy carried practically no political weight, and were therefore unable to affect Hurtado's reputation or ability to govern. Congress, the domestic actor most equipped to sabotage Hurtado's plans for reform, agreed with the executive's intentions and was pleased with his willingness to compromise on the details of the legislation. Business leaders, ordinarily the president's strongest critics, were happy to see him advocating free market reforms. Similarly, the US and multinational firms applauded the liberalization of investment restrictions in Ecuador. This unique expression of national and international policy consensus provided Hurtado with a relatively cost-free legislative process.

It is appropriate, then, to consider the effectiveness of the policy. Even before the laws were signed, an optimistic CEPE general manager, Jorge Pareja, promised potential investors that they could expect a 20-30 percent rate of return on their investments in Ecuador, commensurate with what they would receive in other countries (OGJ 1982a). Congress also sent a special commission to attract foreign participants. By October 1982 administration representatives were attracting global bidders. Eleven blocs were put up for bids. The bidding application process, during which potential investors purchased information required to develop their bids, was open from June through October 1983. A total of twenty-five foreign companies from nine countries bought the materials, which cost $50,000 a piece for blocs in the Gulf of Guayaquil and the

Oriente. This favorable response left Ecuadorans highly optimistic over future investments.

The actual bids were disappointing. Seven companies placed six bids on a total of four blocs in the Amazon and Gulf of Guayaquil. Experiencing the strains of the global recession, many oil companies were cautious in deciding where to invest in risky ventures. Ecuador entered into negotiations and eventually signed exploration contracts with Texaco, Occidental, Esso-Hispanoil and Belco. Although the Hurtado administration worked feverishly to sign the contracts before it left office, numerous administrative difficulties delayed the signing until Febres Cordero took power. The postponement damaged Hurtado's image as the leader of the reform process. Private sector critics claimed that the delay proved Hurtado was not truly committed to the petroleum legislation reform, and that only a strong free-marketeer such as Febres Cordero could enact the new legislation (Pallares Sevilla 1991; Terán Terán 1991).

VI. THEORETICAL APPLICATION

This section applies six theories to two of Ecuador's foreign policy decisions. First, Hurtado's decision that the existent petroleum legislation required reform to attract greater foreign investment is considered. This initiative set the stage for the congressional debate that followed. Second, the compromise laws to which the executive and legislative branches agreed are examined. Congress called for numerous revisions to the administration's reform proposals. For the most part, Hurtado was willing to accept those revisions so long as the essence of the bills remained intact.

A. Compliance

The reform initiative appears to be a case readily explained by compliance. Hurtado, as leader of an economically vulnerable country, developed an initiative that accorded with the preferences of the US and financial institutions in the North. It might be assumed that Hurtado responded to pressure or fear of reprisals from these Northern actors in developing the reforms to investment in the oil industry. Careful scrutiny of this case, however, reveals that the process by which Hurtado called for reform did not follow compliance.

First, a critical element of compliance is that policy-makers in Ecuador act in opposition to their own preferences. Hurtado did not oppose the investment reforms, but instead acted as their primary supporter on Ecuador's political stage during the early 1980s. While he may have preferred that Ecuador were not in such desperate economic straits as to require increased foreign investment, he clearly advocated the reforms as a response to a crisis economy. As Hurtado himself stated, he supported the reforms "totally, completely" (Hurtado 1991).

Second, and in a similar vein, compliance expects that the adopted policy will diverge from Ecuador's national interest and as such will receive a considerable amount of domestic opposition. Again, this was not the case. Although small leftist groups criticized Hurtado's opening of Ecuador's oil fields to foreign interests, on the whole the policy was unique in the amount of domestic political support it received. While many Congress members strove to maintain some Ecuadoran control over oil production and profits, nearly all agreed that foreign investment in the industry had to be increased. If Ecuadoran leaders were forced to adopt the reforms, as compliance suggests, such domestic policy consensus would not have existed.

Third, there is no evidence that the US government or other Northern actors pressured Hurtado to adopt the reforms. Hurtado remembers the political process that led to the reforms as one "in national hands. [External actors] didn't influence us because it was a national initiative. And they knew that I agreed, that I was the party most interested in seeing that law approved" (Hurtado 1991). Northern actors did not need to pressure a government that already saw increases in foreign investment as a necessary economic measure.

Finally, Hurtado's reform initiative, although in general agreement with US preferences, did not specifically favor US investors.

The reforms aimed to attract foreign investors from all corners of the globe, not simply from the United States. Administration and congressional representatives travelled extensively to advertise Ecuador's new reforms. Their trips took them to many countries, including the Soviet Union, Bulgaria, and Britain (J.D. Martz 1987:353). This behavior does not conform with compliance's anticipation that Ecuador, heavily dependent on the United States, would develop specifically pro-US policies. While the Reagan administration did advocate the opening of Latin American economies to foreign investment, it did not receive in Ecuador's reforms any preferential treatment for US investors.

Compliance has even less applicability to the debate between the executive and legislative branches or to the laws' final form. For the most part, Hurtado acceded to congressional demands that he protect Ecuador's autonomy. This action opposed the interests of Northern actors such as the US government and foreign investors, who preferred open access to foreign investment. It is true that, overall, investment regulation did ease up as a result of this legislation. However, given that Caicedo and his colleagues sought to minimize Ecuador's sacrifices to foreign investors, the law would have been more favorable to foreign investors had the Congress not participated in its development. The component of this case in which Congress participated, the laws' generation, therefore does not conform with compliance.

In sum, although Hurtado and other policy-makers in Ecuador did develop reforms aimed at decreasing their own control over the oil industry, this process did not follow compliance. Ecuador during this period was heavily dependent on the United States. But the reforms were less a reaction to dependence per se than to the mere fact that the country was experiencing a financial crisis and desperately needed funds to finance proposed development projects and to pay interest on the foreign debt. Hurtado developed a policy aimed at increasing revenue, but not in a way that ingratiated him to the United States. The link between dependence and policy expected by compliance theory is missing.

It is nonetheless important to recognize that Ecuador, when under financial hardship, developed policies that accorded with general US preferences. Hurtado largely abandoned his 1970s economic nationalism in favor of free market reforms during his presidency. These reforms largely matched what the US and other Northern actors prescribed for Latin America. While Hurtado did not act in direct response to US demands, the fact that his general policy path followed US preferences demonstrates the power of the United States over the regional economy. Ecuador's poverty moved its economic program towards free market reforms, an event indicating that mere economic weakness is sufficient to exact general policy concessions from Latin American states. Indeed, while a high degree of economic dependence on the US did not elicit *specifically* pro-US policies from the Ecuadoran government, economic crisis was sufficient to produce *general* pro-US policies.

This suggests that the notion of US hegemony implicit in compliance theory is inappropriate. Russett's (1985) conception of hegemony as control over outcomes is perhaps a better model for this case. Russett describes a global economy operating by rules that continue to favor the US and other advanced industrialized economies. The continuation of global economic outcomes favoring the US, such as Latin America's adoption of pro-investment policies, is an indicator of hegemony that is more difficult to identify but no less favorable to the United States. Joseph Nye advances a similar thesis. Arguing that the traditional conceptions of power as control over resources have lost their analytical utility, Nye contends that "it is just as important to set the agenda and structure the situations in world politics as it is to get others to change in particular situations" (Nye 1990:181; see also Cox 1987).

B. Consensus

Ample surface evidence exists in Hurtado's reform initiative to support a consensus interpretation of foreign policy. Policy-makers in core and periphery agreed to easing restrictions on foreign investment in Ecuador's petroleum industry. Even before the legislation was signed, CEPE's chief Jorge Pareja was advertising Ecuador's new openness to foreign investors. Hurtado and his advisers emphasized these reforms' mutual benefit to both Ecuador and foreign investors. He abandoned nationalist rhetoric in order to demonstrate his eagerness to receive foreign capital and treat it favorably. As is expected in a consensus-based policy, Ecuador's Chambers of Production supported the reform while many leftist and popular groups largely opposed it.

Missing, however, is the philosophical concordance between the Ecuadoran president and foreign leaders that characterizes a consensual relationship. Consensus theorists claim that peripheral leaders will develop pro-core policies because they share values and ideologies with elites in the core. No such ideological agreement existed between Hurtado and Reagan. Hurtado's political maturation was characterized by a heavy emphasis on economic nationalism, redistribution of wealth, and state control over many aspects of the national economy. Once in office and experiencing a dire economic crisis, Hurtado modified his position on foreign investment and other free market reforms. Nonetheless, towards the end of his presidential term Hurtado sponsored a region-wide conference which attacked the US government and other actors in the North for advancing policies which kept Latin America impoverished and dependent (see chapter 5). This is uncharacteristic of a consensual leader whose personal upbringing and ideology parallel those of capitalists in the North. Hurtado's conditioned agreement with Northern leaders was a result more of economic circumstances and Hurtado's own flexibility than of ideological consensus with US elites.

Consensus cannot account for the legislative outcome. The laws were less favorable to foreign interests than the administration had originally proposed. Congress worked to maintain a sufficient degree of autonomy and earning power for Ecuador, confronting the foreign companies' preferences. Throughout the entire episode, Congress, led by Hugo Caicedo, remained the most counterdependent of all the involved political actors.

C. Counterdependence

Counterdependence does not apply to either Hurtado's initiative or to the laws developed. The key to a counterdependent policy is that it is designed to reduce dependence. Although there were debates as to how much the laws should favor foreign interests, the reforms were always designed to increase the level of foreign participation in Ecuador's oil industry. Though in many arenas a counterdependent leader, Hurtado did not act defiantly in this economic policy. Similarly, while congressional deputies sought to maintain Ecuador's control over the oil industry, they still liberalized the policy in a direction more favorable to foreign investment. Congress acted in a more counterdependent manner than did the president. However, its overall behavior was to increase foreign investment and probable dependence on foreign investors.

D. Realism

The legislative reforms were not designed to increase Ecuador's regional prestige. The fact that Ecuador had to resort to foreign capital to exploit its most precious resource was more a source of embarrassment than prestige. It is more appropriate to ask to what degree the policy fed development, the objective that realist theory expects dependent leaders to pursue.

Hurtado's initiative was designed to foster development, which during his administration was defined principally as economic survival. The president saw increased foreign investment as the only way to acquire oil revenues necessary to maintain the levels of development reached during the 1970s. That development had been financed largely by oil exports. Faced with depleting reserves and CEPE's inability to pay for more exploration, Hurtado's logical reaction was to promote drilling by foreign companies. Hurtado sold the policy as essential for financing the national development plan and, later, to avoid an economic collapse. Concerns for development, then, explain the executive initiative well.

Development also motivated the legislative outcome. Although congressional leaders, particularly Hugo Caicedo, differed with the administration on the specifics of the reforms, they were no less concerned with development. There is little evidence that political rivalries motivated Congress's differences with the president on this issue. Rather, the leftist coalition in Congress was genuinely concerned that the administration's proposals provided the multinationals with unnecessary profit levels and that Ecuador's development prospects would suffer as a result. The compromise legislation signed in August 1982 represented a mix of the administration's and Congress' beliefs. Although different, both sets of views were born in a desire to heighten Ecuador's development.

Both components of this case also meet the condition that Ecuador not overcommit its resources. The reform initiative and legislation required many political resources but few financial commitments. These policies did not require that Ecuador advance any financial, military, or even diplomatic resources beyond its own borders that were not directly designed to earn more funds in the long run. As such, any resources committed to attract foreign investors were seen as a small price to pay for a hopefully large future payoff.

E. Leader preferences

The reform initiative conforms to the leader preferences approach to foreign policy. First, Hurtado clearly demonstrated an interest in this policy. During the campaign and then as vice president, Hurtado was the leader of the administration's call for reforms in oil industry investment. He also remained committed to and in control of the policy through its development and implementation. His willingness to allow Congress to modify certain aspects of the legislation indicates Hurtado's dedication to its passage. That Congress did not attempt to change the essence of the reforms meant Hurtado did not have to sacrifice too much.

Second, the reforms conformed to Hurtado's views. His position on foreign investment in the oil industry is difficult to gauge, because it changed with the passage of time and the deterioration of the country's economic situation. However, Hurtado's behavior indicates he was not a steadfast ideologue but a flexible pragmatist willing to adapt his policy prescriptions according to the exigencies of the current circumstances. In this case, that meant increasing foreign revenues through an expansion of foreign participation in the oil industry.

As was discussed in the compliance section above, it is important to point out that leaders of poor and dependent countries such as

Ecuador are likely to be called upon to be adaptive more often than leaders of wealthy states. Ecuador's economic vulnerability increases the likelihood of its experiencing financial conditions beyond its control. Its leaders therefore are called on more frequently to make difficult adjustments to their beliefs. While Hurtado could have maintained a hard-line nationalist position, this would have invited economic isolation and catastrophe. Hurtado was not afforded the same luxury of ideological purity that leaders of wealthy states have.

Leader preferences does not apply to the executive-legislative compromises which led to the laws. Hurtado demonstrated his willingness to compromise. The final outcome reflected Congress' preferences as much as Hurtado's.

F. Domestic politics

Domestic support for the reform initiative no doubt facilitated Hurtado's decision. A relevant domestic political actor, the business elite, continually supported increased foreign investment in the oil and other industries. However, there is no clear indication that Hurtado's desire to increase foreign investment was a product of business pressure. To an extent, domestic political factors explain the *timing* of the reforms. Upon entering office, Hurtado immediately worked to achieve oil investment reforms, whereas he waited until late 1982 to implement more difficult austerity measures. Overall, however, domestic politics does not explain Hurtado's initiative. The president never publicized the reforms as a policy for which the administration should receive political points from economic elites. Had domestic political considerations motivated Hurtado's reforms, he would have attempted to reap more political benefits of the policy.

Furthermore, there is no evidence that Hurtado's decision to enact the reforms was a reaction to domestic pressure. The strongest domestic pressure emanated from the country's industrial elites. These business leaders would like to take credit for Hurtado's petroleum reform initiative. However, the relationship between the country's capitalist elite and the Roldós and Hurtado administrations worsened throughout the early 1980s. Hurtado had isolated the Chambers from his decision-making circles. His decision to reform the legislation resulted from his calculations that oil revenues would decrease drastically if new exploration projects were not instigated. The Chambers had advocated increased foreign investment throughout the 1970s, when the military government pursued a nationalist oil policy. Hurtado supported the junta's decision in the 1970s, conflicting with the Chambers. That his position later moved closer to that of the Chambers does not reflect his submission to them, but rather was an independent move in reaction to economic necessity.

It might also be argued that congressional support for the reforms prompted Hurtado's call for reform. The flaw in this reasoning lies in the fact that Hurtado could not have known that Congress would support the initiative. Indeed he had many reasons to believe that Congress would oppose him. The reform bills sat in committee for over a year, an apparent indicator of Congressional opposition, or at least apathy. More importantly, Hurtado suffered through the congressional censure and ouster of his trusted minister of natural resources, Eduardo Ortega. If a coalition of left and right forces had joined against Hurtado to oust the minister, they could easily have opposed the investment reforms, which had great potential for political volatility. In the political climate of the time, Hurtado could not have anticipated congressional support.

The legislative outcome, in the form of new laws on taxes and contracts, is explained well by domestic politics. Hurtado's strongest and most powerful opponents on this reform was the legislative bloc headed by ID's Hugo Caicedo. Hurtado's willingness to modify the bills to meet congressional demands indicates his sensitivity to Congress' preferences and power on this issue. Congressional agreement with the thrust of the bills, that foreign investment needed to be encouraged, eased the pain of the administration's compromise. The agreed-upon laws maintained intact the essence of Hurtado's proposals. Nonetheless, the administration gave in to nearly all of Caicedo's demands for change in the terms of the bills, evidence of the role of domestic political actors in the formulation of this foreign policy.

VII. CONCLUSION

Table 9 details the theories' applicability to the two cases presented and reveals that realism is the only single theory that explains both the reform initiative and the legislative outcome. Realism accounts for both, but only in very gross terms. It tells us that policy-makers in Ecuador were concerned with development and acted accordingly. As we have seen in other cases, realism alone cannot explain the *content* of the policies. In both cases, additional theories, leader preferences and domestic politics respectively, are required to explain Ecuador's behavior fully.

Table 9: The Two Reform Decisions

	Compliance	Consensus	Counter-dependence	Realism	Leader preferences	Domestic politics
Initiative	no	no	no	yes	yes	no
Legislative outcome	no	no	no	yes	no	yes

Hurtado's reform initiative presents an intriguing theoretical challenge. He developed an essentially pro-core foreign policy in increasing foreign investment, but neither of the dependent foreign policy theories (compliance and consensus) that anticipate pro-core behavior explains his position. Neither theory describes the process through which Hurtado changed his views as the economic situation worsened. Realism can explain the general policy approach, but leader preferences best accounts for Hurtado's initiative. His behavior mirrored his evolving views on how best to manage the economy. However it is important to remember that his preferences were under pressure. He was not able to implement the perhaps idealistic nationalist economic program he had advocated as a party leader during the economic boom of the 1970s. By the 1980s, he concluded that the adoption of measures that weakened Ecuador's control over its natural resources was preferable to risking the country's financial collapse. While Hurtado's decision was his own, it is better seen as a choice between evils than a reflection of his pure ideological preference.

Realism can account for the legislative outcome, inasmuch as it expects poor countries to generate laws that foster development. However, it tells us little about what specific processes led to those laws. A theory of domestic politics expects that the executive will bend to domestic opposition in foreign policy. While this was the case, the theory does not provide information on the policy's substance. Under what conditions will the executive be willing to give in to domestic political pressure? This is impossible to determine with a single case, but the compromise legislation on petroleum investment provides some tentative answers. Hurtado gave in to Congress on this piece of legislation for two primary reasons. First, he needed congressional approval of the bills. The reforms could not have been passed by executive decree. The necessity of congressional approval led to Hurtado's compromise. Second, the demands from Congress were not very threatening to the administration's proposals. While Congress wanted to place greater restrictions on foreign investment, it remained committed to the broader national goal of increasing investor participation in the oil industry. This general policy consensus combined with Hurtado's urgency to pass the reforms further explain his willingness to compromise with Congress.

Two conclusions emerge from this case. First, it is apparent that, contrary to what compliance theories expect, Ecuador was not forced to adopt specifically pro-US behavior, even during a time of extreme dependence and economic crisis. However, dire economic straits did push Ecuador's leaders towards a generally pro-US position in the adoption of foreign investment reforms. This provides evidence that the United States exerts strong influence over policy outcomes in Latin America even when it does not directly use dependent ties to lobby the region's governments (Russett 1985).

Second, Ecuador displayed two contradictory behaviors. On one hand, the country was pulled in a pro-core direction by economic circumstances largely outside of leaders' control. The severity of the liquidity crisis and the few options for escaping it urged Ecuador's policy-makers to increase foreign investment. At the same time, however, domestic actors, principally in Congress, worked to maintain Ecuadoran control over the oil industry. Externally produced pro-core forces combined with internally generated anti-core forces to produce a reform legislation that increased foreign investment but maintained a high degree of local jurisdiction over the terms of oil investment contracts. That the Ecuadoran government responded to both pressures may be regarded as policy confusion. However, Hurtado's willingness to call for increased investment while at the same time permitting Congress to check the expansion of foreign investment is better judged as adaptability than ambiguity. As a leader of a highly dependent country, Hurtado simultaneously faced demands from external sources calling for economic liberalization and internal sources seeking to maintain Ecuador's control over its own economy. The resultant response to these forces was legislation that incorporated both of their demands.

5   La Conferencia Económica
Latinoamericana

I. INTRODUCTION

IN JANUARY of 1984, the Ecuadoran government under the leadership of Osvaldo Hurtado sponsored the Conferencia Económica Latinoamericana (Latin American Economic Conference, CEL).[1] Presidents, foreign ministers, and their representatives from all corners of Latin America and the Caribbean attended the two-day conference convened to create a united solution to the region's foreign debt crisis. The CEL may appear to the casual observer as just one of many regional diplomatic efforts that quickly fade into obscurity for all but the immediate participants. However, the conference has had a sustained influence on the debt debate in the hemisphere. The CEL was the first in a series of regional debt conferences that maintained pressure on the North for structural change in creditor-debtor relationships.

The Conferencia also presents a considerable challenge to dependent foreign policy theorists. Hurtado's initiative was much more complex than it first appears. At the same time that the Ecuadoran leader implemented a strongly anti-creditor policy, he privately and bilaterally negotiated with creditors, promising them

---

1. Information on the background and chronology of the CEL process, the content of the documents and the participation of different actors is outlined in SENDIP (1984a), and J.D. Martz (1987:327-30).

that the CEL would not threaten debt servicing. This dual policy makes difficult both the implementation of the CEL's declarations and the classification of the policy into a single theoretical category. This case illustrates the competing demands placed on Latin American leaders who simultaneously must appease powerful economic centers in the industrialized bloc and implement policies at home that will reduce economic dependence. These competing demands often lead to contradictory policies such as the one examined in this chapter.

II. INITIATION OF THE CONFERENCE

The CEL was conceived in a February 1983 letter from Osvaldo Hurtado to the executive secretaries of the UN Economic Commission on Latin America (Comisión Económica para América Latina, CEPAL) and the Latin American Economic System (Sistema Latinoamericano Económico, SELA) (SENDIP 1984b:45; J.D. Martz 1987:327). Hurtado later sent the letter to all heads of state in Latin America and the Caribbean, calling for "a renewed economic mindset" to confront the regional economic crisis (Hurtado 1990b:149). Nearly a year later, from 12 to 14 January 1984, the CEL convened in Quito. This section evaluates the global, regional, and domestic political and economic environments that facilitated the conference's enactment. These environments were crucial to the CEL's success. However, without Hurtado's personal motivation and initiative, the CEL would not have occurred.

A. The International environment

On the global front, an increasingly hostile confrontation between North and South was brewing. The South suffered the economic repercussions of the North's recession and correspondingly called for changes in the global economic structure. Such appeals were not new, but arrived with greater intensity in the early 1980s as Third World states found themselves mired in debt and facing a contracted global economy. Numerous groupings of

Southern states convened throughout 1983 to address the global economic crisis. Most notable was the meeting of the Group of 77, a coalition of Third World states, in Buenos Aires in March. The Southern bloc called for a constructive dialogue between the poor and rich nations of the world. The industrialized world, led by the United States and also suffering the effects of a global recession, responded by entrenching its opposition to calls for reform. In May 1983, the world's most powerful industrialized states met in the annual Group of Seven meeting in Williamsburg, Virginia. The US vehemently opposed both reductions in interest rates on loans to the developing world and a cutback on protectionist measures against Third World imports (SENDIP 1984b:138). The confrontation climaxed at the June 1983 UNCTAD (United Nations Conference on Trade and Development) meetings in Belgrade. The industrialized bloc rejected flatly nearly all of the Third World's requests for structural change (SENDIP 1984b:51-52, 139). While the reaction of an industrialized group led by Ronald Reagan and Margaret Thatcher was perhaps not unexpected, it solidified the confrontation that characterized North-South relations in the mid-1980s. From Osvaldo Hurtado's point of view, the North's reaction intensified the need for Latin American unity to manage the economic crisis. The increasingly visible friction between North and South also provided him an opportunity to make his mark on a highly publicized concern among other Third World states.

B. The Regional environment

The regional environment was highly conducive to the debt conference's success. Latin America had become the showcase for the foreign debt problem. By 1983, the total Latin American debt had exceeded US$350 billion (SALA 1989:74). CEPAL labeled 1983 the worst year Latin America had experienced economically in half a century (*El Comercio* 1983k). Latin American leaders realized they were facing more than a short-term liquidity crisis that could be managed with new loans or shuffled off to future administrations. Rather, the problem's resolution necessitated systemic and long-term measures. The CEL was the beginning of Latin America's united effort to manage the region's economic disaster. Some leaders remained reluctant to endorse drastic measures, but nearly all agreed that the situation required integrated regional action. Thus, the economic and political environment in Latin America and the Caribbean favored Hurtado's initiative.

That Hurtado chose to work with SELA and CEPAL leaders on the conference is indicative of the tone the CEL would take. Both organizations were strong proponents of regional and radical strategies to hemispheric problem solving. CEPAL, in particular, had developed into the region's strongest supporter of Latin American economic nationalism. Leaders of advanced industrial states have consistently rejected CEPAL's dependency-based views, considering them statist, harmful to private enterprise, Marxist, and too demanding of Western industrial economies (Klarén 1986:15; Skidmore and Smith 1989:354). Hurtado's cooperation with CEPAL and SELA meant that the Quito conference would be influenced by those who largely blamed Northern actors for Latin American economic difficulties. This approach was endorsed by most of the region's debtors, and increased Hurtado's ability to win wide regional participation in his conference. Raúl Prebisch, CEPAL's first secretary general, participated in the CEL as part of Argentina's delegation, further reinforcing CEL's image as a meeting designed to confront Northern banks and governments (*El Comercio* 1984c).

Latin America had united on issues of importance before. Examples include the founding of regional free trade agreements and the acceptance of John F. Kennedy's Alliance for Progress scheme of development and anti-communism for the Western Hemisphere. Ecuador had never acted as a leader in these or other regional efforts. Why did Ecuador assume responsibility for allying its neighbors in a foreign debt strategy? The success of Hurtado's CEL would undoubtedly prove more difficult than either the Alliance for Progress or the free trade agreements. In those instances, Latin Americans had negotiated and united from positions of strength. In 1983, Latin America was clearly an economic subordinate (SENDIP 1984b:49-50).

The answer lies in Ecuador's status as a "typical" Latin American country and as one that did not suffer from extreme political chaos at the time. First, Ecuador was attractive to outside governments as a nascent, yet firmly established, constitutional democracy (J.D. Martz 1987:329-30; Conaghan 1988:127; Fitch and Fontana 1991:16). The CEL came at the end of Hurtado's administration, nearly five years after the military ceded power. As an example of the region's move towards electoral democracy, Ecuador assumed a legitimacy in international fora that many of its neighbors could not have attained. Second, Ecuador has no reputation, regionally or globally, for extremism on either side of the political spectrum (Corkill and Cubitt 1988:1). It would therefore not present a threatening image to regional participants or international observers. Third, Ecuador's own economic and political history reflected reasonably well the region's recent experiences. Politically, it had experienced military dictatorship but was able to build a strong democratic foundation. Transition to democracy was among Latin America's strongest political themes during the late 1970s and early 1980s. Economically, the country had accumulated a tremendous debt, but was not considered a "basket case" with no prospect for survival. Ecuador's experiences not only illustrated Latin America's problems at the time, but also offered an example of hope for their resolution. Finally, other regional presidents who might have assumed leadership for the continent's debt crisis were consumed with problems at home that inhibited their ability to sponsor such an initiative or damaged their international legitimacy. Argentina still reeled in the wake of its loss in the 1983 Falklands/Malvinas War and was working to consolidate its transition to constitutional rule. Chile, Brazil, and Uruguay, among the most cosmopolitan of the Latin American states, all remained under military dictatorship. Besides the fact that their leaders did not favor multilateral approaches to regional economic problems, their status as military dictatorships undermined their legitimacy on the regional and global scene. Venezuela and Colombia, which at the time could have launched an initiative similar to the CEL, dedicated their diplomatic efforts to the Contadora process for peace in Central America. Mexico, ordinarily famous for its regional leadership, suffered from an economic crisis of enormous proportions that prevented its exercising much influence in the debt area (Lernoux 1987:712). It was Mexico's near default in 1982 that had triggered the regional debt crisis (Atkins 1989:261; Spero 1990:180). To a large extent, then, there was a regional leadership vacuum in which, according to a principal aid to Hurtado on the CEL, "it was easy for Ecuador to take leadership" (Narváez 1991).

C. The Domestic environment

The best Hurtado could hope for from Ecuador's domestic political actors was that they not oppose his initiative. The fact that Ecuador's domestic political actors rarely involve themselves in foreign policy matters not immediately related to their interests facilitated Hurtado's initiation of the Quito conference. Hurtado developed the idea for the conference towards the end of his administration, when most of his opponents were dedicating their efforts to the 1984 presidential elections rather than to opposing Hurtado on matters of little consequence in their view. At a November 1983 meeting of Latin America's Chambers of Industry in Santiago, Quito's representative agreed with the organization's declaration that debt renegotiation should be performed on a bilateral basis. The statement was an apparent warning to CEL leaders against the radicalization of the conference. However, there was no specific reference to the Quito conference (*El Comercio* 1983a). Furthermore, Ecuador's industrial leaders, Hurtado's most likely opponents on this issue, did not feud with the president over the CEL.

The conference was clearly designed to appeal to a regional and global audience. Hurtado exerted very little energy selling it on the domestic scene. Except for grumbling from his most fervent opponents in the private sector, Hurtado's efforts to develop the conference in the way he chose were unhindered (Aspiazu 1991; Hurtado 1991; Terán Terán 1991). The Ecuadoran press was somewhat skeptical of the conference's potential for success, but praised Hurtado for his pursuit of a regional initiative on a critical economic problem (*El Comercio* 1983f; Jervis 1983; Larrea 1983). Congress, labor groups, and the military all remained uninvolved and uncritical.

D. Hurtado's views

That Hurtado's most enduring foreign policy legacy is an attempt to resolve the region's debt crisis reflects his priorities. As vice president, and even more strongly as president, Osvaldo Hurtado had made clear his concern about the debt crisis. The gravity of the country's economic situation had been the principal theme of his first national speech as president. Despite fierce opposition from business and labor groups, Hurtado instituted austerity packages aimed, at least in part, at diminishing the country's debt burden. Hurtado had always advocated a two-tiered approach to the country's economic woes. On one hand he believed that Ecuador and other individual Latin American states needed to enact more economically responsible policies that diminished waste and fostered a healthy balance of payments. On the other hand, Hurtado consistently maintained that the international sector was much to blame for the crisis. In a January 1984 interview, Hurtado said that it was "absurd to think that since 1980 all the Latin American countries fell into the hands of incompetent governments. There must be some international factor, common to all of the continent's states, that is causing the [economic] crisis" (*El Comercio* 1984a). Heavily dependent on export markets and credit sources in the North, he argued, Latin America necessarily suffered from the recession in the industrialized states. Furthermore, it was wrong for creditors to demand foreign debt payments without considering the harsh repercussions it implied for the Latin American people. Hurtado claimed that *both* creditors and debtors were accountable for the region's economic troubles and therefore were both responsible for its resolution (SENDIP 1984b:7-9; J.D. Martz 1987:328; Hurtado 1990b:149-50). While this approach appears reasonable, it earned the president criticism from popular groups that claimed he was submitting to the imperialist creditor states as well as from creditors who opposed his blaming actors in the core for problems the Latin Americans brought on themselves (J.D. Martz 1987:316-19).

In addition to Hurtado's sense of co-responsibility for periphery and core is his belief in integration as a necessary means to regional economic health. The combination of these pieces of economic philosophy is the Conferencia Económica Latinoamericana. As Hurtado envisioned it in early 1983, the conference would be an attempt by Latin American and Caribbean states to coordinate their efforts at resolving the debt crisis. While he pointed out the many areas in which the industrialized world should modify its policies, there was never any mention of a moratorium on debt payments or other measures a more radical leader might have suggested. The CEL, particularly at its inception, was a clear reflection of President Hurtado's views on appropriate responses to the debt crisis.

E. Debt renegotiation

One event which coincided with the development of the CEL could have damaged the conference's success and Hurtado's image as its leader. In December 1983, less than one month before delegates from across the region arrived at the Quito conference, Hurtado's economic advisers travelled to New York City to renegotiate Ecuador's $600 million debt with private creditors for the following year. Three key members of Hurtado's economic team made the trip: Central Bank chief Aberlado Pachano, Minister of Finance Pedro Pinto, and Monetary Board president José Antonio Correa. Their agenda included requests for an extended payment scheme, grace periods, and more favorable interests rates on Ecuador's debt, as well as $500 million in fresh loans (*El Comercio* 1983g, 1983h). They returned to Quito with a refinancing package for the first half of 1984. Refinancing for the second half of the year was conditioned on an IMF stand-by loan, left to be negotiated by a new administration which would assume power in August 1984. Creditors refused to discuss the request for $500 million, claiming that progress should be made on the refinancing before new disbursements were discussed (*El Comercio* 1983j).

It is somewhat ironic that the leader of a multilateral debt convention would bilaterally renegotiate his country's debt so shortly before the conference convened. Ecuador's renegotiation with creditors can be interpreted in two ways. It could be argued that

Ecuador was confronting the banks at a crucial juncture. That Hurtado chose to hold the conference at a time when his own debt problem was publicly evident could be seen as a bold move, an act of defiance in a time of weakness. By meeting with bank leaders at a time when Ecuador was making news as a regional leader on debt, the banks' insistence on bilateral negotiations and their refusal to provide fresh loans would be revealed as unfair and indicative of a need for structural change. On the other hand, it could act as a message to the banks that, despite regional proclamations to the contrary, Latin America's debt would remain a bilateral matter until the banks chose to handle it differently. According to this logic, the banks would have little reason to worry about the conference's repercussions.

The first interpretation falters under scrutiny. The renegotiation was kept quiet in the news. Hurtado and his ministers made no mention of it during the conference. Had Hurtado intended to use the talks with creditors to embarrass them or expose their unfairness, he would have publicized it during the conference and afterwards. To the extent that the second argument views Ecuador's renegotiation as a planned message to world bankers, it also fails. That the debt negotiations occurred so shortly before the conference appears to be more of a coincidence than a planned event. As 1983 came to a close, the Hurtado administration became aware that it could not pay 1984's debt as it was then financed. Short of announcing that Ecuador would not pay, which Hurtado never considered, only a renegotiation could ease the country's debt burden. Those talks had to occur before the end of 1983. Hurtado had originally scheduled the CEL for mid-1983, but could not arrange for the participation of important regional actors until January 1984 (Hurtado 1991). That the bilateral renegotiation occurred nearly at the same time as the multilateral conference is indeed a fluke. But it underscored the weakness of the debtors. Although Hurtado did not intend the bilateral negotiations to act as a message to creditors, it contributed to assuaging creditors' fears that Latin Americans would refuse to pay.

III. ELABORATION OF THE CEL AND THE DRAFTING OF THE DOCUMENTS

A. Pre-conference positions

1. Conference participants

Once President Hurtado had made the initiative for the regional conference, his aides and other regional actors prepared for it. In August 1983 Quito was officially chosen as the CEL's site at a meeting with CEPAL and SELA leaders in the Dominican Republic (SENDIP 1984b:140; J.D. Martz 1987:328). A Follow-Up Committee (*Comité de Seguimiento*) was established to organize the conference and worked to attract as many high-level participants as possible. The effort was led by Hurtado, his special envoy, Eduardo Santos, CEPAL's executive secretary, Enrique Iglesias,[2] and SELA's executive secretary, Sebastián Alegrett (*El Comercio* 1983d; SENDIP 1984b:53-54). Facing these men was the task of organizing the participation of all the region's leaders, from Cuba's Castro to Chile's Pinochet (Hurtado 1990b:150).

The region was essentially divided into two ideological camps (SENDIP 1984b:85; Narváez 1991). The majority, following the strong leadership of CEPAL and SELA, advocated a united front against creditors (*El Comercio* 1984b). They considered the debt a North-South issue brought on by the structural inequalities controlled by power centers in the North. Their solution, therefore, lay in policy changes in the industrialized world. Specifically, this group called for longer payment plans, debt forgiveness, lowering of interest rates, an end to protectionist policies in the North, and an increase in financial flows to Latin America. Hurtado and Ecuador's delegation philosophically belonged to this group.

Opponents to this view included Brazil, and to a lesser extent Mexico, which was financing its economic recovery through a large aid package from the United States. These states, the region's largest

---

2. Iglesias assumed a particularly prominent position in the Latin American debt scene in 1987 when he was elected as president of the Inter-American Development Bank (IDB). His election was conditioned on, and tempered by, the simultaneous appointment of James Conrow, former undersecretary of the US Treasury, as the IDB's vice president (Cypher 1989:71-72).

debtors, worried that the CEL would take on the image of a "debtors' club" and that creditors might punish them for participating (Pérez 1990). A debtors' club could demand that member countries' debts be renegotiated as a group, depriving creditors of their significant leverage over individual debtors. The North also viewed a debtors' club as a threat because of its potential for instituting a payment moratorium (*Wall Street Journal* 1983a).

Neither Hurtado nor his allies in the conference's development ever sought to create a debtors' club (*El Comercio* 1983d, 1983i; Tussie 1988:282; Hurtado 1991). Their proposals called on creditor states and institutions to bear a larger share of the regions' debt burden. They did not propose the measure that would have defined a debtors' club: that renegotiation efforts with creditors proceed on a multilateral basis. Rather, Hurtado suggested that Latin American debtors construct a set of common guidelines to employ in their individual renegotiation procedures. This important distinction meant that each debtor still faced its creditors alone, without its neighboring debtor nations to boost its bargaining power. The difference between supporters of the CEL and those originally reluctant to endorse it was that the latter group demonstrated intense concern that the conference would be perceived as a debtors' club by the North. Wholesale rejection of the debtors' club idea at regional financial meetings in 1983 eased their fears significantly (*Wall Street Journal* 1983a, 1983b, 1983c, 1983d).

It is necessary to recognize that 1983 was still an early point in what later became a clearly chronic debt problem. The Quito conference was the first in a series of regional debt conventions. Debtors in 1983, however, had no experience by which to gauge how their participation would be accepted in the international community. Individual countries had been approaching their mounting debts as short-term liquidity deficits. Creditors had been content to manage the cash flow problems with "rescue packages" (Tussie 1988:283). When Hurtado proposed that a more long-term and coordinated solution be sought, Latin American leaders had to reevaluate their strategy quite significantly. Most states were willing to couch their discourse in the language of Third World unity, comfortable that they would find security in numbers. The region's two largest debtors, however, were wary of incurring the wrath of creditors. This was particularly true of Mexico, which had maintained a strict bilateral approach to renegotiation since its near-default in 1982 (Tussie 1988:284). Brazil's military government was wary of multilateral strategies to regional problem-solving (*El Comercio* 1983d; Kuczynski 1988:151). Like Mexico, Brazil had been saved by an IMF package and emergency loans from the US in 1982 (Tussie 1988:283). Bilateral financing to these states had kept them from bankruptcy and made them wary of regional debt initiatives that creditors might perceive as hostile. Furthermore, the biggest debtors were aware that the sheer enormity of their debts gave them leverage over creditors that smaller debtors such as Ecuador did not have. As Hurtado's financial adviser Alfredo Bergara stated at the 1983 IDB meetings in Panama, "big shots" such as Brazil "knew banks had to support them" and as such were likely to receive favorable treatment from creditors (*Wall Street Journal* 1983a). This reality made the largest debtors even less likely to support a debtors' club which might jeopardize their expected preferential treatment. As it happened, creditors had little or no reaction to the conference. However, the Latin American debtors could not have predicted this at the time they were contemplating their participation in the meetings.

In his original letter, Hurtado encouraged all the region's leaders to participate regardless of their ideological, political, and territorial differences (SENDIP 1984b:48). Santos, Iglesias, and Alegrett travelled extensively, persuading reluctant leaders to attend. Brazil was the most intransigent. Brazil's military government asserted that each states' debt was unique, and therefore should be treated bilaterally. Brazilian leaders agreed to send the foreign minister after the three diplomats assured them the CEL would not constitute a debtors' club (*El Comercio* 1983d, 1983e). By the close of 1983, Hurtado and his aides had secured the participation of all the major Latin American states and most of the remaining countries.[3] Foreign Minister Luis Valencia Rodríguez was instrumental in the

---

3. A list of the participant countries and their representatives is provided in SENDIP (1984b:205-6).

final stages of this effort. At the November OAS General Assembly convention in Washington, DC, Valencia successfully lobbied the region's foreign ministers to send representatives of the "highest political level" to the CEL (*El Comercio* 1983b).

2. Creditors

One would expect that the region's private creditors would be Hurtado's greatest opponents in this endeavor. The US government and the IMF, frequent defenders of creditors' interests, were also anticipated antagonists. Hurtado and his advisers on the CEL were aware that these powerful financial actors were not pleased about the prospects of a regional debt conference (Salvador 1991). Power centers in the North never directly communicated their displeasure to Ecuador's executive office (Pérez 1990). "It was never documented," Hurtado commented, "it was just known" (Hurtado 1991). Luis Narváez, undersecretary of foreign affairs for economic issues and principal aide to the president on the CEL, stated that "there are always subtle ways of doing things," a reference to the method by which the US government and creditor banks communicated their disapproval. Northern actors had made known their views against multilateral approaches to debt negotiations, frequently in international fora such as the recent UNCTAD conference in Belgrade (SENDIP 1984b:139). The presence of a US delegation at the 1983 OAS meetings in Caracas made a strong statement. Creditor banks, the US government, and the IMF had remained on the margins of the regional debt debate in an effort to depoliticize the issue. The Reagan administration remained adamant that the debt was a technical and financial, but not political, problem (Roett 1989:63). The US government had originally decided not to send a delegation to the Caracas meetings in which a united approach to the debt was on the agenda, claiming that the OAS meetings were to be misused for "political or speculative purposes." But the Reagan administration changed its decision when rumors of a debtors' cartel and a moratorium on payments circulated. Representatives of international creditor banks also made their first appearance at a regional economic convention to ensure that the Latin Americans' discussions on debt did not become too radical (*Wall Street Journal*

1983d). These types of activities conveyed the North's opposition to a united Latin American front on debt. It was unnecessary for the US and other actors to risk the political fallout associated with a direct intervention in Ecuador's foreign policy affairs.

Furthermore, actors in the North had little reason to worry about the CEL's prospects. The South's failure at the recent UNCTAD conference to create a cohesive and effective trading bloc against the North was indicative of the Third World's inability to effect global economic change. The Latin Americans were less organized in 1983 than were the UNCTAD leaders. The recent renegotiation with Ecuador was an ideal example of creditors' ability to demand that debt be managed bilaterally. Additionally, key Latin American states' hesitancy to participate in the conference or to endorse strong anti-creditor language indicated that the region was insufficiently united to threaten the North's economic interests. The mainstream press in the North also hindered the CEL's chance for success. Most major US newspapers failed even to mention the conference.[4] The *Wall Street Journal's* coverage was limited to the pre-CEL meetings in which the debtors' club idea was suppressed. The *Journal* portrayed the organizers of the conference, particularly the Ecuadoran government, as weak adversaries of the creditor states. Articles covering the early stages of the CEL's development used the words "debtors' club" in the title, even though Hurtado had consistently rejected that terminology (*Wall Street Journal* 1983a, 1983b, 1983c, 1983d). This type of press coverage denied the Latin Americans favorable access to the financially powerful audience in the North. Furthermore, it portrayed Hurtado's plans as significantly more ambitious and radical than they were.

A final measure weakening the CEL was Ecuador's quiet assurance to the US government, the IMF and private banks that the CEL was not intended as a debtors' club that would institute a payment moratorium. Immediately after sending his February 1983 letter proposing the conference, Hurtado travelled to the US to explain his initiative to government and bank officials. According to

---

4. The only notable coverage of the conference by a major US newspaper were two brief articles in the Los Angeles Times (1984a, 1984b).

a Ministry of Foreign Affairs' annual report, Hurtado told creditors that the CEL "was not about a united front against any country in particular, but [an attempt to find] a favorable solution to the problems of the region, which is in the interest of all and not only in the interest of the Latin American states" (MRE 1984:53). Hurtado and his aides kept their communication with creditors relatively quiet in order to avoid undermining Ecuador's reputation as leader of the CEL. "Nothing was ever written down," explained one of Hurtado's chief aides in the CEL planning stages, "but we told [the creditors and their representatives] verbally that [the conference] was not about not paying the debt, but rather it was about finding a solution to making [the debt payments] possible" (Narváez 1991). Some of Hurtado's public statements also served to allay creditors' fears. For example, in a television interview two weeks before the CEL convened, Hurtado described the conference as political rather than economic, pointing out that heads of state, not ministers of finance, were invited. The distinction meant that Hurtado intended few concrete economic decisions relating to debt payments to emerge. Rather, Hurtado said, the conference was intended to "seek a consensus among Latin American countries that we have common problems, that are more or less equivalent. Upon this foundation we can *later* establish a North-South dialogue" (emphasis added; *El Comercio* 1984a). These assurances further eased creditors' concerns about the CEL and made unnecessary a significant effort to oppose it.

3. Summary

The Quito conference's preparatory stages were therefore characterized by two distinct policy positions on the part of the Ecuadoran government. The high-profile policy was to work with Latin American and Caribbean leaders to acquire significant regional participation. Hurtado was very committed to this part of the policy; that twenty-seven states attended the CEL is evidence of that commitment. However, he simultaneously enacted a second policy of appeasing creditors and their government leaders. Hurtado was fearful that the CEL would not go forward without these assurances and probably worried that Ecuador might receive punitive treatment for its leadership. Hurtado's willingness to allay creditors' fears contributed to their rather subdued response to the conference.

B. Drafting the documents

The government of Ecuador assumed responsibility for drafting two documents to be signed at the CEL. The "Declaration of Quito" stated the participants' views on the debt's origin and resolution. The "Plan of Action" outlined the measures required to resolve the crisis. Hurtado included all regional actors who wanted to participate in the drafting process. His success in generating documents that all participants agreed to sign was largely a function of the fact that this crucial stage was open to a free exchange of ideas. Delegates to the Follow-Up Committee convened in the first week of January 1984 to establish the convention's procedural rules. They agreed to establish two special committees that would debate the trade and financial aspects of the "Plan of Action" draft. These committees met the following week at the Technical Level Meeting (*Reunión a Nivel Técnico*). Furthermore, the Follow-Up Committee agreed that during the two-day general conference, the first day would be dedicated to debate in which only heads of each delegation would speak, while the second day would be spent adopting and signing the documents. The Technical Level Meetings were devoted specifically to the modification of Hurtado's draft documents. Few changes were made (SENDIP 1984b:204-5). Hurtado had designed the documents with sufficient sensitivity that all agreed to sign with little protest. However, the fact that all delegates were welcome to participate in the pre-conference meetings was probably the most significant facilitator of the process.

The conference went smoothly. Twenty-seven countries were represented, nine by heads of state. The region's four largest debtors, Argentina, Brazil, Mexico, and Venezuela, all sent foreign ministers (SENDIP 1984b:206). The secretary general of the Organization of American States and the president of the UN General Assembly also attended. Hurtado's opening speech set the tone for the conference. He situated the region's debt crisis firmly within the context of the international recession and placed primary responsibility for the problem's resolution on banks and governments in the North. Hurtado argued that the North must change its financial, trade, and investment policies (SENDIP 1984b:207). Subsequent speeches by other delegates echoed Hurtado's sentiments. Even Brazil's foreign minister, whose participation had been under question, used the opportunity to remind the world that "the weight of adjustment should not fall exclusively on the debtor countries," and that the primary cause of the crisis was recession in the North (SENDIP 1984b:221-22).

The "Declaration of Quito" and the "Plan of Action," signed during the second day, spoke of an economic crisis of immense proportions and assigned a series of tasks to their creditors (SENDIP 1984b:264-91). First, lenders were told to lower their interest rates and to extend debtors' payment periods. The documents made particular mention of the significant increase in interest rates, and the extent to which interest payments cut into funds that could otherwise be used for development and economic recovery. Second, debtors called for fresh financial resources to ease the pain of austerity programs. Third, they asked for a linkage between debt payments and receipt of development financing from the North. Fourth, they called for the industrialized world to reduce its protectionist trade barriers so that Latin American exports would be more readily received. Increases in trade revenues, the participants argued, would improve the debtors' ability to pay. Fifth, they called for an increase in the lending resources of the IMF and greater accessibility for Latin America to that institution. Finally, the industrialized world was called upon to provide more funds to the United Nations and the Inter-American Development Bank. These lending institutions accept the South's economic and political arguments more readily than do the IMF and the World Bank, and are therefore more likely to be generous with troubled Latin American economies (Payer 1986).[5]

---

5. Indeed, in April 1986 the Reagan administration called for modifications in the IDB's loan-granting structure. The US called for an increased role for the US government and demanded that loans be granted on terms similar to those used by the IMF and World Bank, namely that the recipient countries institute pro-market economic reforms and liberalize their trade policies (Payer 1986). This pressure peaked in 1987 when the Reagan administration's failure to support the IDB led to a cut in the bank's

For their part, the Latin American leaders agreed to strengthen regional economic cooperation, hardly a measure likely to impress creditors. They promised not to increase intra-regional trade barriers, and developed a list of products for which Latin American commercial partners would receive preferential tariff treatment. They also committed themselves to reviving already extant regional trade institutions such as the Andean Pact and the Latin American Free Trade Association (LAFTA). In light of these rather modest and sacrifice-free measures, it could be argued that the Latin Americans made no concessions to their creditors. They merely demanded better treatment from the North while agreeing to unite their efforts at home. But the reality remained that each delegate returned home to a country still under the obligation to pay its debts, mostly according to the terms established in bilateral talks with lenders (Fishlow 1985:136).

C. Post-conference negotiations

During the CEL it was agreed that President Hurtado would assume responsibility for ensuring that the documents were distributed to "those who have high-level international decision making ability" worldwide (SENDIP 1984b:315; J.D. Martz 1987:329). Hurtado took this task very seriously. He dispatched his Foreign Relations minister, Luis Valencia Rodríguez, to European capitals to announce and sell the CEL proposals. The more important trip, to Washington, Ottawa, and the United Nations, was made by former Ecuadoran president, ambassador to the United States, and OAS general secretary Galo Plaza Lasso. As a diplomat educated in the US and with a pro-US reputation, Plaza was a non-threatening messenger, a person with whom Northern leaders could negotiate (Carrera 1990:51). Plaza delivered the documents calling for radical change in creditor behavior. His speeches, however, couched the

loans by $700 million from the previous year. At the same time the US promised new funds to the IDB if the bank agreed to condition its loans on recipients' structural adjustment. After an administrative restructuring which included the acceptance of former US secretary of treasury official James Conrow as IDB vice president, the bank decided in 1988 to condition 25 percent of its loans in the manner desired by the US (Cypher 1989:71-72).

harsh message in rather acquiescent terms. Above all, he communicated, the CEL was not born in a spirit of confrontation. Rather, its developers hoped to generate a constructive dialogue between creditor and debtor states. Plaza did not back down from the language of the CEL documents. He reiterated the need for creditors to ease their interest rates and terms of payment. But the atmosphere surrounding his discussions with leaders in the US was significantly less conflictual and accusatory than conversations during the CEL had been (MRE 1984:336-37).

The response to Plaza in Washington was cool. President Reagan refused to meet with him; Secretary of State Shultz received him instead. Hurtado attributes the brush-off from Reagan as a response to Hurtado's insistence on reestablishing relations with Cuba in 1981. Hurtado had disregarded a personal telephone call from George Shultz urging him not to reinstate diplomatic ties with Havana, an action he believes spurred Reagan's rejection of Plaza (Hurtado 1990b:153; 1991). Shultz diplomatically called the CEL useful and productive, but failed to agree to any policy changes. Plaza's reception in Canada was more favorable. Prime Minister Trudeau agreed that the debt problem required a global effort, as opposed to the strictly bilateral approach favored by the US. Foreign Minister Valencia received a warm, but non-committal response from leaders in industrialized Europe. As expected, the response from Eastern Europeans and Third World leaders was positive (J.D. Martz 1987:329). This most enthusiastic group, of course, had no power to change the structural relationship between Latin America and its creditors.

IV. EXAMINATION OF THE DECISION

The extent to which the CEL both failed and succeeded was a function of Hurtado's simultaneous catering to the initiative's supporters and opponents. From beginning to end, Hurtado attempted to please most Latin Americans with strong North-South and anti-creditor language. At the same time, he made sure that those same creditors did not feel threatened. The strong pro-South language in the CEL documents was permitted because Hurtado had already assured creditors that Ecuador would not encourage its neighbors to cease payments. Once the creditors were placated with this assurance, Hurtado was free to proceed with a political line that would gain wide popularity throughout the region.

The positive consequences of such an approach were that the conference took place with little interference from outsiders. Hurtado was commended for his ability to unite the region on a question of such sensitivity and great importance. He displayed regional leadership during a time when multilateral approaches were gaining favor as a means to confront the United States on crucial hemispheric matters. The Contadora Group had organized a front against the Reagan administration's policies in Central America. Hurtado began a similar movement to weaken the power of creditors in his debt-ridden region. The very fact that he united the region in its first effort to pressure for structural modification in the hemisphere's financing was worthy of considerable recognition.

However, placating both creditors and debtors also had negative repercussions. By letting the North know that Latin America would not create a debtors' club or threaten a payment moratorium, Hurtado essentially precluded any real success for the CEL's proposals. The conference's participants clearly indicated that creditors and their representative governments bore responsibility for the crisis and its resolution. Their willingness to modify their behavior and expectations was a requisite for the Latin Americans to achieve the structural change demanded. Such behavioral modification was highly unlikely from creditors who were promised beforehand that they would be paid regardless of what was decided at the CEL. Hurtado's assurance to creditors denied the Latin Americans any leverage over their creditors. The behind-the-scenes negotiating may have helped the CEL to run smoothly, but it essentially relieved creditors of any responsibility and guaranteed that the CEL documents would have little more than rhetorical impact.

The contradictory policy was necessary for the CEL to convene. However it was also an expression of Hurtado's somewhat contradictory beliefs on the debt question. He consistently maintained that the industrialized world holds significant responsibility for the debt problem, but also argued that debtors need to act more responsibly. Hurtado was undoubtedly displeased with having to negotiate privately with creditors on the CEL. However, if this had not been necessary, it is unlikely that he would have called for a payment moratorium or other measures that would have outraged lenders in the North.

The contradictions in the way Hurtado approached the CEL are also illustrative of Ecuador's status as a dependent state. In order to remain economically viable, at least in the short-term, Ecuador could not alienate the United States or its private creditors. To do so would risk being cut off from financial resources or preferential trade treatment, leaving Ecuador vulnerable to potential economic ruin. As a person who considered himself a responsible leader, Hurtado would not have imagined such an approach. On the other hand, as a leader of a dependent state, Hurtado was also responsible for diminishing that dependence whenever possible. The CEL was an attempt to unite regional actors so that together they would comprise a more powerful negotiating bloc. In the long-term, this policy would serve Ecuador's interests. Hurtado's simultaneous pursuit of his country's short-term and long-term interests generated a debt policy that contradicted itself.

V. CONSEQUENCES

A. Direct consequences

The Quito conference brought about very little direct and noticeable change. Concrete results in the form of modifications in the industrialized world's behavior were nonexistent. Nor did creditors enact any punitive measures against Ecuador or other participants. Latin America's debt continued to be negotiated on a bilateral basis (Fishlow 1985:136; Payer 1986; Tangeman 1988). There was some strengthening of intra-regional economic cooperation and trade barrier reduction, but for the most part the CEL achieved little beyond the fact that it occurred.

A primary reason for the lackluster performance is the conference's timing with respect to Ecuadoran domestic politics. The CEL took place less than a month before Ecuador's first round of presidential elections and only seven months before Hurtado left the presidency. The new president, León Febres Cordero and his foreign minister, Edgar Terán, were among Hurtado's staunchest detractors and political rivals. Both were wary of multilateral activity and objected to the Quito meeting. The success of the CEL proposals required an extended commitment from its participants, particularly its leader. Not only did Febres Cordero fail to follow up on the CEL, he disallowed any mention of the conference in Foreign Ministry meetings and documents (Hurtado 1990b:152; Pérez 1990). Without any mention of it in the press and lacking continued leadership from Ecuador, the CEL fell relatively quickly into national and regional obscurity.

B. Subsequent debt meetings

The most important of the CEL's accomplishments was that it began a process by which Latin American leaders conferred and cooperated on debt questions. Shortly after the Quito conference and in response to its minimal impact on creditor behavior, the leaders of Argentina, Brazil, Colombia, and Mexico called for a second conference to discuss the region's debt. Additional participants included Bolivia, Chile, the Dominican Republic, Ecuador, Peru, Uruguay, and Venezuela (Atkins 1989:262). The conference was held in Cartagena, Colombia and occurred simultaneously with the June 1984 Group of Seven meeting in London. Most noteworthy of the meeting's accomplishments was a letter sent to the leaders of the industrialized countries in London in which the Latin American leaders called for a summit meeting to establish a "constructive dialogue" between debtor and creditor states (Roett 1989:60). Leaders in London responded that they would under no circumstances enter into such negotiations. Undaunted, the Latin leaders formed the Cartagena Group (also known as the Cartagena Consensus) and agreed to meet regularly to treat the region's debt in a multilateral manner.

A mere two months remained of Hurtado's presidential term when the Cartagena meeting was held. Ecuador's delegate participated in the formation of the Cartagena Group and signed the documents calling for modifications in creditor behavior. The language of the Cartagena Consensus was nearly identical to that of the CEL.

During the meetings, Ecuador's delegates worked to keep the CEL fresh in participants' minds and reminded them that Hurtado's initiative began the process of regional cooperation on debt. The CEL certainly facilitated the Cartagena process and to that extent was successful in fostering continued regional cooperation on foreign debt matters. Hurtado, however, was angered and frustrated by the Cartagena meetings. He felt that Cartagena happened too quickly after the Quito conference, robbing his own initiative of its deserved regional impact. Hurtado claimed that the Cartagena Consensus began as a "simple meeting about financing," which its formulators turned into a debt conference because it would enhance their regional reputations and political careers (Hurtado 1990b:151-52, 1991). Hurtado's desire to be remembered as the region's foremost leader on the debt question denied him the capacity to champion the CEL as a successful beginning to a series of regional debt conferences.

Hurtado's distrust of its members' motives notwithstanding, the Cartagena Group demonstrated commitment and creativity towards improving Latin America's bargaining position on the debt throughout 1984 and 1985. Like the CEL, the Cartagena Consensus avoided language of a debtors' cartel. This generous concession to creditors made clear, leaders in Cartagena made specific proposals for improving the outcome for individual debtor negotiators (Tussie 1988:288-91). The Cartagena Consensus faded away in 1986 and was replaced by the Group of Eight.[6] The group, which first met in Acapulco in November 1987, comprised Latin America's "big three" (Argentina, Brazil, and Mexico) but conspicuously did not include Ecuador. Those familiar with President Febres Cordero's disdain for multilateral action knew not to expect Ecuador's participation in the Group of Eight. Like the CEL and the Cartagena Consensus before it, the Group of Eight failed to unite in a demand for multilateral debt rescheduling, but it did agree to advance a common set of objectives to be followed in individual negotiations (Tangeman 1988; Roett 1989:61).

As this discussion reveals, Hurtado's Conferencia Económica

---

6. The Group of Eight's members include Argentina, Brazil, Colombia, Mexico, Panama, Peru, Uruguay, and Venezuela.

Latinoamericana was the forerunner of an impressive regional movement to unify around debt policy. To evaluate the impact of Hurtado's initiative, then, it is necessary to consider the effectiveness of the Cartagena Consensus and the Group of Eight. The over-whelming academic response is that such multilateral initiatives have had little or no impact on the share of the burden between creditors and debtors (see, e.g., Feinberg 1988:60; Kuczynski 1988; Roett 1989; Schmitter 1989; and Golub 1991:200). Numerous books, edited volumes, and articles covering the Latin American debt crisis fail to mention these efforts.[7] The almost universal critique is that Latin American debt initiatives have rarely moved beyond rhetoric to meaningful proposals that creditors would sincerely consider. Worried about angering creditors and reluctant to subordinate national interests to regional concerns, the debtors have been unwilling and unable to effect real change (Kuczynski 1988:151). Under this interpretation, it is difficult to commend the multilateral initiatives or Hurtado for starting the process.

This type of sweeping dismissal of Latin American debt initiatives is inappropriate. A closer look at Latin American debt politics in the 1980s reveals that the CEL and its successors did have an impact on rescheduling outcomes and on the nature of the debt debate in three important areas. First, Hurtado deserves credit for adding a new player to the regional debt cast. When Mexico chose not to rely on its neighboring debtors during its crisis in 1982, a strong precedent was established by which debtors would reschedule individually (Feinberg 1988:59). This contrasted with the creditors, who joined together in steering committees and international organizations such as the Paris Club during negotiations (Tussie 1988:285). The CEL brought a new player to the game—regional debtor associations that proposed pro-debtor negotiation terms (Walton and Ragin 1989:216). Their mere existence shifted the balance of power towards a more equal distribution between creditors and debtors.

Second, the Quito conference for the first time made an unequivocal statement that the region's debt was a political problem. Before

7. Examples include special issues of Latin American Perspectives (1989) and Journal of Interamerican Studies and World Affairs (1986). Also see ECLAC (1985); Wiarda (1987); Brock, Connally, and González-Vega (1989); and Stallings and Kaufman (1989).

1984, creditors had succeeded in maintaining that the debt was a financial and technical problem to be handled by bankers and economists, not political leaders (Griffith-Jones and Sunkel 1986: 113; Tussie 1988:286). That the CEL, the Cartagena Consensus, and the Group of Eight were attended by high-level *political* leaders strongly communicated Latin America's message that technocratic approaches would no longer suffice. The groups maintained constant pressure on creditors and their governments and kept the debt question active in the political hemispheric agenda (Van Klaveren 1990:114).

Finally, and most important, the various debt conferences led to some distinguishable changes in individual countries' debt rescheduling. The Cartagena Consensus is credited with making it difficult for creditors to provide favorable rescheduling terms to one debtor and not the others (Griffith-Jones and Sunkel 1986:113; Tussie 1988:296). Diana Tussie convincingly argues that debtors used the multilateral initiatives as a back-up threat to extract favorable concessions from creditors during negotiations. Worried that a debtor might resort to a debtors' cartel if rescheduling terms were not generous, creditors were more likely to sweeten their offers to keep individual debtors from resorting to a moratorium (Tussie 1988:297; see also Feinberg 1988:59). Pedro-Pablo Kuczynski, a former World Bank official, disagrees, arguing that the threat of a debtors' club made creditor concessions less likely. Kuczynski contends that creditors would not extend special concessions to an individual debtor for fear they would have to do the same for the rest of the region (Kuczynski 1988:151). That creditors softened the terms of rescheduling in the mid-1980s provides evidence in support of Tussie's argument.[8] The most visible effect of the multilateral initiatives was US secretary of treasury James Baker's debt plan. The Baker Plan, instituted in 1985, called for commercial banks and international development organizations to disburse a total of $29

---

8. Creditors appeared to have heard the calls of the CEL and the Cartagena Consensus in 1985. Rescheduling agreements in that year were characterized by a decrease in interest rate spreads, a reduction in the cost of credit, a significant drop and, in some cases, the elimination of costly rescheduling commissions, and longer amortization periods (Tussie 1988:293).

billion in new loans to the world's fifteen largest debtors, most in Latin America. Loans were conditioned on economic adjustment policies by recipient states. However, Baker's plan differed from previous IMF-sponsored packages in that it acknowledged that economic policy should promote economic growth, not merely austerity aimed at maximizing debt service (Payer 1986; Roett 1989:61; Tussie 1988:295). This concession was seen as a direct response to the Cartagena Consensus' emphasis on the need for growth and development within the region.

C. Summary

The CEL's directly tangible consequences, positive and negative, were few because few immediate changes resulted from the conference. Few analysts or regional leaders remember to mention that the Quito conference preceded the Cartagena Consensus and the Group of Eight. President Hurtado continues to contradict himself on the conference's success. On the one hand, he states that it was very important, the innovative agreements reached having wide-ranging implications. On the other hand, he concedes that the conference achieved very little, given that his successor refused to support the policy (Hurtado 1991). Nonetheless, the CEL was the first in a series of regional meetings that has contributed to keeping Latin America financially afloat. It also remains a rare example of Ecuadoran leadership in Latin American integrative efforts. As such it continues to be a source of pride within the Foreign Ministry and for former president Hurtado, who called the conference "perhaps the sole foreign policy initiative in Ecuador's diplomatic history that has been successful" (Hurtado 1990b:149).

VI. THEORETICAL APPLICATION

What appears to be a straightforward and uncomplicated regional conference emerges as the result of a series of complex foreign policy decisions. This section examines three distinct policy choices that resulted in the Conferencia Económica Latinoamericana. First is Hurtado's initiative to hold the conference. Second is the method he used to design the documents that were signed at the conference. Finally, this section considers the quiet policy of appeasement to creditors and their representative governments in the North. This element of the policy makes the CEL as a whole impossible to classify as a single type of dependent foreign policy. At the same time Hurtado was pursuing a bold regional initiative that decried the unfair practices of lenders, he promised those same lenders that the CEL would not generate a payment moratorium.

A. Compliance

Hurtado's decision to hold the Conferencia Económica Latinoamericana does not conform with compliance theory. While there was a clear conflict of interests between Hurtado and creditor states, the decision to hold the conference did not favor creditors or their representative governments. Similarly, the CEL's documents do not conform with compliance. The region's leaders expressed solidarity in confrontation with the North. Hurtado allowed all Latin American and Caribbean delegates to participate in the document drafting, but did not invite representatives from the North. He clearly sent a message that this was a regional initiative designed to challenge the creditor states, not to include them.

The fact that Ecuador privately promised creditors no drastic action would be taken maintains a number of elements that accord with compliance's preconditions and expectations. First, the issue was salient to both parties. Hurtado felt strongly about the debt problem, as is evidenced in his many public addresses and his policy priorities throughout his administration. The US government and others creditors were becoming increasingly concerned with the prospect of a Latin American debtors' club, as evidenced primarily in their attitudes at the 1983 UNCTAD meeting in Belgrade and the OAS meetings in Caracas. Furthermore, Latin America's foreign debt is unquestionably salient to creditor banks who together have billions of dollars at stake. There is also some evidence of indirect pressure from creditors to keep the CEL leaders from becoming too radical in their pronouncements. Leaders in Ecuador knew what the US position was without the latter having to proclaim it publicly. The Ecuadoran government's quiet assurances to creditors can be interpreted as a reaction to this pressure.

But for compliance to apply, Hurtado's promises not to threaten the North would have to have been *against his own wishes*. Compliance can only occur if a leader is forced to do what he otherwise would not have done. Hurtado's insistence that his aims never included a generation of a debtors' club, a suggestion for a moratorium on payments, or to threaten creditors undermines this theory's applicability. It is necessary, however, to investigate Hurtado's motives in this regard. To a large extent, his determination not to anger creditors is a function of his vulnerability to them. He undoubtedly would have preferred to move ahead with the CEL without having to placate creditors on the side. To the extent that his policy of appeasement was born in fear of the financial repercussions of angering creditors with his leadership of the CEL, Hurtado indeed complied with those creditors' wishes. The lender-placating element of the CEL is explained well by compliance.

B. Consensus

Consensus cannot account for any of the CEL decisions. The initiative, as well as the elaboration of the documents and the language used in those documents, do not exhibit any of the indicators of North-South elite cooperation. Most importantly, the conference diverged from core preferences. These phases of the CEL were clearly oriented to fomenting South-South cooperation, a concept inconsistent with the consensus approach to foreign policy.

Nor do the Ecuadoran government's promises to creditors that the CEL would not constitute a debtors' club illustrate consensus. These promises were not made from within a context of mutually beneficial economic collaboration. Rather, the Ecuadoran government had to placate lenders to insure against attempts to sabotage the CEL or to punish Ecuador for sponsoring the conference. The relationship between debtors and creditors remained antagonistic throughout the process, and therefore cannot be categorized as an example of the elite accommodation that typifies dependency theory's portrayal of US-Latin American relations.

A possible argument in favor of the applicability of the consensus model to the appeasement is the policy's potential for favoring local economic elites. It could be argued that Ecuador's bourgeoisie favored a policy of appeasement so that they would not be cut off from international credit. According to this argument, domestic elites would lobby the administration to execute the appeasement policy. A brief review of the evidence undermines this notion. There is no indication that domestic economic elites lobbied the administration. Furthermore, the business sector, particularly importers concentrated in Quito, suffered from the country's debt burden and the austerity imposed by creditors and the IMF. No consensus existed among the country's economic elite that Hurtado's CEL proposals were inappropriate. Only a very unified business sector could have influenced Hurtado so late in his administration.

C. Counterdependence

Hurtado's decision to sponsor a region-wide conference on foreign debt conforms well to the counterdependent interpretation of dependent foreign policy. There would have been no need for the conference had Latin America not been dependent and economically vulnerable. Hurtado conceived this policy with the reduction of that vulnerability in mind. His intent was to unite the region so that debtor nations would possess greater bargaining power vis-à-vis creditors. Hurtado publicized the conference as a purely Latin American initiative, one designed to reduce the region's dependence. He made clear that representatives from creditor banks or governments were not invited. Also, there is evidence that actors in the industrialized states resisted the policy in a manner commensurate with the threat posed by the CEL. The US government and many creditor banks communicated their disapproval of the conference in a myriad of ways, including proclamations at global economic conferences. However, bank and government leaders did not forbid the conference, which they perceived as little more than a rhetorical seminar with little power to change the terms of the debtor-creditor relationship.

The manner in which Hurtado constructed the CEL documents was also quite counterdependent. By excluding Northern participants while including all members of the Latin American and Caribbean community in the drafting process, Hurtado communicated a message of independence and defiance. The exclusion of Northern actors also increased the likelihood that the documents would carry a strong anti-creditor theme. Similarly, regional actors were more likely to acquire a sense of unity and strength as a regional group under the drafting conditions Hurtado established. Had Northern actors participated, they could have influenced individual Latin American states to curtail the CEL's objectives and weaken the documents' language. By including only regional representatives, Hurtado increased the probability that the participants would acquire a sense of solidarity and defiance against creditors.

The appeasement component of the policy contradicts counterdependence. Rather than a public act of independence, Hurtado's assurances to creditors privately illustrated the economic dependence that tied Ecuador to Northern banks. These assurances provide evidence that the Ecuadoran government needed to submit to actors in the core precisely because of their dependent relationship. That Hurtado placated creditors indicates his understanding that Ecuador's dependence made it impossible to confront the industrialized world on this issue without risking reprisals.

D. Realism

It would at first appear that realism accounts well for Hurtado's decision to hold the CEL. The policy would benefit Ecuador's regional leadership status and, to a lesser extent, foster development. Closer scrutiny, however, reveals that the CEL was motivated more by Hurtado's *personal* desire to establish himself as a regional leader, than by a concern for Ecuador's national reputation or status. Hurtado has consistently called attention to the fact that the CEL was the product of his personal initiative, rather than publicizing the conference as the result of Ecuador's rightful status as a regional leader. As the forerunner to the Cartagena Consensus and the Group of Eight, the CEL could be considered and promoted as a highly influential regional event. That an Ecuadoran president began that process is a significant achievement for a state that so rarely features in regional and global negotiations. However, Hurtado remains mostly dissatisfied with the outcome of the Quito conference, largely because he perceives that his own role is underappreciated.

Nor did Hurtado sell the CEL to his domestic audience as a measure which would directly enhance Ecuador's development. Surely any resolution to the debt would eventually free up funds for development projects. The CEL language did refer to the fact that debt service constituted an unfair portion of Latin America's financial resources, resulting in a neglect of critical development concerns. However, Hurtado and his aids never stated specifically which development goals the CEL would serve. They also failed to pursue domestic political points by portraying the CEL as a necessary component of Ecuador's development process. Though development was certainly a long term benefit if the CEL were successful, it was not a primary motivator of the policy.

Hurtado did not commit resources beyond his means in initiating the CEL. As a diplomatic initiative, the CEL did not require financial or other resources that Ecuador lacked. Instead, the initiative went forward specifically because the Ecuadoran president was willing to commit his administration's diplomatic resources.

The drafting process similarly did not require resources that Hurtado was unable or unwilling to commit. This is the only realist criterion that the document drafting process adheres to. As a united regional effort, the CEL could not advance Ecuador's development more than its neighbors.' Hurtado's pursuit of a multilateral initiative blocked his ability to serve Ecuador's interests solely. He deliberately included all the region's leaders in the drafting of the documents, thereby diminishing the possibility that the document would cater to Ecuador's specific needs in the debt problem. The document procedure also did little to improve Ecuador's regional status. If Hurtado felt that a policy of inclusion would facilitate the CEL's success, it was because he was concerned with his own regional reputation rather than that of his country. Hurtado, not Ecuador, was praised for being flexible and creative. Hurtado's successor, Febres Cordero, quickly erased that image from the executive office.

The policy of appeasing creditors does not conform to a realist interpretation of dependent foreign policy. The appeasement entailed essentially no resource commitment and thus conforms to the criterion of realism. However, Hurtado's relieving creditors of responsibility for instituting structural changes denied the success of the conference's resolutions. A failed CEL could only damage Ecuador's opportunities for rising as a regional leader or improving its level of development. It could be argued that the appeasement policy was necessary for the CEL to go forward, thereby creating the possibility for Hurtado to achieve regional status. Two arguments reject this reasoning. First, as explained above, such a policy would be aimed at improving the personal reputation of a leader rather than the regional prestige of a nation. Second, Hurtado faced the risk of exposure of his private appeasement policy. Had it been publicized, his stature as leader of the CEL would have suffered. Furthermore, Hurtado's promises to creditors subverted any chances for real pro-debtor change in the region, and therefore damaged Ecuador's long term development prospects.

E. Leader preferences

Hurtado's CEL initiative strongly reflected his personal beliefs. The CEL conformed to his advocacy of multilateral cooperation on an issue that was of central personal concern to him, the foreign debt. Moreover, the president was in control of the policy from beginning to end. Once he formulated the idea for the conference, he and close advisers contacted interested parties throughout the hemisphere. Hurtado personally travelled to the United States to ensure that policy-makers there understood his initiative and its implications. He did not leave the CEL to members of the bureaucracy. One aide to Hurtado on the CEL claimed that most members of the Ecuadoran foreign affairs bureaucracy, accustomed to thinking of their country as a "tiny power," were overwhelmed by the

CEL's ambition (Pérez 1991). The leadership vacuum within the Foreign Ministry increased Hurtado's personal influence over the policy. In addition, the nearly total lack of domestic opposition to the CEL and the fact that the initiative came late in Hurtado's administration helped to generate a policy which clearly reflected his personal beliefs.

Determining whether the document drafting process conformed to the leader's preferences is more difficult. On one hand, all the region's leaders were allowed to modify the document, thereby diminishing the personal impact of the Ecuadoran president on the final draft. However, Hurtado defined the method by which the documents were to be drafted. It was his choice to include all regional actors in the pre-conference meetings. That choice conformed with his beliefs advocating regional cooperation on critical issues. The policy of inclusion therefore did not detract from Hurtado's influence on the CEL, but rather reflected his leadership style. Furthermore, he and his advisers composed the original drafts to be modified during the Follow-Up and Technical meetings in the days before the official CEL. That authorship gave Hurtado considerable influence over the language and resolutions used in the CEL documents. That the drafting process was open calmed regional leaders who originally feared that the CEL language might be too strong and antagonistic towards creditors. The result was that the documents were modified only slightly, resulting in pro-South declarations that conformed to Hurtado's preferences.

Leader preferences accounts well for the CEL's initiative and drafting process. However, it fails on the appeasement element of the policy. The ultimate decision to appease creditors was in Hurtado's hands. Similarly, Hurtado saw this as necessary for the CEL to proceed without difficulty. Despite these indicators in favor of the theory, the decision lacks the vital component of leader preferences. It did not conform with his preferences. His need to placate creditors was a function of his economic vulnerability. In the absence of that vulnerability, he would not have made such promises to lenders. His ideology on North-South relations rejects the subordination that characterized his behavior in appeasing the North. This element of the policy was an unwanted necessity dictated by a power structure Hurtado did not appreciate.

F. Domestic politics

Neither Hurtado's initiative to hold the CEL nor his decision to include regional leaders in the drafting of the documents was influenced by domestic opposition groups. The CEL was unique in its nearly total independence from domestic political pressure. Hurtado did not seek to cater to, confront, or receive the blessing of his political opponents. As they perceived little threat from the CEL and their efforts were dedicated to the upcoming presidential campaign, opposition groups essentially left Hurtado alone on this policy. The conference was designed for and required the cooperation from an international audience, not a domestic one.

It is possible to argue that by appeasing creditors Hurtado intended to pacify the domestic bourgeoisie that so continually harassed the administration. To the extent that Hurtado promised that the CEL would not grow into a debtors' club, he eased fears the Ecuadoran business community might have held about the CEL. However, by 1984, Hurtado was finding it impossible to please Ecuador's private sector. Business leaders would interpret each presidential action, no matter if it was born in the spirit of reconciliation or cooperation, in the most malicious terms. The way in which Edgar Terán, Febres Cordero's foreign minister, depicted the CEL is indicative of the business community's approach to Hurtado. When questioned on Hurtado's motives, Terán responded, "the conference was, politically speaking, of the most malicious nature, because it occurred in the days right before the election. Hurtado's motive was total propaganda. He wanted subliminally to swing the vote towards Borja" (Terán Terán 1991). Terán refers to the upcoming election which pitted León Febres Cordero against Rodrigo Borja, a Social Democrat. Terán claims that Hurtado waited until late in his term to hold the CEL so that the voting public, impressed with the conference, would elect Borja, whose philosophies accorded more with Hurtado's than with Febres Cordero's. Terán's argument is unsubstantiated. Hurtado had originally attempted to hold the conference in 1983. Scheduling difficulties postponed it until 1984, Hurtado's final year in office. Furthermore, Hurtado is hardly a political supporter of Borja; he promoted his own party's candidate, Julio César Trujillo, in the election's first round (Ayala Mora 1989:88). Finally, it is difficult to argue that domestic political concerns motivated Hurtado when he committed so little energy to selling his policy to the Ecuadoran population.

VII. CONCLUSION

Table 10 depicts the applicability of each theory to the three decisions examined. A number of observations and tentative conclusions can be drawn. First, only three of the theories discussed come into play in the CEL case: compliance, counterdependence, and leader preferences. Both realism and consensus, among the leading theories of North-South international relations, performed poorly. The rational behavior by a unitary actor expected by realists was as absent as the elite consensus anticipated by dependency theorists. To the extent that realist and dependency theories have often been juxtaposed as the two principal competing approaches to international relations,[9] the CEL case provides one example of their mutual deficiencies in explaining dependent foreign policy.

Table 10: The Three CEL Decisions

	Compliance	Consensus	Counter-dependence	Realism	Leader preferences	Domestic politics
Initiative	no	no	yes	no	yes	no
Drafting process	no	no	yes	no	yes	no
Appeasement	yes	no	no	no	no	no

Second, with regard to each theory tested, both Hurtado's initiative for the conference and the manner in which he drafted the documents were explained by the same theories, counterdependence

---

9. An example of this juxtaposition is in Bradshaw and Wahl's (1991) study of Third World debt. While the authors do not explicitly address realism, their view of "monetarist" approaches to the debt involves the type of power relations and outcomes expected of realists who focus on global distributions of power. The authors then contrast this view with a dependency-based analysis. Other studies that pit dependency against realism include Moon (1983, 1985) and Gilpin (1987:25-64).

and leader preferences. This indicates that Hurtado was in control of the policy from its inception through its conclusion. Although the drafting process involved actors from all corners of the region, the Ecuadoran president did not submit his authority or influence over the CEL. Unlike other cases examined in this study, the CEL does not require different theoretical approaches to explain its inception and implementation.

Third, these decisions demonstrate that counterdependence and leader preferences co-occur. In this instance, both were necessary for the CEL initiative and processing. Without the leadership and motivation of Osvaldo Hurtado, the conference would not have taken place. However, in the absence of a dependent environment Hurtado would have had no purpose in designing such a policy. The Ecuadoran leader implemented a counterdependent policy because his personal motivations and dependent conditions combined to warrant that action. Mere dependence alone will rarely necessitate counterdependence. The initiative of a leader inclined to manage that dependent relationship in a confrontational manner is also required. Together, Hurtado's personal motivation and Latin America's dependent status generated the necessary and sufficient conditions for the CEL initiative.

Finally, table 10 reveals that the appeasement component of the policy conforms to an entirely different theoretical process from the rest of the policy. Theories of leader preferences and counterdependence that account so well for the initiative and the drafting of the document cannot explain why Hurtado promised creditors they need not fear the conference's outcome. Counterdependence is the theoretical opposite of compliance, which explains the appeasement. That such contradictory theories are needed to explain different elements of the same policy is consistent with the highly contradictory substance of the CEL's different components. Hurtado chose not to risk his own counterdependent policy preferences by also complying, if quietly, with the creditors' wishes. He was able to implement the highly visible and combative CEL only because he had complied with creditors' most important objective, that they continue to be paid. The CEL is an ideal example of a Latin American leader managing the two competing demands of dependence: the need to counteract dependence and the responsibility not to increase one's vulnerability to powerful economic actors. Explanation of this substantive duality requires the use of at least two theoretical approaches, counterdependence and compliance.

It is useful, nonetheless, to ask whether one of these two countervailing forces prevailed over the other. Overall, was the CEL more counterdependent or compliant? Some may claim that Hurtado's promise to continue debt payments and not to institute a debtor's club indicate a victory for compliance. Creditors were awarded what was most important to them and debtors lost their only bargaining tool. However, the wave of debt conferences that the CEL initiated may also indicate a victory for counterdependence. Contrary to core wishes, the politicization of the debt has not ceased. Latin American and other debtors have maintained pressure on creditors for better rescheduling terms and debt forgiveness. That pressure has at times translated into more favorable renegotiation terms for Third World debtors. Hence, while Ecuador's capitulation on some important issues surrounding the CEL is crucial, it is not necessarily clear that compliance was more powerful than counterdependence in this case.

6   The Contadora Support Group and Febres Cordero's Relations with Nicaragua

I. INTRODUCTION

IN OCTOBER 1985 Ecuador became the only Latin American country to rupture diplomatic relations with revolutionary Nicaragua. The break was made all the more dramatic by the fact that earlier the same week, Ecuador had joined the Contadora Support Group. The Support Group, originally comprised of Argentina, Brazil, Peru, and Uruguay, combined efforts with the Contadora Group (Colombia, Mexico, Panama, and Venezuela) to mediate a peaceful resolution to the conflicts in Central America. Contadora and the Support Group clearly accepted revolutionary Nicaragua as a welcome member of Latin America (Bagley 1987: 182). The Reagan administration consistently scolded Contadora for failing to criticize Nicaragua's Sandinista government (Bagley and Tokatlian 1987). Thus, the fact that Febres Cordero broke relations with Nicaragua contradicts greatly his joining the Contadora Support Group.

II. THE CONTADORA SUPPORT GROUP

Ecuador's incorporation into the Support Group began with talks at the United Nations (*El Comercio* 1985b). The foreign ministers of Costa Rica, Honduras, and El Salvador approached Foreign Minister

Edgar Terán in New York regarding their desire to "amplify" the Contadora Support Group. Terán agreed and spoke with the Dominican Republic's president, Jorge Salvador Blanco, about the prospect of joining the mediation group Terán sarcastically referred to as "famous": "I suggested to the leader of the Dominican Republic, that Ecuador as well as his own country had no reason not to participate in this famous group, [especially] since international mediation, according to international law, is a voluntary act" (Terán Terán 1991).

Although Costa Rica, Honduras, and El Salvador were not members, they extended a formal invitation to Ecuador and the Dominican Republic to join the Support Group. Officially, the Central Americans' invitation was extended because Ecuador and the Dominican Republic were (1) committed to democracy, (2) wanted to participate in the resolution process, and (3) could exert a "great political weight" within Latin America that would contribute to Contadora's success (*El Comercio* 1985a). These motivations were undoubtedly supplemented by another reason for inviting Ecuador. The three inviting governments represented the right-wing bloc in Central America (Lincoln 1985; Whitehead 1988:457-58; Hey and Kuzma 1993:111). In Febres Cordero, they hoped to find an ally in their attempt to isolate Nicaragua and to keep the Sandinistas from winning too much international recognition, respect, and support (L. Carrión 1991).

Terán's account of the process conforms with this analysis. He claims that the four original Contadora Support Group members, Argentina, Brazil, Peru, and Uruguay, "curiously were all from the so-called social democratic tendency" (Terán Terán 1991). He is especially suspicious of Alán García, the Peruvian president who first initiated the Support Group.[1] Terán portrays Ecuadoran and Dominican participation in the Group as a counterweight to the leftists who controlled it. He describes the then foreign minister of

---

1. Terán is suspicious of the entire Support Group process, portraying it almost as a Social Democrats' plot: "It's obviously strange that a 'support group' would exist, the language itself is mysterious. This meant that these eight Contadora and Support Group countries would meet very frequently" (Terán Terán 1991). Given that they were all in the Social Democratic "orbit," they would undoubtedly frame the mediation of the Central American conflicts in a pro-Sandinista manner, according to Terán.

the Dominican Republic as "very neutral, very central, a person who, like me, would not participate in any [of the] political games" in which the Social Democrats so often engaged (Terán Terán 1991). The foreign ministers of Ecuador and the Dominican Republic, as well as diplomats from three Central American states who invited them to join, all had in mind the deradicalization of the Contadora process. Table 11 details the different groups of countries that participated in Contadora and the extension of the Support Group.

Table 11: Players in the Contadora and Support Group Process

	Contadora	Support group	Amplifiers of the Support Group[a]
Members	Colombia, Panama, Mexico, Venezuela	Argentina, Brazil, Peru, Uruguay	Costa Rica, Honduras, El Salvador
Objective	Peace in Central America; demilitarization of conflict	Same as Contadora	Obtain more right-wing participation in the Support Group
Political Orientation	Varied	Social Democrat	Right-wing

[a] This was not a formal political group, but the states that joined in the UN to encourage Ecuador and the Dominican Republic to join the Support Group.

Although the Support Group members' view on the Central American conflicts was very different from Febres Cordero's, they also had an interest in including Ecuador under Febres Cordero and Terán in their efforts. Many in the US and in Latin America believed that Contadora was too accepting of revolutionary Nicaragua and made insufficient demands on its democratization process. Despite rhetorical support for the Contadora process, which called specifically for the demilitarization of the Central American conflicts, the Reagan administration maintained military support for the *contra* army and for the government in El Salvador. Thus, one would expect that the Support Group, committed to the Contadora principles of demilitarization and non-intervention, would reject the participation of an Ecuador governed by a very pro-US president. Despite the assurance that he would be antagonistic to many of Contadora's goals, Febres Cordero could provide the Support Group with a significant advantage. As a respected friend of the Reagan administration, Febres Cordero could act as a source of information and influence that governments less friendly to the US could not achieve (L. Carrión 1991). Contadora and its Support Group necessarily attempted to influence US policy in their quest to demilitarize the region. Having a friend of Ronald Reagan among them could only enhance their stature and leverage in Washington.

Convincing Febres Cordero to join the Support Group promised to be difficult. Given his lack of interest in and distrust of multilateral diplomatic efforts, one would not have expected Febres Cordero to join the Support Group. His administration was marked by antagonism towards the Andean Pact, OPEC, and other such institutions. In fact, during the same week that negotiations for Ecuador's incorporation in the Support Group were taking place, Ecuador's delegation to the annual OPEC meetings in Vienna departed early in protest of OPEC's refusal to increase Ecuador's production quota. Rumors circulated that Ecuador would quit the organization (*El Comercio* 1985c). Nor had Febres Cordero shown any interest in aiding revolutionary Nicaragua. While many other Latin American executives expressed their solidarity with Nicaragua during its battle against US economic, diplomatic, and military assaults, Febres Cordero maintained a strained and sometimes antagonistic relationship with Nicaragua. He sent a low-level Foreign Ministry official to Ortega's 1984 inauguration and delayed until May 1985 appointing an ambassador to Managua. In December 1984, Febres Cordero expelled the Nicaraguan consulate for having delivered a speech advocating revolution in Latin America. The Ecuadoran government charged that the consulate had intervened in its "internal political activities" (MRE 1985:24; Rivadeneira 1985; Villacís 1991:2). During the March 1985 inauguration festivities in Brazil, Febres Cordero met with Daniel Ortega. While publicly the meeting is characterized as "cordial" and "reserved" (Rivadeneira 1985), Febres Cordero and Terán describe a "harsh" confrontation in which Febres Cordero attacked Ortega for infiltrating Ecuadoran society with leftist activities (Terán Terán

1991). Finally, Febres Cordero's anti-communist and free market ideologies made him an unlikely supporter of the Sandinistas.

Why, then, would Febres Cordero, uncommitted to multilateral efforts and suspicious of Nicaragua, join the Support Group? It must first be understood that Ecuador's participation in the Support Group was not an initiative of the president, but of the Ministry of Foreign Relations. Foreign Minister Terán acted as the primary instigator of the activity as well as the primary defender of the decision to leave the Support Group after the break with Nicaragua. Febres Cordero's brief incorporation into the Support Group must also be understood within the context of Ecuador's historical struggle with Peru. The Ministry of Foreign Relations maintained an ongoing policy of "balancing Peru's foreign policy" (L. Carrión 1991). Bureaucrats within the Ministry of Foreign Relations advised the president to join the Support Group so as not to lose regional prestige and influence relative to Peru. As one diplomat put it, "it wasn't because [the Foreign Ministry officials] were interested in the Central American problems. No, instead it was to balance the Peruvian presence within the Latin American context" (L. Carrión 1991). Bureaucrats in the Foreign Ministry, aware of Peru's presence in the Support Group, advised Febres Cordero to join. As career diplomats, the members of the Foreign Ministry also wanted to ensure that they did not "remain outside of the international current" (L. Carrión 1991). The executive was essentially uninterested and considered the Contadora Group unimportant and ineffectual. In his mind, the decision to follow the advice of his advisers did not carry significant costs, risks, or responsibilities.

Lack of domestic opposition further facilitated the decision to join the Support Group. Quito newspaper editorials, though doubtful of Contadora's eventual success, supported Ecuador's incorporation into the Support Group as an extension of the country's historical adherence to the principles of non-intervention, self-determination, and peaceful resolution of conflict (L.Carrión 1985; El Comercio 1985f). The Support Group gave political parties an opportunity to support Latin American unity with little effort beyond verbal pronouncements. The military was the only domestic actor, other than the president, at all likely to oppose an effort that could be construed as supportive of the Sandinistas. By 1985, however, the military was sufficiently depoliticized in international matters, focusing on economic consolidation and leaving diplomatic matters to the executive and the Ministry of Foreign Affairs (Aguirre Asanza 1991; L. Carrión 1991).

The remaining potential opponent was the Reagan administration, which did not display the opposition one might have expected. First, the administration had always rhetorically supported Contadora to counterbalance the effects of military and economic aid packages for Central America which specifically violated the Contadora accords. Contadora allowed Washington to appear to support peaceful resolutions in Central America while continuing a military strategy. Second, Contadora by late 1985 was struggling to survive. Continued violence in Central America weakened the Group's credibility. Ecuador's participation in the Support Group was unlikely to revitalize the moribund organization. Third, Febres Cordero's influence over the Support Group could only weaken the Group's endorsement of the Sandinistas (Narváez 1991). Hence, the Reagan administration had little reason to risk the diplomatic outcry that would accompany its opposition to Ecuador joining the Support Group.

The decision to join the Support Group remained at high policy-making levels within Ecuador. It flowed through the Foreign Ministry channels and to the president's office without being subject to national debate. Observers and Foreign Ministry officials hoped that, despite the president's anti-multilateralism, Ecuador was setting out on a path towards greater regional diplomatic presence. These hopes were dashed very promptly when Febres Cordero broke diplomatic ties with Nicaragua.

III. FEBRES CORDERO BREAKS RELATIONS

The news that Febres Cordero had severed relations with Managua only days after he had joined the Contadora Support Group was both dramatic and puzzling, especially to the Foreign Ministry (L.

Carrión 1991). Febres Cordero severed relations with Nicaragua on a whim, without consulting any advisers and without consideration of the effect such a startling action would have on Ecuador's standing within the Contadora Support Group. No negotiations with congressional leaders or international actors preceded the decision. Debate over the propriety of the rupture could occur only in its aftermath.

Events leading up to the break in relations developed quickly. On Wednesday 9 October 1985, the same day Ecuador officially became a member of the Contadora Support Group, Febres Cordero delivered a speech which included attacks against the Nicaraguan government. That Febres Cordero would so openly attack Nicaragua, the country on which the Contadora effort focused, demonstrates his very superficial commitment to the Support Group. One diplomat suggests that Febres Cordero essentially forgot about the Support Group and went ahead with an anti-Sandinista speech that conformed with his political and economic ideologies (L. Carrión 1991). Febres Cordero's undersecretary of Finance explains that "Febres Cordero didn't give a damn about Nicaragua or the Sandinista Government because he has contempt for mediocre governments" (Juez 1991).

The president claimed that the conflict in Central America could only be resolved when Nicaragua held "legitimate popular elections" in which "clubs, sticks and violence" were not used (quoted in Rivadeneira 1985). Daniel Ortega responded the next day with accusations that Febres Cordero was "an instrument of the United States, which wants to divide the Latin American community and obstruct its efforts for peace in Central America" (*El Comercio* 1985i). He further claimed that "the US wants to occupy the Government of Ecuador so that it can be the rotten apple in the Support Group." Ortega also stated that Febres Cordero had no legitimacy to discuss Nicaraguan democracy given that Febres Cordero had violated the Ecuadoran constitution by postponing elections (*El Comercio* 1985k).[2] Febres Cordero, apparently forgetting the Foreign

---

2. This latter accusation is an apparent reference to Febres Cordero's attempts to postpone provincial elections, a move designed to boost representation of Febres Cordero supporters in Congress. At the time, the request had yet to be approved by Congress.

Ministry's efforts in achieving Ecuador's membership in the Contadora Support Group, responded to Ortega's verbal assaults with a break in diplomatic relations on Friday, October 11.

There is some discrepancy as to who provoked whom in the exchange between the two presidents. Most commonly, Febres Cordero is portrayed as the instigator and Ortega's remarks are considered a reaction to the former's provocations. Chronologically the exchange did begin with Febres Cordero. However, Foreign Minister Terán, perhaps not unexpectedly, claims that Ortega, still angry about the exchange in Brazil earlier that year, purposefully provoked Febres Cordero so that Ecuador would leave the Support Group: "[in Brazil] Febres Cordero was tremendously hard on Ortega. Febres Cordero has a much more dominant personality than Ortega. Ortega was overwhelmed. He had what was probably personal hatred for Febres Cordero. I think that [Ecuador's incorporation into the Support Group] was unpopular to the Sandinista government. The Sandinista leader deliberately made public insults against León Febres Cordero so that he would leave the Support Group" (Terán Terán 1991). In response to the fact that Febres Cordero's statement's predated Ortega's, Terán explains, "I'm sure that Febres Cordero said something critical about the lack of democracy in Nicaragua. He continually said that. But Ortega's response was insulting. If what Febres Cordero said measured a ten, what Ortega said was one hundred" (Terán Terán 1991). Terán dismisses Febres Cordero's statements as components of his everyday discourse, whereas Ortega's accusations were clearly inflammatory and designed to subvert Ecuador's participation in the Support Group.

Febres Cordero himself dates Ortega's anger against him to his denial of a Nicaraguan request for Ecuadoran oil at a favorable price. According to Febres Cordero, Ortega publicly claimed that Ecuador's refusal to sell oil below market rates was in response to orders from the US government. In Brazil, Febres Cordero told Ortega that any discussion between them was contingent on Ortega's rescinding "the barbaric statements" he had made against Ecuador's independence in oil sales. Ortega agreed but never forgot the humiliation he had experienced (Febres Cordero 1991). Febres Cordero's account, like Terán's, places all the blame on a Daniel

Ortega presumably overwhelmed with shame for not having stood up to Febres Cordero in Brazil and waiting for an ideal opportunity to punish the Ecuadoran leader.

These representations of the event are undermined somewhat by their failure to mention that Daniel Ortega was as accustomed to making inflammatory statements against the US and against those he considered US puppets as Febres Cordero was to criticizing Nicaragua. Thus, Ortega's statements seem no more provocative than Febres Cordero's. At the very least, Febres Cordero could have remained uncritical of Nicaragua for a few days after Ecuador's incorporation into the Support Group. While Febres Cordero knew that Ortega was generally critical of the US and its followers, once that criticism was aimed directly at Ecuador, the president could not tolerate it.

After Ortega had accused him of acting as "an instrument of the United States," Febres Cordero, still in Guayaquil and far from his foreign policy advisers, reacted quickly. He called Terán and informed him of the need to respond immediately to the offense with a break of diplomatic relations. Terán disagreed and scheduled an immediate flight to Guayaquil, asking Febres Cordero to delay any official action until Terán arrived. Terán reached Guayaquil to find Febres Cordero completely decided on the decision to break relations. "He had been influenced and advised by his friends in Guayaquil. There were absolutely no members of the Foreign Ministry there," Terán later reflected (Terán Terán 1991). These "friends" were, according to Terán, Febres Cordero's business and party colleagues such as Social Christian (Febres Cordero's party) presidential pretender Jaime Nebot. Other sources state that Febres Cordero was intoxicated when he decided that a break in relations was the only just response to Ortega's offense against him.[3] Although the minister of Foreign Relations as well as the diplomatic corps of the Ministry were in total disagreement with the decision, Febres Cordero refused to be dissuaded (L. Carrión 1991; Terán Terán 1991).

Once the decision to break relations was made, Foreign Minister

---

3. Three sources in Ecuador, including one from the Ministry of Foreign Relations, claim that Febres Cordero was drunk when he broke relations with Nicaragua. Terán, who was not in Guayaquil at the time the decision was made, denies it.

Terán was faced with two alternatives: to resign or to support the president's decision. He decided to support the decision publicly, though personally he felt it was a "drastic and entirely inappropriate action that gave Ortega exactly what he wanted" (Terán Terán 1991). Febres Cordero could not have hoped for a better spokesperson than Terán. The foreign minister immediately went on the offensive, trying to justify what a Foreign Ministry official described as "an illogical event, impossible to explain" (L. Carrión 1991).

Through the press, Terán explained to the domestic and international communities that the break in relations was necessary to "safeguard the dignity and the sovereignty of the nation," in face of such a "grotesque and provocative" offense as Ortega's. He accused Ortega of trying to keep Ecuador's voice of democracy from being heard in Central America. He announced that obviously Ecuador would leave the Support Group as a consequence of the break in relations but that Ecuador would continue its solidarity with the Nicaraguan people and its concern for a peaceful solution to the conflicts in Central America (*El Comercio* 1985h, 1985n). Observers would not have guessed that Terán personally opposed the break in relations. As Terán explained later, despite sincere reservations about the policy, "I looked totally convinced" (Terán Terán 1991). Despite his efforts, Terán's explanations remained obviously full of rhetoric and clearly weak defenses for a policy that was very difficult to justify.

IV. THE POLITICAL DEBATE

A heated debate erupted among national and international actors over the propriety of Ecuador's rupture of relations with Nicaragua. Initially, Febres Cordero allowed his cabinet members, particularly Terán, to speak for him. Terán made it clear that there would be no effort to reestablish relations and that Nicaragua would be given no opportunity to apologize (*El Comercio* 1985v). The break was portrayed as permanent, and in fact remained so until the end of Febres Cordero's term. Terán and Government

Minister Luis Robles Plaza were at pains to assure the public that this was not a political or ideological decision, enacted because Febres Cordero disagreed philosophically with the Sandinistas, but instead a necessary action to maintain intact Ecuador's "dignity" (*El Comercio* 1985s, 1985w). Domestically, the government was supported by Febres Cordero's Social Christian party and by the editors of Quito's principal newspaper, *El Comercio* (*El Comercio* 1985l). These actors accepted the fundamental bases on which Febres Cordero had justified the break: that the 1984 elections in Nicaragua through which Ortega had remained in power were not legitimate, and that Ortega's offense to Ecuador was sufficiently strong to warrant a break in diplomatic relations.

Febres Cordero benefitted slightly from a fragile majority coalition backing him in the legislature in October, 1985. This majority was not very vocal in its support for the policy, but its existence probably kept the opposition from utilizing the break in relations as a basis for the president's impeachment. Members of the opposition parties in Congress all opposed the policy vehemently. The more leftist groups such as the communists and socialists criticized the policy for breaking solidarity with the Nicaraguan people and accused the Social Christians of complicity during the Somoza years (*El Comercio* 1985m, 1985y). Centrist parties, particularly Hurtado's Democracia Popular, used the occasion to disparage Febres Cordero's foreign policy in general (*El Comercio* 1985y).

Furious at congressional reaction to his policy towards Nicaragua, Febres Cordero personally responded. He claimed that his detractors formed part of an international alliance of leftist forces aiming to keep Daniel Ortega in power against the Nicaraguan people's will. A communique from the presidential office ravaged Febres Cordero's political opponents:

> When the national government, in defense of Ecuador's sovereignty and dignity, severed relations with the government of Nicaragua, it knew that it would create an opportunity for a minuscule group of traitors who work for known international political groups, against Ecuador and in favor of Comandante Ortega, who unlawfully holds power in Nicaragua. While those who fight for freedom in Nicaragua applaud the position of President Febres Cordero, who

called for free elections in Nicaragua, in our own country, paradoxically, the leaders of creole communism, [the party] leaders of ID
and DP, cross swords against Ecuador's dignity in order to further
their stingy, sectarian, shameful interests. (quoted in *El Comercio*
1985x)

During the public debate in October of 1985, Febres Cordero
referred primarily to Ortega's offense against Ecuador as justification for his action. While Febres Cordero did accuse Ortega of
dictatorship and denying the Nicaraguan people their freedom,
these references were not employed as direct reasons for the break
in relations. Nor did he directly accuse the Nicaraguan leader of
interference in Ecuador's affairs. In more recent conversations
about the incident, Febres Cordero cites Sandinista attempts to
subvert Ecuadoran democracy as an additional justification for the
diplomatic break. Febres Cordero claims that Ecuadoran military
intelligence had proof that leftist guerrillas in Ecuador were
financed and trained by the Nicaraguans. This, Febres Cordero
explains, in conjunction with Ortega's offense, motivated him to
break relations (Febres Cordero 1991). Febres Cordero's claim that
Nicaragua financed the guerrillas is rather shaky in the absence of
public evidence. It is likely that, if there were even the slightest evidence that such training and financing were being carried out, the
Reagan and Febres Cordero administrations would have publicized
it extensively.

Few other domestic actors expressed their concern over the policy. The Chambers of Industry and labor unions were silent, focusing their efforts at the time on domestic policy. The military
adhered to its policy of leaving matters of diplomacy to the executive (Aguirre 1991; L. Carrión 1991). The strongest anti-administration cry outside of the Congress came from faculty and students at
the Central University. Claiming that Febres Cordero's policy was
inconsistent with public opinion, the university council called for a
national plebiscite in which the voters could reinstate relations with
Nicaragua (*El Comercio* 1985aa). Backed by his constitutional power
to implement foreign policy single-handedly and consistent with
his disdain for political opponents, Febres Cordero did not
respond. As one of the president's advisers and strongest support-

ers put it, Febres Cordero simply "ignored them all" (Manrique Martínez 1991).

Internationally, Febres Cordero received the most support from the expected actors within Nicaragua. Nicaragua's Christian Democrats, opposed to the Sandinistas, claimed that Ecuador's position reflected all of Latin America's concern about democracy in Nicaragua (*El Comercio* 1985n). Nicaragua's opposition newspaper, *La Prensa*, also took advantage of the opportunity to criticize the government for believing it could insult any other country with impunity (*El Comercio* 1985u). Other Latin American states were more hesitant to applaud Febres Cordero's action. Unexpectedly, the foreign minister of Venezuela reacted favorably, stating that other countries in the region also were concerned about elections in Nicaragua (*El Comercio* 1985t). Venezuela nonetheless supported a reestablishment of relations. In general, Latin American states, including all the Contadora members, called for a resumption in relations between Ecuador and Nicaragua (*El Comercio* 1985p).

More interesting is the unanticipated reaction, or lack thereof, from the United States. Many speculated about Washington pressure on Febres Cordero to break relations with the Sandinistas. Certainly many after-the-fact observers portrayed the policy as part of Febres Cordero's strategy to ingratiate himself to Washington (Zuckerman 1986:386; Corkill and Cubitt 1988:80-81; J.D. Martz 1990:24; Villacís 1991:2). There is no evidence that Febres Cordero ever discussed breaking relations with anyone in the US. Febres Cordero made no time for consultation with his own foreign minister, much less international actors. While the Reagan administration expressed reserved contentment over the rupture, it never publicly applauded Febres Cordero or rewarded him financially or otherwise for expelling revolutionary Nicaragua from the Ecuadoran political scene.

The Reagan administration did state the diplomatic rupture was "the inevitable result" of Sandinista politics "exemplified by the absence of democracy in the country." A State Department communique declared that Ecuador's decision "didn't surprise us" but explicitly asserted that the US had in no way encouraged the break nor had any previous knowledge of Febres Cordero's intentions (quoted in *El Comercio* 1985o). The Febres Cordero administration joined the US in affirming the independence of its decision. In a document distributed in the United Nations, Ecuador stated that its break in relations with Nicaragua was the decision "of a free state, never subject to tyranny or any imperialism" (*El Comercio* 1985z). United States assistant secretary of state Elliot Abrams visited Ecuador two weeks after it had severed relations with Nicaragua. Abrams failed even to mention the break in his prepared speeches, claiming he had no authority in this area because it was "a sovereign act adopted by Ecuador" (quoted in *El Comercio* 1985dd).

So, while Febres Cordero could be assured that Washington approved of the policy, the vocal support and recognition one would have expected from the anti-Sandinista Reagan administration was never forthcoming. Indeed, Abrams's behavior in Ecuador reveals that Reagan's team was especially concerned about making clear that the US had *not* influenced the Ecuadoran decision. Washington could generate more negative publicity against Nicaragua if it appeared that Ecuador had taken the decision independently of the US. Ecuador's isolation of Nicaragua was more powerful as an independent decision than if it had been the result of US pressure.

V. CONSEQUENCES

The most immediate consequence of the rupture was Ecuador's withdrawal from the Contadora Support Group. Outside of this, the consequences for the involved parties were few. Despite the heated national debate, Febres Cordero never considered reestablishing relations (L. Carrión 1991; Febres Cordero 1991; Manrique Martínez 1991; Terán Terán 1991). Febres Cordero's finance minister, Alberto Dahik, reflected the opinion of most political observers in Ecuador when he later described the president's intransigence on this point as part of his characteristic obstinacy (Dahik 1991). Indeed, congressional opposition only intensified Febres Cordero's determination to maintain the policy intact. Rather than focusing his public statements on his own government's action, he called attention to the Sandinista's "betrayal of their own revolution" and to the treason of his political opponents, who would take Nicaragua's side over their own country's dignity (*El Comercio* 1985bb). "It's not a matter of [my] apologizing," Febres Cordero stated, "but of giving liberty and democracy to [the Nicaraguan] people who deserve it" (quoted in *El Comercio* 1985cc). Many congressional members publicly denounced the policy, but were without the constitutional power to overturn the executive's decision.

The furious exchange between supporters and detractors of the policy within Ecuador acted as another chapter in the ongoing political squabbles among Ecuadoran politicians. Public attention to the matter subsided a few weeks after the break. Opponents of the policy were aware of the few tangible repercussions the rupture could bring. No economic embargo against Nicaragua was ever mentioned. It would have been of little consequence as less than 0.5 percent of Ecuador's total trade was with Nicaragua (Benalcázar 1989:370, 384). The inability of opponents to change the policy and the relative insignificance the break meant for most Ecuadorans combined to reduce the policy's impact on national politics.

Shortly after the rupture, Uruguay assumed responsibility for Nicaragua's business in Quito while Venezuela did the same for Ecuador in Managua (*El Comercio* 1985r). As if to remind the world of his persistence, Febres Cordero refused to allow Daniel Ortega to attend the inauguration of Febres Cordero's successor, Rodrigo Borja. Once president, Borja immediately invited Ortega to attend the next day's festivities and reestablished relations with Nicaragua (Conaghan 1990:B129).

The two areas most affected by the rupture were the Febres Cordero administration's foreign policy reputation and Ecuador's Foreign Ministry's operating procedures. The incident earned Febres Cordero an even stronger reputation for regional and global isolationism than he already had. His successor, Rodrigo Borja, has consistently called for the need to "reinsert" Ecuador into global and regional politics after four years of the Febres Cordero administration's isolationism. The break with Nicaragua is always considered foremost among Febres Cordero's isolationist tendencies (Borge 1991:19). However, even this effect is more a political tool of Febres Cordero's domestic opponents than a concrete negative result of the policy itself. Ecuador has never had a reputation as a strong regional diplomatic actor. Therefore, breaking relations with Nicaragua had very little impact on inter-American affairs. The incident was as much consistent with Ecuador's diplomatic track record as it was a strong deviation from it. To this day, Febres Cordero discards the "reinserting" language as pure leftist propaganda and continues to express great pride in his decision to break relations with the Sandinistas while disparaging the efforts of others: "If we look realistically at the results of the Contadora group, what do we see? Zero! If we look realistically at the results of the Support Group? Zero! What was achieved by breaking relations with Nicaragua? That the world became aware that Nicaragua had to have elections. My break in relations spurred the necessity of the democratic process in Nicaragua and that brought peace to Central America" (Febres Cordero 1991).

A more enduring effect has been on the future of Ecuador's foreign relations. With the exception of Febres Cordero and perhaps a handful of extremely loyal supporters, Ecuadorans consider the rupture of relations with Nicaragua an embarrassment to their foreign policy. No one feels this sentiment more strongly than the Foreign Relations Ministry employees who were completely left out of the decision. As one scholar who has conducted interviews with numerous Foreign Ministry officials has commented, the incident has left the Ministry all the more determined to maintain relations with all states, no matter how tense those relations may become (Carrera 1991). As one bitter Ministry official remarked, "the whole thing was stupid. Of course nobody won. Ecuador didn't win, the United States didn't win, and Nicaragua didn't *lose*" (L. Carrión 1991).

VI. THEORETICAL APPLICATION

This section examines both the decision to join the Support Group and the decision to break relations with Nicaragua for their applicability to the six theories analyzed in this study. The Support Group example presents some difficulty because it involved three distinct policy-makers in Ecuador: (1) officials in the Ministry of Foreign Relations, who pushed for the policy, (2) Foreign Minister Terán, who first spoke with other leaders in the UN and proposed the policy in Quito, and (3) the president, who agreed to join. The Support Group case will be analyzed with the participation of both the Ministry and the executive in mind. The Ministry and its chief, Terán, were the principal policy-makers. Their initiative allowed the policy to develop. However, it was necessary for Febres Cordero to agree to it.

A. Compliance

Compliance theory requires a conflict of interest between policy-makers in periphery and core. There was clearly no conflict of interest between Febres Cordero and the Reagan administration. Both would have appreciated Ecuador's right-wing influence in the Support Group. It could be argued that there was a conflict of interest between the Foreign Ministry and the US. To the extent that the Ministry used the Support Group to increase its regional power through the Contadora process, its objectives opposed those of the US, which never supported Contadora in anything other than a rhetorical manner. However, the issue was not salient for either party. While the US undermined the Contadora process, it never attempted to keep states from joining the Support Group. Similarly, Ecuadoran Foreign Ministry officials were mostly interested in joining the Support Group in order to keep diplomatic pace with Peru. They were mostly uninterested in the one component of Contadora, its pro-Nicaragua position, that the US would have most opposed (L. Carrión 1991). Compliance theory is not applicable because the US never opposed Ecuador's policy to join the Group.

A casual observer might conclude that Ecuador's decision to break diplomatic relations with Nicaragua was a case of compliance. It appears to be an example of a Latin American state (Ecuador) betraying its neighbor (Nicaragua) because the US, at the height of its anti-Sandinista campaign, ordered it. Scrutiny of the case reveals that although Washington agreed with the policy, it had no participation in it. Febres Cordero was in complete control of his decision to sever relations and was in no way coerced by the US.

B. Consensus

The coincidence of opinion between core and periphery policy-makers required of the consensus interpretation of foreign policy did not exist between officials in the Foreign Ministry and the US on the Support Group question. Ecuador's Foreign Ministry favored Latin American cooperative efforts much more than did the Reagan administration. Also, the US had little interest in Ecuador's joining the Support Group to counterbalance Peru's regional status. However, there was consensus between Ecuador's executive and US policy-makers. Both favored the participation of a right-wing, anti-Sandinista administration in the Support Group, which at the time was comprised of Social Democrats. Recall that Edgar Terán, the foreign minister who would have been Ecuador's primary spokesperson in the Support Group had the country not withdrawn, had contempt for the Group's members and mission. The fact that Febres Cordero did not initiate the activity weakens the argument in favor of a consensus between policy-makers in the US and Ecuador.

Did Ecuador's participation in the Support Group financially benefit Ecuadoran elites? Certainly no immediate benefits would have come from the diplomatic activity. The Chambers of Production did not involve themselves in the decision whatsoever. Their lack of support for the policy is evidence against consensus in this case. The impact of Ecuador's incorporation into the Support Group can be argued as both favorable and unfavorable to economic elites. The Support Group was committed to aiding the Nicaraguan government, at least diplomatically, in its struggle for survival. Success in this mission would have meant an acceptance of some form of socialism on the continent. From this perspective, the policy clearly would not have benefitted Ecuadoran entrepreneurs interested in a regional free market. However, if we consider that Febres Cordero's participation in the Support Group was truly designed to undermine the Support Group's success, elites would have benefitted from a more secure environment for capitalism in the region. This latter interpretation is far-fetched. Febres Cordero was not strong enough to change completely the agenda of the Support Group. Neither elites in Ecuador nor policy-makers in Washington could have expected that the Support Group would become weak as a result of Ecuador's participation. The criterion that economic elites should expect to benefit from the policy is therefore very weakly present in this case.

At first glance, the break in relations with Nicaragua appears to conform well with consensus. There was general ideological concordance between Febres Cordero and policy-makers in Washington about the evils of the Sandinista government. Both repeatedly stated publicly that Nicaragua lacked economic and political democracy. There were no short-term gains for elites in Ecuador, however. What little trade Ecuadorans had with Nicaragua was jeopardized by the diplomatic rupture. More importantly, this case does not confirm consensus because it did not follow the process outlined by consensus theorists. Consensus expects that foreign policy alignment will result from an ideological compatibility between leaders in periphery and core. Febres Cordero did not break relations because it conformed with his ideology about Nicaraguan socialism. Had that been the case, the rupture would have occurred in a more formal, less arbitrary manner. Furthermore, despite its covert war against Nicaragua, the US never broke relations. Ecuador's doing so conflicted with stated US policy at the time, which encouraged regional dialogue. The break lacked the planning and consistency that characterizes interactions among core and peripheral states operating in a dependency-based relationship (Moon 1983, 1985). It was instead an action taken by an impatient, and perhaps intoxicated, Febres Cordero who felt offended by Daniel Ortega's remarks against him.

C. Counterdependence

The Contadora movement is easily interpreted within the counterdependent tradition. The Contadora states directly confronted the Reagan administration in Central America, attempting to end US military assistance in the region (Hey and Kuzma 1993).

However, Ecuador's participation in the Support Group had little to do with opposing US policy in Central America. The foreign minister was interested in countering the strength not of the US, but of the Social Democratic administrations that comprised the Support Group. Foreign Ministry bureaucrats were specifically interested in countering Peru's power and were less interested in the Central American conflict (L. Carrión 1991). Febres Cordero would have opposed immediately any policy that aimed to alienate the US.

Interestingly, the break with Nicaragua was instigated by Daniel Ortega's accusation that Febres Cordero was a puppet of the United States. The Ecuadoran leader portrayed that offense as so great as to merit a break in relations. Febres Cordero's actions could thus be interpreted as counterdependent in that they sought to reaffirm Ecuador's sovereignty. However, the policy is not counterdependent because it did not counter US policy preferences or Ecuadoran dependence. On the contrary, the policy pleased the US and illustrated the ideological bond between the Reagan and Febres Cordero administrations.

D. Realism

The policy-for-power and prestige view of foreign policy explains well the decision to join the Support Group. All participants in the decision enhanced their view of regional prestige by joining the group. The Foreign Ministry could not publicly acknowledge that its goals were anything less than a desire to give "permanent support to all means of peaceful conflict resolution" (MRE 1988:90). The fact that Ecuador later pulled out of the Support Group meant that the Ministry's annual report could not, without embarrassment, elaborate on its decision to join the Group. At the time of the decision to join the Group, Foreign Ministry bureaucrats were privately pleased at having achieved their goal of checking the advantage gained by Peru's participation in the Group. Joining the high-visibility Support Group also enhanced Ecuador's regional prestige, a constant goal of the Foreign Ministry. The foreign minister and the president, to the degree that they were interested in offsetting the regional influence of Social Democrats, saw an opportunity in the policy as well. Joining the Support Group increased Ecuador's regional prestige from all policy-makers' points of view.

The decision to join the Support Group also holds to realism's condition that Ecuador not overcommit its resources. Joining the Group was a diplomatic decision that cost Ecuador little more than the diplomatic energy foreign ministry officials were willing to exert. That Febres Cordero annulled the policy is not an indicator of lack of resources, but of policy inconsistency within the administration. Had the president not removed Ecuador from the Support Group, the Foreign Ministry would not have had difficulty finding the resources necessary to participate.

The realist approach to foreign policy cannot account for Ecuador's break in relations with Nicaragua. The break, despite Febres Cordero's attempts to justify it as an instigator of Nicaraguan democracy, had a drastically negative impact on Ecuador's regional reputation. All Latin American neighbors, including Venezuela, which criticized Ortega, called for a reestablishment of relations. The 1980s was a time of birth and revival for Latin American integrative efforts. That Ecuador would break relations with its neighbor in Central America was seen as a backward step in the necessary process of regional cooperation. Nor can it be argued that breaking relations with Nicaragua fostered development within Ecuador. Although the policy did not require resources the administration was unable to commit, it does not conform to the realist criterion that it serve either development or regional prestige.

E. Leader preferences

The Support Group case does not conform well with the leader preferences view of foreign policy. Febres Cordero did maintain veto power over the policy, which he exercised shortly after Ecuador had joined the group. However, other criteria needed for this theory's confirmation were not present. Participation in the group was not Febres Cordero's initiative. He remained disassociated with the policy and appears to have forgotten that he had just joined the Group when he broke relations with Nicaragua. He left the policy-making to lower-level bureaucrats. Finally, the decision to join the Support Group did not conform with the executive's views on multilateral diplomatic organizations. While most members of the Foreign Ministry felt them important, Febres Cordero disdained them.

The decision to break relations with Nicaragua, on the other hand, is perhaps the best example of leadership preferences examined in this entire study. Febres Cordero made the decision alone, without even his foreign minister to advise him. The decision accorded with his views of Nicaragua in general and of Daniel Ortega in particular. Febres Cordero and Foreign Minister Terán remained actively involved in the policy throughout the ensuing debate. When he was attacked by Congress and other groups, Febres Cordero personally responded with even more vehement charges. The rest of the bureaucracy, with the exception of cabinet ministers, was too stunned and excluded from the policy to participate in its defense very effectively. Febres Cordero ignored all domestic opposition to the policy, even that originating within his own administration. He flatly refused to reverse his decision. From beginning to end, the decision to break relations with Nicaragua was his alone.

F. Domestic politics

No domestic groups, public or private, participated in the decision to join the Contadora Support Group. It was a diplomatic action left to the executive branch. As the policy carried few costs, interest groups had little reason to oppose it. Even Congress, ordinarily a strong opponent of Febres Cordero's initiatives, was quiet on the subject. This can be attributed to the fact that the decision to join the Group was not an executive decision. Had it been one which Febres Cordero strongly supported and publicized, Congress may well have found something unsuitable about it.

Similarly, domestic groups did not participate in the decision to break relations with Nicaragua. Febres Cordero acted too quickly for even his closest advisers to counsel him. The fact that Febres Cordero acted before any domestic groups had an opportunity to express an opinion on the issue essentially precludes domestic politics from explaining this case. Domestic opposition in the after-math of the rupture was significant, but not heeded. In the face of protests from all segments of society, Febres Cordero refused to change his policy. The domestic politics view of foreign policy is thus not confirmed in this case.

VII. CONCLUSION

The two decisions examined in this chapter represent two ends of a policy-making continuum. The decision to join the Contadora Support group is an example of a policy which flowed through the appropriate channels. Foreign Ministry bureaucrats and the foreign minister participated in the development of a policy that served numerous interests. The president, at the top of the policy process, signed on. Interestingly, perhaps the best foreign policy model to account for that decision is bureaucratic politics, a theory rarely applied to dependent foreign policy behavior (Van Klaveren 1984:14; Ferguson 1987:150-51). The break in diplomatic relations with Nicaragua, on the other hand, is an example of foreign policy as made by a single individual, serving his interests alone.

Table 12: The Decisions to Join the Support Group
and Break with Nicaragua.

	Compliance	Consensus	Counter-dependence	Realism	Leader preferences	Domestic politics
Join Support Group	no	no	no	yes	no	no
Break with Nicaragua	no	no	no	no	yes	no

As Table 12 illustrates, realist theory best explains Ecuador's entry into the Support Group. All actors involved in the policy were motivated by a desire to improve Ecuador's regional status, as defined by each actor. The policy did not depend on a visionary leader or a mission to expand Ecuador's regional influence. Instead it was born in a bureaucratic body, the Foreign Ministry, which has a perpetual interest in obtaining and preserving Ecuador's regional status. The Foreign Ministry, led by Terán, took advantage of the offer to join the Support Group as an opportunity to take part in a highly visible diplomatic effort. The executive, perhaps initially reluctant to join a regional diplomatic group, could not deny the regional status benefits derived from Ecuador's participation in the Support Group. It also held the promise of political benefits, in the form of counteracting the influence of Latin American left wing parties in Central America, an area crucial to Febres Cordero's friend, Ronald Reagan. Policy-makers acted rationally. The Support Group incurred no costs and brought Ecuador heightened prestige.

This case also supports realist theory in that it is not necessary to know about individual actors to predict the outcome. Realists reject the type of analysis performed here. They claim that it is unnecessary and futile to enter the "black box" of domestic politics and decision-making because we can assume that all states seek to increase global power and status. Knowledge of the situation confronting Ecuador at the time is sufficient to explain its response. Ecuador was faced with an opportunity to join a regional group. There were no costs, but the benefits included heightened diplomatic visibility and an opportunity to influence regional events. The logical decision was to join the Support Group. An understanding of Febres Cordero's personality or the dynamics of Ecuadoran politics is not needed to explain the policy outcome.

Febres Cordero's decision to rupture diplomatic relations with Nicaragua is an extreme example of a leader having his own way in foreign policy. No one in Ecuador, save Febres Cordero's personal friends, agreed with the policy. Even advisers within his administration were not heeded. This case demonstrates the power of the leader in Ecuadoran foreign policy. Not only could he implement a very unpopular foreign policy and stick to it, he was able to reverse the Support Group policy, which had evolved through the normal foreign policy channels. With one action, the executive reversed all the work that his Foreign Ministry officers had performed in the preceding weeks. In the end of the entire saga, which began with the Support Group and ended with the break in relations, Febres Cordero's personal will prevailed.

Blazing Trails

I. INTRODUCTION

IN MAY of 1987, US troops arrived in Ecuador to participate in a
road construction project in the country's eastern jungle province
of Napo. Code-named Blazing Trails, the operation was designed to
repair earthquake damage to current roads as well as to provide
quality access routes to the remote jungle area. The troops accomplished very little in the road construction project, but their presence spurred a public controversy that led to a tense confrontation
between the administration and Congress.[1] This case sheds light on
the relations between the Reagan and Febres Cordero administrations as well as the dynamics of Ecuadoran domestic politics during the Febres Cordero years.

II. THE BLAZING TRAILS OPERATION

Before the March 1987 earthquakes, Ecuador and the United States
had designed a plan through which US military personnel would

---

1. Most of the information on the Blazing Trails operation, as well as the debate
among Congress and executive branch members, was collected from a classified file in
Ecuador's Congressional Archives. The file was compiled by Congress and includes documents signed between the US and Ecuador establishing Blazing Trails, transcripts of
congressional debate, correspondence between administration officials and Congress
members, and international congressional memos. Given the sensitive nature of the
source, reference to specific documents is omitted.

travel to Ecuador to aid in the upgrade of an existing road in Manabí Province, on Ecuador's coast. In a February 1987 document signed by Ecuador's minister of defense, General Medardo Salazar Navas, and the US commander in Ecuador, Colonel Paul Scharf, the two militaries agreed to a six-month exercise in which US troops would construct a twelve kilometer section of road connecting the coastal populations of San Vicente and San José de Chamanga. The US agreed to send 600-man teams, each on two-week rotations, amounting to a total of 6000 troops. The forces consisted of unarmed national guard and army reserve troops. Also included were approximately 150 active troops from all branches of the US military and 100 Ecuadoran troops, which remained throughout the six-month period. Blazing Trails was significant from a US military standpoint in that it was the first major operation on the South American continent to employ US national guard troops (Little 1988:12).

While the road construction itself was a joint venture between Ecuador's Ministry of Defense and the Pentagon, the initiative came from non-military sources. US ambassador in Quito, Fernando Rondón, who would remain an active player throughout the Blazing Trails saga, offered President Febres Cordero the services of the US military in road construction. It made sense for US reserves to work in Ecuador, argued US officials, because the troops could fulfill their annual two-week training requirement while aiding in Ecuadoran development (Aguirre Asanza 1991). Febres Cordero was "absolutely in agreement" with the proposed road construction plans and saw in this project a unique opportunity for Ecuador to build a low-cost road (Febres Cordero 1991). The Ministry of Foreign Relations did not participate in the agreement (Valencia Rodríguez 1989a:140).

The agreement signed in February was not a formal treaty, but rather a "memorandum of understanding" between the military bodies in both countries. It called for the United States to provide labor and some heavy equipment free of charge. It was later revealed that included in the heavy equipment were six Black Hawk military helicopters. The US also provided (but with compensation from the Ecuadoran government) medical assistance, food and supplies, repair parts, and explosives. Ecuador provided construction materials, some construction equipment, and fuel for vehicles and equipment. In addition, the Ecuadoran government managed all landowner conflicts and exempted US forces from customs, duties, and other charges normally associated with foreign travel. The exemption meant that the US soldiers travelled without passports, an issue that became a significant point of contention in the political debate that ensued after the troops arrived. In addition to the road, the Ecuadoran government expected to benefit from a transfer of construction technology as well as the troops' aid in local health projects, school development and repair, and the opening of a new area to agricultural and forest production.

In early March, a series of earthquakes decimated much of the Ecuadoran countryside, destroyed the national pipeline that transported oil to the coast for export, and changed the fate of Blazing Trails. An estimated 1000 individuals died (*Los Angeles Times* 1987; Ribadeneira 1987). Repairs and losses were estimated at $926 million (Corkill and Cubitt 1988:94). For six months, Ecuador ceased to export petroleum, its greatest source of revenue for national development and debt payments. International emergency assistance arrived in numerous forms. Among them was a modification in the Blazing Trails proposal. Vice President George Bush, during a brief visit to Ecuador shortly after the earthquake, suggested that Blazing Trails move its operations to Ecuador's Oriente, or eastern jungle zone, where the damage was most extensive (Little 1988:12). Approximately 100,000 inhabitants of the region's Napo Province had been cut off from supply routes as a result of the earthquake. The Oriente is also the source of most of Ecuador's petroleum. Febres Cordero, concerned about the damage in the Oriente, and not one to argue with an offer from the Reagan administration, agreed. In April, the same signatories of the original Blazing Trails agreement signed an amendment which called for the road to connect the towns of Hollín, Loreto, and Coca, in Napo Province. The troops began construction in May 1987. In addition, they provided local residents with school desks and other educational supplies donated by the governor of Tennessee. US troops also administered vaccinations to local residents and provided air transport for supplies to isolated communities.

III. THE POLITICAL DEBATE

Opposition to the presence of US troops on Ecuadoran soil began instantly. Numerous observers (e.g., Little 1988:12; Morejón Pazmiño 1991:1; L. Carrión 1991; Carrión Mena 1991) cite general public discontent with the policy. No public opinion surveys were administered on the issue. Evidence of public dissatisfaction includes an increase in "Yankee Go Home" graffiti on the nation's streets and university walls (Little 1988:13; Primack 1988). However, university activities do not necessarily reflect national public opinion. Opponents also cite discontent on the part of residents of the area in which the road was being built. Napo residents were concerned about an increase in prostitution and sexually transmitted diseases in the region (Little 1988:13). However, Congress members who visited the construction site in May concluded from their interviews that, while the local people weren't necessarily happy with the presence of the troops, they cared little about whether they stayed or left. US ambassador Rondón and former president Febres Cordero insist that the local population adored the troops and highly appreciated their work (Febres Cordero 1991; Rondón 1991).

Stronger opposition came from more organized political groups. More than twenty youth, Christian, and women's organizations formed the Committee for National Sovereignty. The Committee organized a petition drive and a protest march calling for immediate withdrawal of troops (Little 1988:13). Leaders of Ecuador's principal indigenous organization, CONAIE, sent a letter to congressional president Andrés Vallejo arguing that the presence of US soldiers was a form of "neocolonialism" and a "violation of our dignity and national sovereignty." They further complained that the sole beneficiaries of projects such as Blazing Trails were multinational corporations representing petroleum, forestry, and agroindustrial interests. The Ecuadoran Federation of Indians called for the troops' ouster on constitutional grounds. An emerging women's group, Women for Democracy, labeled the US presence anti-democratic because the agreement had been designed outside of public debate. These sentiments were supported by the more radical of Quito's two principal newspapers, *Hoy* (*Hoy* 1987a).

But it was Congress with its opposition majority that led the campaign to expel the US troops from the Oriente. In May, members of the Special Committee on International Affairs travelled to the construction site. Their ensuing report, citing previous Reagan administration attempts to use Ecuador as a base from which to prepare for invasions in Nicaragua and Panama, called for the immediate withdrawal of the Blazing Trails troops. The Special Committee, however, cannot legislate; its powers are limited to recommendation. So, opponents of the policy within the Committee, as well as in Congress and in Ecuadoran society, pressured congressional president Vallejo to call an extraordinary session of the entire Congress, to debate and decide on Blazing Trails' legality. An extraordinary session was required because a standard legislative session could not constitutionally address matters of inspection and control of executive programs. However, the constitution did allow the legislature to meet in special sessions to engage in non-legislative activities such as an examination of Blazing Trails.

As an opposition bloc controlled Congress, there was little doubt that the extraordinary session would be called. The administration and its supporters within Congress argued that the extraordinary session was unnecessary and unconstitutional, citing among other reasons the executive's constitutional privilege to create and implement foreign policy. Opponents countered that Blazing Trails had never been subject to popular debate and had not been sufficiently explained to the Ecuadoran people (*El Comercio* 1987a). When Vallejo did decide to call the extraordinary session, he emphasized his desire that the session not last more than a single day. Congressional blocs agreed that only their leaders would speak during the session, thereby minimizing the time spent on debate. Vallejo's restraint in establishing the terms and mood of the extraordinary session belies his image among Ecuadoran conservatives as a leftist instigator who would have done anything to undermine Febres Cordero's authority.

Despite Vallejo's efforts, the extraordinary session held on 15 July lasted 13 hours. While Febres Cordero's partisans defended the policy eloquently, the majority remained in opposition. Congress passed a resolution that called for the immediate withdrawal of the US troops based on the following considerations and arguments:

1. That the presence of the US forces had caused severe concern among ample sectors of the Ecuadoran population;
2. that the "Memorandum of Understanding" on which this presence was based was in violation of Ecuador's Constitution and Administrative Code;
3. that no Ecuadoran law allowed for the presence of foreign troops on Ecuadoran soil under any circumstances, and that even foreign aircraft were disallowed from flying over Ecuadoran territory without the express permission of the Ministry of Foreign Relations;
4. that it was unacceptable that foreign troops could enter and leave Ecuador freely, without submitting to immigration procedures;
5. that it was detrimental to international relations that the foreign assistance to a country devastated by a natural disaster would take the form of military exercises;
6. that the presence of foreign military troops added elements of tension to the current domestic political situation, particularly given that the country was on the verge of an electoral campaign; and
7. that the Corp of Engineers of Ecuador's Armed Forces was capable of constructing this type of road.

The document added that the work completed in the two months since the troops' May arrival was insignificant and that no transfer of technology to Ecuador had occurred. Indeed, the document stated, Ecuador's military had supplied the US troops with valuable experience in construction in jungle terrain. The Congress further reminded the administration that the US could not be trusted to uphold its treaty commitments with Latin America, citing particularly Washington's failure to support Argentina during the Malvinas War. In other fora, including congressional debate, internal congressional documents, and public pronouncements, members cited more serious concerns, including references to Washington's desire to open a School for the Americas in Ecuador to replace the one which had closed in Panama. There were also accusations that the US was using this opportunity to train its troops in anti-narcotic and counterinsurgency tactics (*Hoy* 1987c). Opposition bloc member Rene Vargas spoke extensively during the extraordinary session on the excessive cost of supplying fuel and other necessities to such an ill-conceived project. Vargas is a former high-ranking officer in the Ecuadoran military and the brother of Frank Vargas, who led the military coup attempt and kidnapping of Febres Cordero earlier the same year. As such, his message carried particular impact.

An internal congressional document further articulated Congress' fears that the proposed road project was merely a front for a training mission in which US troops would prepare for warfare in the Andes. Evidence cited included the fact that the proposed road site had specifically been rejected by Ecuador's Ministry of Public Works because of its too-soft terrain. Also, the road connected rather small towns. If the US troops were sincerely concerned with aiding Ecuador, why, the document asked, did they not build a road to connect larger population centers left isolated by the earthquake? The Black Hawk helicopters incited particular consternation. The document concluded by accusing the US of using the operation to establish a base in Ecuador from which, in case of a leftist presidential victory the following year, the US could initiate battles if necessary. These more radical explanations of the US presence were largely left out of the congressional resolution, but maintained high visibility in public debate.

Febres Cordero did have supporters in the Congress. The vote to expel the US troops was not overwhelming, with thirty-five votes in favor and twenty-eight opposed (*El Comercio* 1987h). Guayas Provincial deputy and member of the Committee on International Affairs, Nicolas Lapentty had argued strongly that the Committee's report was illegal, given that some Committee members had not participated in its formulation. As such, Lapentty argued, the congressional resolution based on information from the Committee report was also void. His arguments were not heeded, but gained significant publicity in Quito's most widely read newspaper, *El Comercio*. The newspaper consistently supported Blazing Trails and accused Vallejo of bending to pressure from "communists and pro-communists" when he agreed to call the extraordinary session (*El Comercio* 1987f).

Febres Cordero's problems were further complicated when the Tribunal of Constitutional Guarantees (TGC) met the day after the congressional session to look into the constitutionality of the operation. The TGC censured Febres Cordero and Foreign Minister Rafael García Velasco for having violated the constitution in allowing foreign troops on Ecuadoran territory. The Tribunal did not censure the defense minster, citing the executive's responsibility to oversee this type of operation (*El Comercio* 1987j).

Facing a national mandate for the troops' expulsion, US ambassador Fernando Rondón stated that, out of respect for democracy, they would leave when their contract expired in November if that was what the Ecuadoran people truly desired (*El Comercio* 1987d; *Hoy* 1987b). Rondón did not offer to dismiss the troops immediately, which was what the Congress, the TGC, and organized opposition groups had specifically demanded. Rondón also added that the troops would have liked to remain beyond November in order to complete a larger section of road and would be willing to return if the political climate were more favorable to their presence the following year (Little 1988:12).

Charges that the troops' mission was to build a School for the Americas, train for jungle warfare, and establish a military presence in the Andes were never verified. In the absence of US military documents, it is difficult to ascertain if the Pentagon secretly used Blazing Trails for other than the expressed purposes. There is no mention of any suspicious proposals or plans in the agreement signed between the US and Ecuadoran military officials. Ambassador Rondón concedes that "from a training and logistical point of view, [Blazing Trails] was invaluable for the US military." The harsh conditions in the Ecuadoran jungle were difficult to replicate in the United States and therefore provided the soldiers with unique challenges and experience. He nonetheless describes claims that US troops were performing secret projects as "so ridiculous" that they do not merit a response (Rondón 1991).

However, placing the operation in historical context does lend credence to theories suggesting Blazing Trails was more than a construction project. Given the history of US covert and overt intervention in Latin America, as well as the more immediate circumstances surrounding the Blazing Trails operation, it is not unreasonable for Ecuadorans to believe that Blazing Trails was a front for a strategic or intelligence operation. At least two interrelated and plausible scenarios regarding US intentions emerge. First, Blazing Trails, although officially established as a six-month operation, could have been conceived as the initiation of a long-term US presence in the Andes. Geographically, Ecuador lies between Colombia and Peru. Colombia throughout the 1980s was besieged by leftist guerrillas and increasingly violent and powerful drug cartels. The Peruvian military, despite significant exertion and firepower, seemed to be losing its battle with the Shining Path and Tupac Amaru insurgents. Ecuador itself was experiencing a rise in guerrilla activity with the recent arrival of the Alfaro Vive Carajo (AVC) insurgent force. The Ecuadoran jungle provided the US military with a strategically critical location from which to examine the Andean situation, train troops in counterinsurgency tactics, or prepare for intervention (Little 1988:12). Blazing Trails could operate as a testing ground by which US planners analyzed the environmental and political climate for an extended US military presence in Ecuador.

Second, Blazing Trails formed part of a historical trend by which the US established a low-level military presence in Latin America. A similar road project had taken place in Honduras three years before. The Blazing Trails code name had been used in a US war games operation in Panama in 1985. Like Ecuador's Blazing Trails, the Honduras and Panama ventures employed US National Guard troops. Road construction and other "humanitarian" projects, also form part of the Pentagon's low-intensity conflict strategy. Cognizant that conventional military confrontations in Latin America were improbable, US military planners developed the low-intensity conflict strategy to defeat the more likely and less visible opponent of leftist guerrillas (Salmon 1990). Included in the political, economic, psychological and military strategies employed in low-intensity conflict are development projects aimed at winning "the hearts and minds" of local populations. The construction project in Ecuador conforms with the "humanitarian" assistance component of low intensity conflict strategy. The US military was also acutely aware of leftist movements throughout the South American continent, particularly in the Andes, where AVC had recently surfaced and Colombian and Peruvian guerrillas already flourished. Blazing Trails could have been part of a US low-intensity conflict strategy to confront these groups.

If it is difficult to know the Pentagon's plans in Ecuador, it is similarly difficult to gauge the extent of its commitment to the project. On one hand, the US did not comply with the Ecuadoran congressional call for an immediate withdrawal. On the other hand, US ambassador Rondón did not insist that the troops remain in Ecuador beyond November, though he had expressed his wish that they would. This limited commitment could be a sign either that the operation was designed solely as a construction project and nothing more, or that the US had learned that Ecuador's jungle zone was an inhospitable territory in which to carry out strategic operations.[2] Blazing Trails was a failure from any standpoint. As road builders, the troops completed only six kilometers, spending most of their time stuck in the mud. As initiators of an extended US military presence they also failed, having established no training center or regional listening post. Their short stay and limited success also made it impossible to win the hearts and minds of the local population.

Rondón made it clear he would not press for the troops to stay without support from Ecuador's executive branch. By the middle of July, Febres Cordero was faced with a congressional resolution and TGC censure. Both bodies demanded the immediate withdrawal of the Blazing Trails troops. The president was faced with three options: call for the troops' withdrawal, allow the troops to remain until the contract expired in November, or make an agreement with the US allowing the troops to remain beyond November. Febres Cordero chose the second option, announcing that the troops would leave by the designated date, 16 November 1987. Not once, of course, did the president make it appear that this was any type of concession. He publicly criticized Congress, declaring that the legislative body had no constitutional basis for action in this area (*El*

---

2. Rondón was clearly the most visible and vocal advocate for the United States throughout Blazing Trails. However, if the US had been using the operation for purposes other than road construction, it is possible that Rondón was unaware of it. The US ambassador is not always told about covert operations. For an example of this practice in US foreign policy towards Ecuador, see Agee (1975:106-316) and Blum (1986:170-74).

Comercio 1987i). This claim was made in spite of the Constitutional Tribunal's ruling against Febres Cordero. Since July 1987, Febres Cordero has called his congressional opponents on this issue "communists" who would undermine the development of Ecuador to further their wicked interests. He denies that his decision was a submission to domestic pressure. It was exactly *because* he would not bend to his congressional opponents on issues such as this, Febres Cordero claims, that they made his life miserable throughout his administration (Febres Cordero 1991).

His cabinet fully supported Febres Cordero. Foreign Minister García acted as an eloquent and persistent administration spokesperson in Congress and the TGC. García sent numerous letters to Congress reminding its members of the executive's right to design and implement foreign policy. He gave a detailed speech to the TGC, in which he argued that Blazing Trails was neither illegal nor an offense to national sovereignty according to the constitution (*El Comercio* 1987e). The Defense Ministry did its part when called upon, but otherwise participated little in the defense of its own project. When requested by Congress, Defense Minister Salazar Navas wrote a letter of justification for the US troops' presence. He cited the military's constitutional role in national development as well as treaties of mutual assistance and cooperation Ecuador had signed with the US. For the most part, however, the Defense Ministry, consistent with its recent tendency to stay out of visible political debates, was willing to allow the executive and the Foreign Ministry to lobby for Blazing Trails. Key players in the administration were so united on their position that the US troops should not be expelled that congressional president Vallejo appealed directly to the US government for their dismissal. Vallejo explained that Congress fully expected Febres Cordero to ignore its order; it was therefore necessary for him to take it upon himself to see that the US understood congressional opinion (*El Comercio* 1987b).

IV. EXAMINATION OF THE DECISION

There is no obvious victor in the battle over Blazing Trails. Opponents of the administration claim they forced Febres Cordero to expel the troops. Febres Cordero counters that he remained committed to the original agreement and did not submit to domestic pressure. The executive decision to allow the troops to stay until, but not beyond, November 1987 was something of a compromise. It reflected a balance of power between a strong executive and a very vocal opposition Congress. Febres Cordero's strength was born in his constitutional privilege to design and implement foreign policy and his willingness to disregard congressional votes against him. Congress, on the other hand, stirred significant anti-administration publicity. During the same month Congress called for the troops' dismissal, congressional vice president Enrique Ayala went on an anti-Febres Cordero campaign throughout Europe. Ayala warned his European hosts that Febres Cordero was an autocrat and leader of the "most corrupt regime in history." He added that Febres Cordero was unlikely to cede power if the victorious candidate in the following year's presidential elections were not to his liking (quoted in *El Comercio* 1987c).[3]

A. Febres Cordero's victory

Febres Cordero's victory was his defiance of the immediate-withdrawal order. Even in facing the congressional and TGC resolutions, this decision was not as difficult as it appeared, for three reasons. First, as is discussed in more detail below, the relationship between Febres Cordero and Congress was extremely strained by 1987. Congressional condemnation of the executive's policies was as expected as Febres Cordero's disregard of it (Corkill and Cubitt 1988:94-95). Febres Cordero had learned that he could ignore congressional resolutions with few or no consequences. Later the same year, for example, Congress impeached Febres Cordero's interior minister and voted to dismiss him. Febres Cordero simply ignored the procedure and vetoed the minister's expulsion (EIU 1987:3; Conaghan, Malloy, and Abugattas 1990:21). Thus, Febres Cordero

---

3. Ayala was proved wrong. Ecuador in 1988 experienced a peaceful transition of executive power. Rodrigo Borja, the incoming president, is intensely hated and mistrusted by Febres Cordero. While Febres Cordero did not disrupt the transition, it is widely believed that his irresponsible economic behavior in the last year of his administration was done in part out of a desire to make governing difficult for his successor.

was reasonably confident that he could defy the congressional order with impunity.

Second, few Congress members were sufficiently committed to the troops' immediate expulsion to pursue the issue. Once satisfied that the troops would leave in November, most legislators turned to other projects. The only remaining political actors strongly committed to the troops' withdrawal were leftist groups operating outside of Congress. These groups carry little influence in Ecuadoran politics in general, and were particularly weak during the Febres Cordero administration. As a Ministry of Foreign Relations official explained, the left in Ecuador has a great capacity to mobilize around issues concerning national sovereignty and US imperialism. However, policies on these politically charged issues have little impact on the more critical matters of economic development and survival. The Febres Cordero administration was therefore willing to allow leftist protest against Blazing Trails. The opposition could be readily ignored and even served the purpose of distracting attention away from the dismal economic conditions Ecuador suffered throughout 1987 (L. Carrión 1991).

Finally, Febres Cordero's decision not to expel the troops was facilitated by Congress' failure to provide any concrete evidence for its accusations. Charges that the troops were planning a School for the Americas and training in jungle tactics lost force in the absence of proof. When Rene Vargas, perhaps Febres Cordero's most forceful opponent on Blazing Trails in Congress, was asked to provide evidence for his accusations, he resorted to shaky reasoning. The evidence, Vargas asserted, lay in the fact that the troops had achieved so little in the two months they had been working in Napo Province. They were therefore obviously spending their time on other projects (*El Comercio* 1987l). The simple counter-argument was that the working conditions were so poor and the US troops so unaccustomed to the jungle heat and rain, that their work progressed very slowly. The administration had also allowed members of the press and of Congress to visit the work site. That they could travel freely to the area denied opponents the opportunity to claim Febres Cordero was hiding a covert operation from them. They also returned without a shred of evidence that would support their claims. The lack of evidence equipped Febres Cordero with strong ammunition with which to combat his opponents on Blazing Trails.

B. Congress' victory

Despite Febres Cordero's achievements, Congress accomplished a great deal as well. Indeed, Febres Cordero agreed to dismiss the troops in November despite the factors bolstering his position described in the preceding section. The victory of Congress and other opponents on this issue was Febres Cordero's failure to extend the US troops' stay. Despite the road's unfinished status and an offer from the US for the troops to remain, Febres Cordero announced in July of 1987 that the troops would leave in November. The president's compromise on this point should not be underestimated. Ambassador Rondón explains that the limited success on the road was a function of the troops' needing to adjust to difficult working conditions.[4] Ecuadoran and US military planners both felt the project was improving with time and should be extended. An extension beyond November would also allow the project to be undertaken during Ecuador's dry season, significantly increasing its chances for completion. Rondón admits that "because of the political controversy," the US decided to leave in November and that he was very disappointed that the mission was not extended (Rondón 1991). Congressional opposition to Blazing Trails ceased once Febres Cordero had promised the troops would leave in November, indicating that Congress' primary concern was that the US not establish an *extended* presence in Ecuador. Congress achieved a significant victory in creating a political environment hostile to US military operations. That victory denied that Blazing Trails could act as the precursor to future US military maneuvers. Congress thus achieved its strongest objective *even though* it had no proof to back up its claims that Blazing Trails was more than a construction project.

---

4. Febres Cordero claims that a US military officer working in the jungle told him that the conditions in Ecuador were worse than he had faced in Vietnam (Febres Cordero 1991).

V. CONSEQUENCES

The political consequences were minor for all parties involved. The Blazing Trails controversy was one scene in the tense confrontation between the executive and legislative branches. By mid-1987 that confrontation was public and active. Ambassador Rondón described the political climate as "ballistic" (Rondón 1991). Thus it was expected that Congress would oppose Febres Cordero, particularly on a subject related to his strong relationship with the Reagan administration. As he neared the end of his term, Febres Cordero demonstrated an increasing tendency to ignore congressional opposition, exemplified in his direct defiance of the resolution calling for the troops' expulsion. Congress, reasonably satisfied in having publicly embarrassed the president and reassured that the troops would not remain beyond November, saw little political profit to be gained by continuing the debate. The matter was essentially abandoned two weeks after the congressional resolution had been signed.

The episode also produced no discernible damage to US-Ecuadoran military or diplomatic relations. Beyond Ambassador Rondón's expressions of discouragement and frustration, the US expressed no public disappointment or anger over the congressional decision to expel the troops. This perhaps is attributable to the fact that the jungle road construction was an extremely difficult and laborious task to which the troops were not accustomed (L. Carrión 1991). Also helpful was Congress' express assertions that its actions were not intended to insult or undermine the US in any way. Juan Pablo Moncagatta, DP's national vice president and a leader in the anti-Blazing Trails campaign, made clear in his speeches that the Congress' desire to expel the troops had nothing to do with Ecuador's relations with the US. It was simply a matter of maintaining national sovereignty. Moncagatta went so far as to liken the situation to the original colonies' attempts to expel British troops from American soil in 1774 (*El Comercio* 1987g). Given that the colonies, not a sovereign state at the time, deliberately acted with hostility towards Britain, Moncagatta's analogy is rather weak. Nonetheless, while Moncagatta's interpretation is perhaps farfetched, his desire not to inflame US wrath is unquestioned.

The most significant consequence of the Blazing Trails debate is the improbability that US troops will return to Ecuadoran soil. The political difficulties associated with the road construction project were sufficient to convince future administrations that the costs of hosting US troops in Ecuador outweigh the benefits. US military assistance will most likely remain in the form of financial aid and the limited participation of military advisers. Ecuadoran laws guard against the extensive presence of foreign troops. For example, when the US lends aircraft to Ecuador, the planes must be piloted by Ecuadorans (L. Carrión 1991). The Blazing Trails experience has increased the resolve of all but the most right-wing political parties to prevent direct US military intervention in Ecuador. Even as US efforts against drug trafficking in South America become increasingly militarized (Wiarda 1990:4), Ecuadoran political leaders remain determined that only national forces will operate on national territory. Recent popular rejection of US troops operating in Colombia demonstrates that Ecuadorans are not alone in these sentiments (*Christian Science Monitor* 1994).

VI. THEORETICAL APPLICATION

This section applies two distinct decisions to the six theories reviewed in this study. First, the decision to bring the US troops to Ecuador to work on the road is considered. This was a primarily elite decision made by high-ranking officials in the US and Ecuador. Second, Febres Cordero's decision that the troops would remain until, but not beyond, November 1987 is applied. This second decision reveals a different theoretical profile because it was subject to intense domestic political debate.

A. Compliance

Neither the decision to allow the Blazing Trails troops into Ecuador nor the decision to permit them to remain until the contract expired in November resembles the compliance model of dependent foreign policy. The conflict of interest required of this theoretical approach did not exist between the Febres Cordero and Reagan administrations on the Blazing Trails initiative. While the project was salient to both parties, there was no need for pressure from the United States to initiate the project because the Ecuadoran government fully agreed with the idea.

There was, however, a conflict of interest on the troops' dismissal. Fernando Rondón made clear to Congress his desire that the troops remain to finish the project. Nonetheless, there is no evidence that he pressured Febres Cordero to keep the troops beyond November. Most importantly, the US position was not implemented.

B. Consensus

Consensus explains well the Blazing Trails initiative. The policy was overwhelmingly marked by a sense of mutual benefit and cooperation. There was a coincidence of opinion between policy-makers in the US and in Ecuador on the desirability of Blazing Trails. Febres Cordero was delighted to have US aid in the road construction project. He remains angry and frustrated with those who would reject such aid simply because it involved a presence of US troops (Febres Cordero 1991). Febres Cordero's approach to insurgency in Ecuador also concurred with the low intensity conflict strategy employed by the US. Febres Cordero had announced a total war on the emergent guerrilla force, AVC (J.D. Martz 1986: B115). In a 1985 speech, the president linked the guerrillas to drug trafficking activities and urged the country to work with "countries like the United States, of whose leadership in this battle we should take advantage." He then publicly thanked the US Drug Enforcement Agency for pursuing joint activities with Ecuador that would eliminate drug trafficking and related illegal activities (SENDIP 1987a:197-98). Febres Cordero appreciated and encouraged any contribution the US military presence could make to the anti-insurgent effort.

Did the Blazing Trails initiative benefit Ecuadoran economic elites as consensus would predict? There is no evidence that economic elites influenced the decision-making process in any direct way. The Chambers of Production, owing to their claims as apolitical organizations, did not involve themselves, at least publicly, in the decision or the national debate. There is little reason to believe that a road in a poor section of Napo Province would materially benefit elites in the short-term. Ecuador's Ministry of Public Works, sometimes accused of corruption in designing its development projects, had not recommended the site chosen by the US (Little 1988:12). The proposed road connected poor and isolated communities. In the long term, however, elites could have expected to prosper from the development project. The road opened up oil-rich Oriente territory to further agricultural and petroleum exploitation which could provide considerable profits for Ecuadoran investors at a future date. Most economic elites, anti-communist and very suspicious of leftist organizations, also would have supported counterinsurgency activities in the jungle, particularly when funded by the US. That popular groups opposed the project provides some evidence of its elitism. Even Indians' rights organizations believed that the road's intended beneficiaries were multinational corporations, rather than local populations. Such opposition from popular groups is expected of a consensus-based policy designed by elites.

Consensus does not explain the president's decision to dismiss the troops in November. True, there was agreement between the US, as represented by Ambassador Rondón, and Ecuador, as represented by Febres Cordero, that the troops should not remain beyond November. However, this decision did not reflect their policy preferences, but instead was a joint decision made out of their sensitivities to the domestic political situation. Furthermore, the decision to dismiss the troops made impossible the road's completion, erasing any benefits that Ecuadoran elites hoped to derive from the project.

C. Counterdependence

The Blazing Trails initiative did not fulfill the most important criterion of a counterdependent foreign policy: that it be designed to reduce Ecuador's dependence on the US. Febres Cordero's opponents, who called for the immediate withdrawal of the troops in the name of Ecuadoran sovereignty, certainly wished for a more counterdependent policy. Febres Cordero's initiative directly defied those wishes.

On the other hand, Febres Cordero's failure to extend the troops' stay is an example of counterdependence. The president yielded to the intense domestic opposition calling for a more counterdependent foreign policy. Repeatedly, opponents of Blazing Trails criticized the operation for undermining Ecuadoran sovereignty and strengthening the country's dependence on the US (L. Carrión 1991; Morejón Pazmiño 1991:1). The congressional resolution calling for the troops' immediate withdrawal was replete with references to Ecuador's diminished sovereignty and autonomy resulting from the presence of foreign troops on Ecuadoran soil. Administration opponents prioritized the restoration of Ecuadoran sovereignty over any development benefits the Blazing Trails operation might have produced. The decision against extending the troops' stay was counterdependent in that Febres Cordero implemented the policy to placate those who sought a more independent and anti-imperialist foreign policy.

D. Realism

As conceived by the US and Ecuadoran governments, Blazing Trails was a development project. It was originally designed to develop the coastal region, and then modified to restore and develop the Oriente region, which had been damaged by the earthquakes. The operation conformed with the road construction plans Febres Cordero had emphasized since the early days of his administration. Speaking in the Oriente region in November of 1984, Febres Cordero announced a detailed and extensive development project for Napo Province, including a network of roads and railways (SENDIP 1987a:16). In his annual address to the nation in 1985, Febres Cordero spent considerable time on the details of road construction successes and plans. He also pointed out the military's role in national development projects (SENDIP 1987b:36-38, 61-62). The fact that the designers of the road worked in conjunction with Ecuador's Ministry of Public Works further adds to its credibility as a development operation. Once the policy came under public criticism, members of the administration repeatedly reminded their opponents that one of the constitutional duties of the Ecuadoran military is to participate in development projects. Hence, Febres Cordero could not be criticized for fabricating a commitment to road construction in Napo, having demonstrated that commitment throughout his years as president. There is therefore ample evidence supporting the theory that the Blazing Trails initiative was designed to further Ecuador's development.

Does the decision to invite the troops fit the condition that Ecuador not commit resources it does not have? This is more difficult to determine. The fact that Congress and other domestic groups were able to force Febres Cordero to dismiss the troops suggests that he overcommitted his administration's resources in initiating Blazing Trails. Important to remember, however, is that the initial operation was planned for six months, and was completed. Febres Cordero was able to carry out the mission with the resources he committed. The initiative therefore conforms with this realist condition.

The resource commitment criterion also holds for the decision to dismiss the troops. The administration had to commit no resources towards the troops' dismissal other than to explain the situation to US officials. However, Febres Cordero's decision to dismiss the troops in November is not supported by references to development. Caught up in political polemics, Febres Cordero referred more to his resolve to see the policy to its end than to its development prospects. The troops' dismissal guaranteed that Blazing Trails would achieve very little in the way of development. The president's failure to extend their stay demonstrates that he was motivated not by development but by a concern for domestic politics. Nor can realism explain the domestic opposition's motives. Congress members and other critics of the policy made no reference to enhanced regional prestige that might result from the troops' ouster. Rather, the opposition sought the troops' dismissal in order to win a political victory against the administration and to reassert Ecuador's foreign policy autonomy.

E. Leader preferences

The Blazing Trails initiative conforms with the theory linking leader preferences to foreign policy behavior. Febres Cordero had demonstrated a commitment to development and anti-insurgency in the region. He had also previously reminded the nation that those projects should involve both Ecuador's military and representatives from US organizations. The means and ends of Blazing Trails clearly corresponded with Febres Cordero's views on development projects and international assistance. He also remained actively involved in the issue once it began to stir controversy. Febres Cordero personally and vehemently responded to his critics throughout the heated debate and stood firm in his decision that the troops would remain until the contract expired. His cabinet's loyalty provides further evidence that Febres Cordero remained in control of the policy. Finally, Febres Cordero firmly resisted the opposition's call for the troops' immediate withdrawal. This last point is particularly important given the weight of that opposition. Not only did the executive withstand demands from private political groups, he blatantly defied motions from the Congress and the Constitutional Tribunal.

The only weak point in this case's applicability to the leader preferences theory is that Febres Cordero most likely did not originally initiate Blazing Trails. It is somewhat unclear in which camp the proposal for the project began. The memorandum signed by both militaries makes no reference to the initiator. Febres Cordero's critics claim that he "invited" the US troops (Hurtado 1991; Salvador 1991). However, Febres Cordero explains that it was a North American initiative with which he completely agreed (Febres Cordero 1991). The Congress' internal documents claim that Ambassador Rondón was the first to present the proposal. It was George Bush who officially suggested that the project move to the Oriente after the March earthquakes. Other evidence supports the view that the US first proposed Blazing Trails. Febres Cordero's opponents have consistently criticized him for being too close to the Reagan administration. In the absence of any clear information on who initiated the project, the opposition would tend to assume it was Febres Cordero. However, it is unlikely that Febres Cordero would have thought of inviting US military personnel to participate in a development project. US troops had not before been involved in development projects in South America. Although a similar project had taken place in Honduras three years earlier, that operation was easily explained as part of the US commitment to fighting insurgency and communism in Central America. There was little reason for Febres Cordero to believe the US would have sent troops to fight insurgency in Ecuador when no US forces had arrived in Colombia or Peru to battle insurgents, who were clearly a greater threat than those recently emerged in Ecuador. Additionally, had the initiative come from Febres Cordero, he would assuredly acknowledge it. Never one to be coy about his political ventures, Febres Cordero assumed full responsibility for supporting the policy. He undoubtedly would be delighted to claim the idea for Blazing Trails had it originated in his office.

The fact that the policy initiative came from the United States damages only slightly this case's applicability to the leader preference-based theory. An understanding of President Febres Cordero is crucial to explain the Blazing Trails initiative. Once the US had proposed the operation, Febres Cordero became an active and committed participant in the policy because it so clearly conformed with his ideology and style. Furthermore, the policy could not have gone forward without his approval.

The president's decision to keep the troops until November did not conform with his preferences. Febres Cordero's refusal to expel the US forces in July 1987 as his opponents demanded appears to be an indication that the policy remained under the executive's control despite widespread opposition. However, Febres Cordero did submit to domestic rivals in not extending Blazing Trails beyond November. That the troops were required to leave denied Febres Cordero the fulfillment of his goal of completing the project. Leader preferences fails to account for the president's significant compromise.

F. Domestic politics

It is difficult to determine whether a relevant domestic political actor maintained a policy preference in the Blazing Trails initiative.

Because the policy was conceived behind closed doors, domestic groups had no opportunity to develop or to express an opinion. There is clearly no evidence that the regime, in designing the operation, considered potential criticism from domestic opponents. The fact that the agreement between the Pentagon and Ecuador's Ministry of Defense was never subject to public debate became one of the opposition's primary complaints against the policy. The question, then, is whether Febres Cordero submitted to opposition in his decision not to extend the troops' stay. There is significant evidence that he did. First, Ambassador Rondón stated clearly that the disappointing decision against extending the project was a response to the "political controversy." Rondón remains extremely bitter over the Congress' handling of Blazing Trails, stating that Congress members "demonstrated so much immaturity" and prevented the US from helping Ecuador (Rondón 1991). Second, the opposition significantly subdued its barrage against Febres Cordero on Blazing Trails once the president promised the troops would leave in November. This demonstrated that Congress was most concerned that the US not establish an extended presence in Ecuador, a presence Febres Cordero would happily have accepted. Febres Cordero's dismissal of the troops therefore subordinated his own desire to that of his opponents. That the president refused to dismiss the troops immediately allowed him to camouflage his compromise on the more important issue to Congress. The most enduring effect of the Blazing Trails experience is that US troops will almost assuredly not return to Ecuador. Hence, Febres Cordero's opponents achieved a great deal.

VII. CONCLUSION

Table 13 details the applicability of the six theories to Blazing Trails initiative and the decision to dismiss the troops at the end of their six-month contract. Which of the theories reviewed best explains the Blazing Trails initiative? Table 13 demonstrates that three of the six can account for the foreign policy behavior exhibited: consensus, realism, and leader preferences. The reason that three interpretations simultaneously explain the initiative lies in the fact that their defining components do not conflict. Ecuador developed a policy that concurrently served the interests of the executive, the US, and development. Febres Cordero fits ideally with the consensus description of most Latin American elites as confidants in a North-South agreement. In this case, he could serve that agreement while also implementing his own preferences and furthering national development.

Table 13: The Two Blazing Trails Decisions

	Compliance	Consensus	Counter-dependence	Realism	Leader preferences	Domestic politics
Initiative	no	yes	no	yes	yes	no
Dismiss in November	no	no	yes	no	no	yes

Consensus theorists concerned with foreign policy expect that core and peripheral leaders will agree on foreign policy principles and therefore develop similar and cooperative policies. Blazing Trails conforms to this description well. Military and civilian leaders in the US and Ecuador saw this project as an ideal opportunity for both countries to benefit. Febres Cordero, with his personal ties to US culture and business, is an ideal-typical leader according to consensus. Unlike many of his contemporaries in Latin America, Febres Cordero did not oppose US military presence in his country. His ideology and policy preferences conformed much more with those of US leaders. Policies like Blazing Trails are expected to emerge under pro-US administrations which play a crucial role in dependency theory's vision of US-Latin American relations.

Leader preferences also accounts well for the initiative. Febres Cordero's philosophy was necessary for Blazing Trails to occur. US actors could propose Blazing Trails specifically because they knew that Febres Cordero would accept the idea wholeheartedly. Once the troops were in Ecuador, the president assumed personal responsibility for the policy and defended it forcefully. Leader preferences is subordinate to consensus here only because Febres Cordero did not make the first initiative and because he could not have implemented the policy alone. Blazing Trails required significant activity from the United States. However, had Febres Cordero not been president, it is very unlikely the operation would have been initiated.

Blazing Trails can certainly be interpreted as a policy-for-development of the kind realist theory expects leaders of an economically weak country to implement. The theory only works, however, if one focuses solely on the executive branch. While Febres Cordero appeared fully committed to development in Napo Province, numerous actors within Ecuador fiercely opposed him. Ecuador was not a unitary actor in this case. Furthermore, Febres Cordero failed to cite development as the primary reason for which he wanted to maintain the policy. Once it came under fire, his references to development goals all but disappeared. Instead, he insisted that he personally would not submit to his opponents in Congress or elsewhere in society. Even today he cites the incident as one about which he is proud for defying such intense opposition. This "personalization" of the policy undermines the realist approach. Also, a focus on development alone cannot explain the Blazing Trails initiative. Without an understanding of the Ecuadoran leader and his relationship with the United States, realism cannot predict what type of development policy Ecuador would have designed.

Table 13 reveals that there is no theoretical competition for explaining Febres Cordero's decision to allow the troops to remain only until November. Domestic political considerations were the only force that caused the president to operate against his will. A number of factors contributed to Febres Cordero's willingness to dismiss the troops. Congress made Blazing Trails a high-profile national issue. The extraordinary session and the call for the troops' dismissal damaged the president politically. That pressure was sufficient to make him dismiss the troops in November even though his friends in the US wanted them to stay. Congress was willing to accept the troops until November because of Febres Cordero's promise they would not remain past that date. Having achieved its primary goal of preventing an extended US military presence in Ecuador, the opposition eased its campaign against the administration. Febres Cordero was able to keep Blazing Trails alive until the end of the original contract's terms, thereby allowing him to save face, claiming that he had fulfilled his policy and not submitted to the opposition. Nonetheless, the final outcome favored the opposition's preferences over the president's. That the troops were not allowed to stay and are prohibited from returning is a substantial victory for the opposition.

8   Febres Cordero Signs the OPIC Agreement with the United States

I. INTRODUCTION

IN NOVEMBER 1984, only three and one-half months after assuming power, the Febres Cordero administration signed an investment agreement with the Overseas Private Investment Corporation (OPIC). OPIC, an agency of the US government, insures private investors against investment losses in participating countries. The agreement played an important role in the Febres Cordero administration's aggressive neo-liberal economic plan. In generating the accord with OPIC, Febres Cordero communicated to investors around the world, and particularly in the United States, that Ecuador's doors were open to foreign investment.

OPIC provides risk insurance to US firms operating in less developed countries. For a modest fee, investors are protected against revolution, expropriation, nationalization, and sudden shifts in currency values that could jeopardize profit returns. OPIC was ostensibly designed to generate both development in the Third World as well as growth for US-based multinational corporations. However, by the 1970s, OPIC had gained a reputation for protecting investments in well-established and low-risk industries in countries enjoying relative political stability. The Reagan administration revived the US government's commitment to promoting foreign investment and targeted OPIC as a primary vehicle for attaining that goal. Under Reagan, numerous OPIC agreements were signed with Third World governments. In addition to insuring private investments, OPIC funds were also invested directly (EIU 1985a:8; J.D. Martz 1986:B117; Molineu 1990:99).

The agency's relationship with Ecuador began in 1955. OPIC's contracts with Ecuador and other members of the Andean Pact were nullified when in 1970 the subregional economic association implemented its controversial Statute on the Common Treatment of Foreign Capital and Technology, most commonly known as Decision 24 (Ferris 1979:45). Among Decision 24's most restrictive regulations were the requirement that foreign enterprises become "mixed" companies (i.e., more than 51 percent controlled by local capital) and the 20 percent limit on repatriation of profits (Ferris 1979:51-52; Cherol and Nuñez del Arco 1983:411). Decision 24 made the investment climate sufficiently hostile to warrant OPIC's withdrawal and eventually led to Chile's departure from the Andean Pact in 1976 (Ferris 1979:55). Febres Cordero's reinstatement of Ecuador's relationship with OPIC required that he violate Decision 24's conditions on foreign investment, an infringement the Ecuadoran president was more than willing to commit (EIU 1985a:8; J.D. Martz 1986:B117; Molineu 1990:99).

II. THE FEBRES CORDERO AND REAGAN ADMINISTRATIONS

The signing of the OPIC agreement was among the first manifestations of a strong and cooperative economic and political relationship between the Reagan and Febres Cordero administrations. This section details the Reagan and Febres Cordero administration officials' positions on foreign investment in general, and on the OPIC agreement specifically. It reveals that leaders in both countries supported fully the OPIC signing, a consensus that led to a smooth negotiation process.

A. León Febres Cordero

President Febres Cordero's clear support for the OPIC agreement greatly facilitated its smooth passage. He championed foreign investment as a necessary element of economic growth for Ecuador since he entered public life. In his 1984 inaugural address, the new president promised to open Ecuador's doors to foreign investment (SENDIP 1987a:17). His 1985 Foreign Ministry report captures the administration's policy position on foreign investment: "The policy of the Ecuadoran Government with respect to foreign investments is clear: it seeks to channel foreign investments towards Ecuador in all those areas where it is considered useful. In petroleum, mining, agro-industry, [and in] certain branches of services, [foreign investment] is considered indispensable" (MRE 1985:35).

Febres Cordero's embrace of foreign investment was accompanied by a distrust of multilateral institutions that would seek to restrict international corporations' ability to earn and repatriate profits. Foremost among the objects of his disdain was the Andean Pact, particularly its Decision 24 (Corkill and Cubitt 1988:78; J.D. Martz 1990:24-25). For many in the Andean region, the Andean Pact is as much a political body as an economic one. Economically, the Pact has sought to plan development and industrial projects, as well as to encourage intra-subregional trade. However, the Pact has also advanced the notion that political unity is necessary for the Andean countries to gain visibility on regional and global stages. Former presidents Roldós, Hurtado, and Borja often treated the Pact as a political matter, worthy of loyalty even when the economic benefits it generates are impossible to detect (L. Carrión 1990). For example, Roldós's foreign minister, Alfredo Pareja, took advantage of a 1979 Pact meeting to gain support for Roldós's human rights policy (MRE 1980:148).

In direct contrast to his contemporaries, Febres Cordero saw the Andean Pact as merely an economic organization. He accordingly evaluated its progress solely in economic terms and deemed that it failed miserably. He explained his frustration with the organization's Decision 24 in a 1991 interview: "If we don't have sufficient national funds [for investment], we have to seek out foreign capital. But the subregion was isolated by this famous leftist idea. The Decision 24 turned us into an island where nobody wanted to invest because they weren't allowed to extract their own profits!" Febres Cordero went on to claim personal responsibility for ridding the subregion of the absurd Decision 24 ruling (Febres Cordero 1991). Indeed, the Febres Cordero administration did lead the

Andean effort at modifying Decision 24. Ecuador under Febres Cordero signed bilateral trade agreements with Pact members Colombia, Peru, and Venezuela (EIU 1986:19). Such agreements would have been unnecessary had the Andean Pact functioned properly as a trade organization. Febres Cordero's hostility towards the Andean Pact made it quite easy for him to violate Decision 24 in signing the OPIC accords.

B. Presidential advisers

The president's position on foreign investment was bolstered by the strong agreement of his economic and foreign policy-making team. Since 1980, Febres Cordero had consulted with three members of Guayaquil's business community who were to become the core of his future economic team and negotiators in the OPIC agreement: Carlos Julio Emanuel, Francisco Swett, and Alberto Dahik. All were trained in the US (Conaghan 1989:5; Conaghan, Malloy, and Abugattas 1990; Emanuel 1991). Foreign minister Edgar Terán, an ardent advocate of neo-liberal economic policies, also participated in the OPIC negotiations. This ideological conformity on the foreign investment issue assured President Febres Cordero that there would be no intra-administration dissent on the OPIC matter.

Central Bank president Carlos Julio Emanuel explained the position of the administration's economic team towards OPIC: "OPIC was a clear idea of ours. We wanted to attract foreign investment, particularly US investment, into the country. In order to do that an agreement with OPIC was necessary. The violation of Decision 24 is simply something that has to come along with that decision. We had to give special treatment to this foreign investment" (Emanuel 1991). Edgar Terán fully committed himself to opening Ecuador to foreign investment. As such, he opposed Decision 24, which in a 1991 interview he characterized as viciously restricting foreign investment:

> If you had to take your child to Moscow to see a medical specialist who lived only there, then you would submit yourself to all the bureaucracy of the Soviet Union in order to treat your child. But we

are talking about an international market of money and investments, and if an investor can choose among Indonesia, Spain, Togo,
Argentina, and Ecuador, then these countries must compete.
Unfortunately, an investor won't go to the place that cries against
foreign investment, that is, the place that says "Come, come, come,
but in order to invest here you have to place 18 special requests."
(Terán Terán 1991)

Given his commitment to a free market economy, Terán's frustration with Decision 24's constraints on foreign investment is
understandable. However, his likening the Andean Pact's restrictions to the Soviet bureaucracy reflects his deep-seated resentment
against the "leftists" he feels are responsible for Decision 24. In the
same interview, the former foreign minister expressed extreme disdain for Ecuador's leaders in the 1970s who committed the country
to the Andean Pact, referring to them as a "nucleus of Indian, dirty,
sick, and ignorant integrationists who were enemies of foreign
investment" (Terán Terán 1991). Terán's racist and other excessive
adjectives again reveal what appears to be as much a personal as an
ideological opposition to proponents of the Pact. Whatever the
nature of his opposition to Decision 24, it is clear he was fully committed to dismantling it with measures such as the OPIC agreement.

Febres Cordero assembled a competent and ideologically consistent team of economic and diplomatic advisers that strengthened
the administration's pro-foreign investment position. As is discussed below, this consensus generated a climate in which the OPIC
negotiations proceeded efficiently.

C. The Reagan administration

Fortunately for members of the Reagan administration, the
newly elected government in Quito proposed an economic plan
that closely adhered to policy preferences advanced in 1980s
Washington. In 1983, the Reagan administration released its
"Statement of Governmental Policy on International Investment."
The document stated that direct foreign investment should be the
primary source of new funds for development in the Third World

and that host countries should liberalize their restrictions on such investments. OPIC was targeted as the principal means through which US foreign investment would be encouraged. OPIC required the signing of bilateral agreements with Third World governments, which were obliged to accept international arbitration in instances of disputes between investors and the host countries (White 1988: 154-55). International financial institutions such as the World Bank, the IMF and the Inter-American Development Bank strongly supported the policy statement and implemented similar strategies (White 1988:156-57).

The Reagan administration found in President Febres Cordero a strong supporter of its pro-foreign investment policies. The consensus between the executives in Ecuador and the US led to the signing of an OPIC agreement shortly after the new Ecuadoran president came to office. Before detailing these negotiations, a consideration of the domestic political forces within Ecuador influencing the OPIC policy must be considered.

III. DOMESTIC ACTORS

The Febres Cordero administration's ability to sign the OPIC agreement with the United States was facilitated by the domestic political atmosphere in Ecuador. The administration's position was strong and united, whereas domestic political opponents were relatively weak and insufficiently committed to opposing Febres Cordero on the OPIC issue.

Febres Cordero's most important base of support came from the country's business community. This group had been the president's most ardent supporter during the campaign and expected him to implement foreign investment reform. Furthermore, the business community appropriately saw León Febres Cordero "as one of their own" (Conaghan, Malloy and Abugattas 1990:13). Both as a congressional deputy and as a private citizen leading Guayaquil's Chamber of Industry, Febres Cordero had directed the business community's opposition to the Andean Pact (Hurtado 1990; Pérez 1990; G. Salgado 1990). The skepticism of business elites towards subregional economic integration was two-fold and somewhat contradictory. On the one hand, they criticized the Pact's restrictions on the flow of international funds, citing free enterprise as the guiding principle of an efficient economy. On the other hand, many individuals worried that reductions in protectionist measures within the Andean community would damage particular economic interests (G. Salgado 1990). Clearly, the business community's most fervent opposition to the Andean Pact centered on Decision 24's restrictions on foreign investment. Ecuador's most important negotiator in the Pact, Germánico Salgado, claims that the notion that Decision 24 prohibited foreign investors from financing projects in Ecuador is "mythology." Salgado can recall only one foreign company, Coca-Cola, that decided against investment as a result of Decision 24's restrictions. Otherwise, Salgado adds, Decision 24 was much stronger in words than in deeds (Salgado 1990). Although in practice the restrictions may have been more diluted than they appeared on paper, Decision 24 nonetheless solidified the business community's opposition to the Andean Pact (Conaghan 1988:91-93). This group was therefore delighted when Febres Cordero was elected to the presidency. The Chambers of Production, the primary vehicles of communication for Ecuador's business community, repeatedly stressed their support for the administration's pro-investment policy positions (see, e.g., CIG 1985; CIP 1987:13-15; Pallares Sevilla 1991).

Ecuador's student and labor groups were Febres Cordero's most vocal non-governmental opponents to foreign investment. However, these groups' ability to effect policy changes was "stunted by a combination of internal weaknesses within the movements and the enormous institutional and political powers accrued by the neoliberal teams" (Conaghan, Malloy, and Abugattas 1990:24). Student groups rarely garnered the authority or organization to achieve policy modification. Protests by labor groups in the early months of the Febres Cordero administration were met with harsh measures by the administration. The Frente Unitario de Trabajadores (FUT), the largest and most visible labor organization, was already weakened by internal divisions when it launched its offensive against various aspects of the Febres Cordero administration's neo-

liberal economic program. Febres Cordero successfully used the
national police as well as army troops to put down FUT protests
(Conaghan, Malloy and Abugattas 1990:25).

Febres Cordero was also opposed by Congress' Bloque Progresista
(BP), a coalition of anti-administration forces that vowed to oppose
the president's economic restructuring (Conaghan 1989:6). Despite
its majority in Congress, BP was unable to halt the OPIC signing. A
number of factors explain Febres Cordero's successful resistance to
pressure against his signing the OPIC agreement. First, Febres
Cordero and his team negotiated and signed the OPIC agreement
so swiftly that the opposition forces had little time to organize
against it. Second, the force behind the administration's desire to
sign the agreement, combined with strong support from economic
elites, increased its ability to resist opponents. As Febres Cordero's
Central Bank president chief, Carlos Julio Emanuel explained,
"[Congress and other leftists] criticized the agreement with OPIC,
but that didn't influence our decision because Febres Cordero was
clear on what he wanted to do. He wanted to open up the country
to foreign investment" (Emanuel 1991).

Former president Febres Cordero explained his administration's
ability to proceed with the policy in the face of opposition in a similar way. "The opposition reacted to the OPIC signing with the typical reactions of the left. These we all know from memory. They are
responses that are prefabricated in the communist centers of the
world. But the government has to assume its responsibilities, and it
must confront its problems and resolve them in the face of such
opposition" (Febres Cordero 1991). The administration's strong
sense of mission and disdain for the opposition decreased its vulnerability to criticisms.

A third factor that contributed to Febres Cordero's ability to
implement the policy is the opposition's relatively weak commitment to opposing the OPIC agreement specifically. Labor, student
groups, and the Bloque Progresista made general commitments to
opposing the administration's general economic program, but did
not target its foreign investment component. In fact, the country
had become accustomed to the idea that foreign investment was a
perhaps unfortunate necessity to help Ecuador recover from its

economic crisis (White 1988). Even President Hurtado, an economic nationalist, had promoted foreign investment in the country's most precious petroleum industry (see chapter 4). Febres Cordero's opponents focused on aspects of the economic plan more likely to affect Ecuadorans' standard of living most directly, namely currency devaluations and the lifting of subsidies on basic consumer goods and services. The OPIC agreement was comparably less threatening.

Finally, the Febres Cordero administration skillfully employed constitutional measures to insulate its economic policy from congressional scrutiny. The 1978 constitution allowed the executive to implement economic policy by decree. If Congress did not revoke the decree within fifteen days, it became law (Conaghan 1989:8; Conaghan, Malloy, and Abugattas 1990:20). Furthermore, although Congress repeatedly attempted to legislate economic policy, the administration refused to submit any authority in this area. As Finance Minister Swett explained, "the President vetoed every decision of the Congress that ran contrary to the aim of reordering the economy" (quoted in Conaghan 1989:9). Within this hostile executive-legislative climate, congressional deputies did not deem it worthy of their efforts to attempt to block the OPIC agreement. Febres Cordero's non-compromising approach earned him a reputation as a "civilian dictator" and the leader of a "Rambocracy," but succeeded in enabling the implementation of his economic program (Conaghan 1989:7).

IV. THE NEGOTIATIONS

The regional atmosphere towards investment facilitated the fostering of foreign investment in Latin America by the Reagan administration. The 1980s economic crisis forced Latin American leaders to reevaluate restrictions on foreign investment. As the debt crisis worsened, foreign investment became a necessary source of fresh capital and development funds. Talk of foreign investment as a threat to national sovereignty gave way to its being lauded as a solution to capital flow troubles (EIU 1985a:8; White 1988). Similarly, the Andean Pact suffered a legitimacy crisis in the 1980s as a result of its inability to foster development and intra-subregional trade. During the economic boom of the 1970s, Andean Pact members had agreed to restrict foreign investment in favor of locally-owned industry. However, as economic necessity forced Latin American leaders to seek funds from abroad, the Pact focused on diplomatic, rather than economic, questions. This shift was evidenced in numerous violations of Andean Pact economic rules by all member states during the 1980s (MICIP 1984:47; Pareja Diezcanseco 1990; G. Salgado 1990).

Within this regional trend favoring the acceptance of foreign investment, the US was particularly favored with the presence of León Febres Cordero, a pro-investment conservative. The Febres Cordero administration's clear advocacy of the OPIC signing made the agreement with the United States a smooth process. Foreign Minister Terán described the meetings as one of the most conflict-free negotiations he had experienced during his career as a lawyer. "It was in absolutely no way difficult for me to work with [the OPIC officials]. As I am a lawyer, I have negotiated with many businesses, and this was really simple" (Terán 1991). Terán also stated that the few sources of conflict that did arise were easily resolved. He failed, however, to mention that Ecuador ended in compromising on those issues. The most important concession involved OPIC's requirement that disputes between US companies and Ecuador be subject to international, rather than local, arbitration. The Andean Pact required that disputes be managed in national judicial bodies and that national sovereignty should be a guiding principle in dispute resolution. The Febres Cordero administration hoped to maintain national arbitration of disputes. The US agreed to submit disputes first to arbitration in Ecuador, but if the procedure resulted in a "denial of justice"—to be determined by US investors—the dispute would be advanced to international arbitration (EIU 1985a:8). This was a clear compromise on the part of the Ecuadorans, but one Febres Cordero and his team were willing to make. According to negotiator Alberto Dahik, "these were very minor discrepancies" (Dahik 1991).

Ecuadoran participants in the negotiations described the talks as upbeat. Alberto Dahik described a "mood" in which both sides clearly wanted to sign the agreement. Febres Cordero and Carlos Julio Emanuel agreed, citing OPIC as one of the shining moments of the early days of the administration's economic reforms. Edgar Terán explained that opponents of OPIC highly exaggerated the conflicts between the US and Ecuadoran negotiators.

While there is a high degree of consistency in the description of the negotiations by former Febres Cordero administration officials, it is worthwhile to investigate to what degree they were forced to accept US conditions in order to achieve an OPIC agreement. White (1988:170) claims that the US government had a "unilateral strategy, aimed at imposing changes or ties by means of reprisals or diplomatic protection, as well as the manipulation of multilateral programs" to achieve its economic goals in Latin America. While the Reagan administration may have implemented this aggressive strategy elsewhere, it was unnecessary in Ecuador, where the Febres Cordero government actively sought an OPIC agreement. Furthermore, the Reagan administration was unable to force most Latin American countries to sign bilateral OPIC agreements. Only Colombia and Ecuador agreed. Others refused the conditions that disputes be subject to international arbitration (Bitar 1988:178). It appears, therefore, that Washington's strategy worked only where it was least needed.

V. CONSEQUENCES AND EFFECTS

The OPIC agreement provoked a flurry of business activity. US investors travelled to Ecuador while Ecuadoran business owners in search of joint ventures visited the US in the months following the agreement (J.D. Martz 1986:B117-18). The Ecuadoran Chambers of Production also sponsored numerous investment missions in the US (El Comercio 1985j; CCQ 1986:56-57). In 1985, the Ecuadoran government officially nullified its commitment to Decision 24 and announced new regulations by which foreign companies exporting more than 80 percent of materials produced in Ecuador were no longer obliged to seek local partners. All limits on repatriation of profits were also removed (EIU 1985c:1; CCQ 1986:31). The OPIC agreement initiated the process by which Ecuador's business community and the government fiercely courted foreign investors.

Did the OPIC agreement lead to increased foreign investment in the Ecuadoran economy? The Febres Cordero administration was able to release impressive investment figures in 1984 that appeared to demonstrate that OPIC had indeed generated increased foreign investment. Total direct foreign investment in the Ecuadoran economy increased from $674.8 million in 1983 to $752.3 million in 1984 (EIU 1985c:1). It is misleading to attribute this improvement to the OPIC agreement which, signed in November 1984, could not account for new investment in 1984.

It is more appropriate to evaluate *US investments*, those covered by OPIC, throughout the entire Febres Cordero administration. Table 14 provides figures for total US direct investment in Ecuador during those years. It reveals that during 1985, the first year after the OPIC agreement was signed, there was in fact a $10 million *decrease* in US investment in Ecuador. In 1986 and 1987, however, Ecuador did enjoy an expansion of US investments. Those investments began to decline during Febres Cordero's final year in office (Acosta 1990a:31).

Table 14: Total US Investments in Ecuador, 1984-1988

Year	1984	1985	1986	1987	1988
Total US investments	371	361	413	466	448

Source: United States Statistical Abstracts (1990:797)
Note: Figures are in millions of US dollars.

Former president Febres Cordero boasts that his administration's efforts caused huge increases in foreign investment. While the difference between the 1985 and 1986 figures is impressive, it is necessary to examine their relationship to the OPIC agreement. The majority of these investments financed Ecuador's petroleum industry. According to Febres Cordero's Central Bank manager, Carlos Julio Emanuel, US investors would have been attracted to the oil industry whether OPIC was operating in Ecuador or not. Legislation enacted during the Hurtado administration encouraged foreign investments in the petroleum industry through the liberalization of restrictions on those investments (J.D. Martz 1987:346-55; also see chapter 4, above). Investment in non-petroleum areas remained weak. Former finance minister Alberto Dahik explained that structural economic reforms needed to complement the OPIC agreement were not enacted swiftly enough to attract investors to non-petroleum industries (Dahik 1991). Perhaps the most important factor contributing to low foreign investment in Ecuador was the general trend against foreign investment in Latin America. Latin America's political and economic profile during the 1980's was unattractive to most investors in non-mineral industries. Latin American economies suffered huge debt burdens and deep recessions. Austerity measures were accompanied by political and social discontent, often reflected in hostile relationships between executive branches committed to austerity and legislatures resisting it. Ecuador during the Febres Cordero administration exemplified this executive-legislative tension. OPIC agreements were insufficient to overcome foreign investors' concerns that investments in Latin America would be unwelcome and unprofitable (Schodt 1989:187).

Disappointing foreign investment was more a reaction to the general financial climate than a lack of commitment on the part of the Febres Cordero administration to attract investment. Febres Cordero signed the agreement with OPIC, but it was up to private investors to decide whether to take advantage of the OPIC insurance. However, private investors' response to OPIC opportunities is not the sole measure of the benefits of the agreement. It is also appropriate to examine the US government's reaction to the Febres Cordero administration's signing the OPIC agreement. Did the Reagan administration use the means at its disposal to reward Febres Cordero for inviting US investors into his country?

There is a general consensus among policy analysts that the US government and Ecuador's creditors reacted favorably to Febres Cordero's overall economic liberalization program (Zuckerman 1986; Schodt 1989:187; J.D. Martz 1990:23; Grindle and Thoumi 1991:56; Morejón Pazmiño 1991). The most obvious reward came in the 1985 debt rescheduling package, the terms of which granted

Ecuador a three-year grace period on payments and extended repayment over twelve years beyond that. By all accounts, the package was quite favorable to Ecuador (J.D. Martz 1986:116; Schodt 1989: 187). Similarly, President Reagan called Febres Cordero a "model" of leadership in implementing the necessary economic reforms to pull Latin America out of its debt crisis during the Ecuadoran president's trip to Washington in January 1986 (Grindle and Thoumi 1991:56). Finally, Ecuador was targeted as a primary recipient of Baker Plan funds. The Plan, designed by US secretary of the treasury James Baker, called for private banks and international lending institutions to disburse new loans to Latin American debtors, who in turn promised austerity measures and a reduction of the state's role in the economy (EIU 1986:6; Zuckerman 1986:484; Corkill and Cubitt 1988:77; Acosta 1990b:321). Febres Cordero's willingness to remodel the Ecuadoran economy, including inviting foreign investment and abandoning the Andean Pact's Decision 24, awarded his country a special place in the Baker Plan.

Rewards directly traceable to signing the OPIC agreement are few. Instead, OPIC formed part of an overall economic policy that earned the Febres Cordero administration favorable treatment by economic actors in the United States. President Febres Cordero was one of the pioneers of Latin America's shifting away from economic nationalism, particularly in the realm of foreign investment. As one of the first to open his country to foreign investment and to implement other liberalization measures, Febres Cordero earned a positive reputation among economic actors in the North, who lauded his economic policies and rewarded him with favorable terms on debt repayments.

VI. THEORETICAL APPLICATION

A. Compliance

As is the case with other instances of Febres Cordero's foreign policy alignment with US preferences, a casual observation of the OPIC case might lead one to conclude it to be an example of compliance. However, a crucial defining element of a compliant foreign policy, a conflict of interests between periphery and core, is not present here. There is no evidence that US policy-makers pressured their counterparts in Ecuador on this issue. Such pressure was entirely unnecessary. Members of the Febres Cordero administration were as eager to sign the OPIC accords as were members of the Reagan administration.

Interestingly, in other Latin American states whose leaders did not view OPIC favorably, the US was largely unsuccessful in producing an OPIC agreement (Bitar 1988:178). It appears that despite Reagan administration efforts, the OPIC issue does not lend itself to the successful imposition of pressure to produce a compliant foreign policy.

B. Consensus

The consensus model of dependent foreign policy much more adequately captures the OPIC agreement between Ecuador and the United States. This model anticipates that ideological agreement between policy-makers in the US and Ecuador will lead to policy alignment. The OPIC accords emerged from just such a process. This is a clear example of ideological concordance between political leaders in North and South. Both Febres Cordero and Reagan, hard-core free marketeers, had targeted foreign investment as a necessary and appropriate means to stimulate growth in Latin America. Another element of a consensus foreign policy, the expectation of mutual benefit, characterized the mood of the OPIC negotiations. The OPIC policy also conforms to the expectation that a consensus-based foreign policy will benefit economic elites in Ecuador. The Chambers of Production, the primary political vehicle for the business sector, fully supported OPIC in the anticipation that new funds would be channeled through existing corporations in Ecuador.

C. Counterdependence

Febres Cordero's signing of the OPIC agreement in no way corresponds to counterdependence. This model requires that leaders seek to diminish a state's dependence on the United States. Arguably, the OPIC agreement increased Ecuador's dependence on US sources of foreign investment. Furthermore, the United States is expected to resist a counterdependent foreign policy. Clearly, the US was a primary supporter of the agreement. As a strongly pro-US leader, Febres Cordero would not willfully design a counterdependent policy.

D. Realism

In its expectation that states will design policies to promote regional status, realism fails to explain the OPIC policy. Breaking with the Andean Pact and aligning with US investors did more to damage than to improve Febres Cordero's reputation in Latin America. However, the OPIC accords do conform with realism's expectations that Third World leaders will advance development concerns. The Febres Cordero administration targeted foreign investment as the best means of attracting needed development funds. The economic team's entire development strategy centered on a free market system relying on private sector growth, a fundamental basis of which was increased foreign investment. To the extent that OPIC formed part of Febres Cordero's development strategy, realism can explain the policy.

The OPIC initiative also conforms with realism's expectation that leaders will not embark on policies for which they have insufficient resources to implement. Signing OPIC required that Febres Cordero meet criticism from domestic and regional actors who opposed violating the Andean Pact's Decision 24 and who feared loss of local economic autonomy. Febres Cordero's confrontational style and belief in the need for investment equipped him with more than sufficient diplomatic and political resources to manage that opposition. This was particularly true during an economic crisis, when most Latin American political actors realized the need for increased foreign investment.

E. Leader preferences

Leader preferences can also account for Febres Cordero's signing of the OPIC agreement. The policy clearly conformed with the president's personal views towards the role of foreign investment in the Ecuadoran economy. He demonstrated an active interest in pursuing the agreement, evidenced by the fact that the accord was signed less than four months after he took office. The president also remained an active participant and observer of the policy and negotiations. He gave only his very top economic and foreign policy advisers authority over the OPIC negotiations, allowing no dissent within his staff. Had Foreign Ministry bureaucrats participated in this policy, for example, many would have opposed the violation of the Andean Pact's Decision 24. The Ministry had been involved in Andean Pact operations since the late 1960s and viewed the organization favorably (G. Salgado 1990; L. Carrión 1990). Febres Cordero's hand-picked negotiators were all government outsiders with no allegiance to the Andean Pact that might weaken their commitment to OPIC. These men ensured that the president's preferences were fully implemented.

F. Domestic politics

What domestic political opposition there was to OPIC was largely ignored by the Febres Cordero administration. Domestic opponents, such as labor and student groups, were weak and not steadfastly committed to criticizing the OPIC agreement in particular. These opponents can be considered a relevant opposition group, paving the way for domestic politics to explain this case. However, other conditions allowed the executive to disregard his domestic detractors on this issue. Febres Cordero's dedication to OPIC, combined with the weakness of his opponents, enabled him to dismiss domestic critics in pursuit of the OPIC agreement. The only domestic actors whose interests were favored by OPIC were those who fully supported Febres Cordero on this issue. The Chambers of Production provided the Febres Cordero administration strong domestic political backing on OPIC. However, the president in no way had to alter his own preferences to satisfy this group.

VI. CONCLUSION

The OPIC agreement between Ecuador and the United States is an example of a policy in which leaders in both countries were able to implement their preferences. This ideological consensus produced a smooth negotiating process and an outcome favorable to both parties. It also negated any policy impact by domestic opponents, who were too weak to stand up against a Reagan-Febres Cordero coalition favoring foreign investment.

Table 15 demonstrates that three dependent foreign policy approaches, consensus, realism, and leader preferences, can account for the OPIC agreement. Of these, consensus explains the policy most fully. The policy conforms exactly with the consensus model's explanation of dependent foreign policy development (Moon 1983, 1985). Ideological agreement among elites in the US and Ecuador led to policy alignment characterized by an expectation of mutual benefit. That the US continued to treat Ecuador favorably throughout the Febres Cordero administration is further evidence that the two administrations shared common views and goals.

Table 15: Febres Cordero's OPIC Policy

	Compliance	Consensus	Counter-dependence	Realism	Leader preferences	Domestic politics
Signing of OPIC	no	yes	no	yes	yes	no

Consensus explains the policy slightly better than leader preferences because the Febres Cordero administration did have to compromise on an important point in the negotiations. The US succeeded in acquiring international arbitration of disputes. Febres Cordero himself nonetheless describes this as a minor concession, and one he was perfectly willing to make in order to achieve the OPIC agreement (Febres Cordero 1991). Otherwise, the president's preferences were implemented. An understanding of Febres Cordero's views on foreign investment and development explains well his pursuit of an OPIC accord.

As in other cases examined in this study, realism can explain this policy, but only in gross terms. Alone it cannot predict that Febres Cordero would have chosen to advance development through foreign investment channels. Realism expects that Third World leaders will pursue development, but an understanding of a regime's ideological orientation is needed to explain what type of development policy will emerge. Indeed, many other contemporary Ecuadoran leaders would have shunned foreign investment as counterproductive to true development. Realism can account for the OPIC agreement, but only in a retrospective analysis informed with an understanding of Febres Cordero's preferences.

The two theoretical approaches that expect Latin American leaders to have anti-US preferences cannot explain the OPIC agreement. Compliance and counterdependence both assume antagonism of interests between the US and Ecuador, and as such cannot account for a policy designed by a pro-US leader such as Febres Cordero. Domestic politics fails in this case because the opposition was weak and did not place a high priority on the foreign investment issue. As such, a united administration easily overcame domestic criticism.

Consensus clearly explains the OPIC policy most adequately. The conditions that facilitated its presence exist in this case. First, the Febres Cordero administration aligned ideologically with the Reagan administration on this issue. Second, both were operating in an area of authority and importance. OPIC was considered a crucial agreement to leaders in Washington as well as Quito. Finally, that commitment and unity allowed the Febres Cordero administration to ignore the relatively weak domestic opposition.

9   Conclusions

I. INTRODUCTION

THE PRECEDING chapters detail twelve of Ecuador's foreign policy cases during the 1980s. This concluding chapter aims to extract the theoretically relevant material from the information provided by the case studies. It also seeks to condense the detail into a series of conclusions about the nature of dependence and its impact on foreign policy.

Table 16 summarizes the six theories' applicability to the case studies. A first glance at table 16 reveals that no single theory accounts for all the cases. Leader preferences and realism perform well, explaining 67 percent and 42 percent of the cases respectively. Still, the majority of the theories fail to command impressive explanatory power. A number of potential explanations for the distribution of explanatory capacity detailed in table 16 should be outlined. It is important to remember, for example, that while great care was taken in selecting cases that represented key aspects of a dependent relationship and its impact on foreign policy, the study only examines twelve cases. Therefore, sample bias cannot be ruled out. This possibility does not negate this study's findings, however. Ecuador during the Hurtado and Febres Cordero administrations was a heavily dependent country and the theories evaluated here should therefore account for these cases.

Table 16: Theories' Applications to the Cases and Issue Area Breakdown

Case	Compliance	Consensus	Counter-dependence	Realism	Leader preferences	Domestic politics
Osvaldo Hurtado						
1a. Rejection of US intervention in Nicaragua (D)	no	no	yes	no	yes	no
1b. Failure to support Sandinistas (D)	no	yes	no	no	yes	no
2a. Invite foreign investment to oil industry (E)	no	no	no	yes	yes	no
2b. Investment reform law (E)	no	no	no	yes	no	yes
3a. Initiate debt summit (D)	no	no	yes	no	yes	no
3b. Summit document generation (D)	no	no	yes	no	yes	no
3c. Appease USG and creditors (E)	yes	no	no	no	no	no
Number and percentage of Hurtado administration cases explained (n=7)	1 (14%)	1 (14%)	3 (43%)	2 (29%)	5 (71%)	1 (14%)
León Febres Cordero						
1. Join Contadora Support Group (D)	no	no	no	yes	no	no
2. Break relations with Nicaragua (D)	no	no	no	no	yes	no
3a. Invite Blazing Trails (E)	no	yes	no	yes	yes	no
3b. Dismiss troops (D)	no	no	yes	no	no	yes
4. Sign OPIC agreement with United States (E)	no	yes	no	yes	yes	no
Number and percentage of Febres Cordero administration cases explained (n=5)	0 (0%)	2 (40%)	1 (20%)	3 (60%)	3 (60%)	1 (20%)
Number and percentage of total cases explained (n=12)	1 (8%)	3 (25%)	4 (33%)	5 (42%)	8 (67%)	2 (17%)
Number and percentage of economic/development cases explained (n=5)	1 (20%)	2 (40%)	0 (0%)	4 (80%)	3 (60%)	1 (20%)
Number and percentage of diplomatic cases explained (n=7)	0 (0%)	1 (14%)	4 (57%)	1 (14%)	5 (71%)	1 (14%)

Note: (D) indicates diplomatic issue area, (E) indicates economic/development issue area.

The failure of any single theory to explain all or the great majority of the cases might also suggest that the search for a grand theory of dependent foreign policy is inappropriate. Perhaps no single theory should be expected to explain this universe. Rather we should seek middle-range theories that are useful under specific conditions. Recall that many of the cases detailed in this study failed to meet the defining conditions (outlined in chapter 1) of many theories. For example, a defining condition of compliance was that the policy-maker in Ecuador disagree with the policy preferences of the US. President Febres Cordero rarely disagreed with the Reagan administration, nullifying the possibility that compliance will explain most examples of Febres Cordero administration policies. They therefore cannot act as critical cases, or worthy tests, of compliance. It is appropriate then, to ask first whether the defining conditions of different theories hold for a set of cases, and then to identify the conditions under which potentially competing theories explain.

Bruce Russett (1983) argues that such conditional theories are needed to explain dependency-based relations in general. Russett demonstrates that analyses of dependence cannot find universal truths across states. Rather, state-level factors such as size, colonial history, and the nature of foreign penetration, condition the effects of dependence on economic growth and inequality within the dependent state (Russett 1983:561). Russett thus concludes that different theoretical approaches are needed to explain dependence in different countries.

If the effects of dependence on growth and inequality vary from country to country, it follows that its effects on foreign policy may also vary. Russett's point can be taken a step further. The high degree of foreign policy variation in 1980s Ecuador suggests that the effects of dependence vary within countries as well as across them. Conditional theories may therefore be needed to explain the foreign policy within a single dependent state. The fact that no theory explains all of the cases while each theory explains some of the cases lends credence to the idea that middle-range theories are more appropriate than grand theories.

An additional possibility that Russett (1983) also discusses is that interaction of two or more theories will best explain dependent foreign policy. Table 16 reveals that only three of the cases are explained by a single theory. The remainder are explained by two or three different theories. This suggests that no single approach can tell the entire story, but that together some theories may be able to provide a fuller account. Interactive theories, then, may also be fruitful for explaining dependent foreign policy.

The ensuing discussion considers these possibilities. Section II evaluates how well each theory explains the cases. It is worthwhile here to review the manner in which it was determined whether a particular theory explained a case. Chapter 1 outlined the defining conditions of each theory. The defining conditions do not alone predict whether a theory does in fact explain. The policy *output* must conform to the theory's expectations in order for a theory to account for a case. For example, the defining conditions of compliance are that the policy-makers in core and periphery disagree on the issue at hand, and that the policy be salient to peripheral leaders. In order for compliance to be a potential contender, these conditions must hold. However, the policy output, that peripheral policy-makers implement a pro-core policy, is necessary to determine whether compliance in fact explains the case. This distinction between defining conditions and policy output will prove essential in the evaluation of the theories. As will be seen, for example, while many cases displayed the defining conditions for compliance, the theory explained only one case.

Because the defining conditions alone cannot predict whether a policy will explain a case, I identify contextual conditions and types of issue areas under which each theory emerges.[1] The contextual conditions, combined with the defining conditions, more fully explain when a theory will account for a case. The strength of these conditions is then scrutinized in both a positive and negative manner. First, do the conditions hold for those cases explained by the theory? Second, do the conditions fail to hold for the cases *not* explained by the theory under consideration? My assessment of

---

1. This study's cases fall exclusively into two issue area categories: economic/development and diplomatic. Its issue area-based conclusions will therefore relate directly to these realms. Examples of foreign policies in the military/security issue area were not examined here. It is of course possible that their inclusion would produce different issue-based results.

whether the conditions hold is based on the detailed information provided in the case study chapters. If there are insufficient data to decide whether a condition holds, I reserve judgment. This scrutinized analysis of the theoretical conditions increases the likelihood that they can be generalized to other examples of dependent foreign policy.

Section III proceeds with a cross-theory analysis. It examines when theories co-occur and considers the propriety of an interactive and middle-range theoretical approach to dependent foreign policy. Section IV treats whole policies, rather than individual components or decision points within the cases. Whereas sections II and III consider the twelve different policy points identified in the case studies, section IV looks at the six general foreign policy areas developed in the case study chapters. Finally, section V summarizes the conclusions developed throughout this chapter.

II. EVALUATION OF INDIVIDUAL THEORIES

A. Compliance

An examination of the compliance column reveals perhaps the most striking element in table 16. Compliance fails to explain all but one of the cases. Recall from chapter 1 that compliance has been the prevailing theoretical approach to the study of dependent foreign policy. The intuitive basis of compliance, that dependent states forfeit their own foreign policy preferences to gratify the core, is found here to be too simplistic to account for Ecuador's foreign policy during the 1980s. That compliance explained only one of twelve dependent foreign policy examples in Ecuador parallels this theory's decline in the literature (DeRouen and Mintz 1991).

Table 17 shows that six of the case studies did display compliance's defining conditions: (1) a policy discrepancy between core and periphery and (2) centering on an issue that was salient to the periphery. However, only one of these six cases also displayed compliance's necessary foreign policy output—that the policy be pro-core. It is therefore necessary to consider what other *contextual conditions* lead to compliance's success in explaining a case.

Contextual conditions are criteria beyond the defining conditions that correspond with a particular theory's ability to explain.

Table 17: Conditions of Compliance

| Case | Defining conditions | | Contextual Conditions | |
	Policy discrepancy between core & periphery	Salient to periphery	Core able & willing to punish	Periphery needs to avoid punishment
Osvaldo Hurtado				
1a. Rejection of US intervention in Nicaragua	yes	yes	no	no
1b. Failure to support Sandinistas	no	no	no	no
2a. Invite foreign investment to oil industry	no	yes	?[a]	yes
2b. Investment reform law	no	yes	?[a]	yes
3a. Initiate debt summit	yes	yes	no	yes
3b. Summit document generation	yes	yes	no	yes
3c. Appease USG and creditors[b]	yes	yes	yes	yes
León Febres Cordero				
1. Join Contadora Support Group	?[a]	?[a]	no	no
2. Break relations with Nicaragua	no	yes	no	no
3a. Invite Blazing Trails	no	yes	no	no
3b. Dismiss troops	yes	yes	no	no
4. Sign OPIC agreement with United States	no	yes	no	no

[a] Insufficient data to determine.
[b] This case was explained by compliance.

It is difficult to base conclusions about compliance on a single case. However, some observations are possible. Compliance's one example emerged in an economic issue area. Hurtado complied with core wishes in the realm of his greatest vulnerability. His behavior in the CEL suggests that he worried creditors would punish Ecuador for convening the conference. That retribution could have taken the form of halted loans or more difficult debt renegotiations. Ecuador in the early 1980s faced severe financial conditions and could little afford difficult renegotiation terms. This was also the area where core actors were most able to influence or punish

Hurtado. The US government and creditor banks controlled credit access. They possessed the instruments to damage Ecuador's economy if they so chose. Furthermore, economic policy was critically important to the Reagan administration. The US was therefore most likely to react to defiant behavior by Ecuador in this realm. It appears that Hurtado understood his country's economic vulnerability and complied in order to avoid retribution from actors who were clearly powerful and interested enough to punish him.

Contrast Hurtado's behavior in this case with that in the diplomatic realm, where he defied the United States repeatedly. In his criticism of US policy in Central America and in his sponsorship of the CEL, Hurtado distinctly did not comply. This contrast suggests that compliance is more likely to emerge in the area of Ecuador's greatest vulnerability and where the core was most able and willing to exact retribution for defiant behavior. These conditions in the 1980s emerged most frequently in the economic area, where US interests were well defined and Latin American states were extremely weak. The diplomatic realm, on the other hand, did not demonstrate these characteristics. While the Reagan administration was clearly committed to its objectives in Central America, it did not exert much effort at gaining regional support of its policies. Similarly, Latin Americans united frequently on diplomatic questions such as US regional policy and the debt. These movements provided Hurtado and other Latin American leaders with some protection against bilaterally-imposed penalties from the US. The US rarely opposed these efforts, deciding instead simply to ignore or to circumvent them. Similarly, the US did not have obvious policy instruments at its disposal to punish Latin Americans in the diplomatic realm. Because the US publicly supported new democracies in the region, overt intervention in diplomatic affairs was undesirable to US policy-makers.

It is appropriate here to make explicit a theme that develops throughout this chapter. In the cases examined in this study, the US prioritized the economic issue area and was therefore more likely to intervene in Ecuador's policy in economic matters than diplomatic affairs. This pattern relates less to economic and diplomatic issue areas per se than it does to US priorities and Ecuadoran vulnerability. Because Ecuador was financially imperiled and the US considered Ecuador's behavior in the economic realm salient, the economic realm was the one in which Ecuador's pro-US behavior was most likely. A different pair of core-periphery actors operating in a different time or place might demonstrate this behavior in another realm. Similarly, because the US did not prioritize diplomatic issues in its relations with Ecuador in the 1980s, Ecuador displayed a high degree of foreign policy autonomy. Under different historical circumstances, the core might not tolerate high degrees of foreign policy variation in the diplomatic arena. Economic issue areas were very critical between the US and Latin America during the 1980s while diplomatic issues were less so. These issue areas could exchange positions under a different core-periphery relationship. Military/security issue areas could also assume high salience under certain conditions. The key factor is not the content of the issue area, but its salience to the core and the periphery's vulnerability in that realm.

A consideration of Hurtado's example of compliance leads to the tentative conclusion that compliance will explain when, in addition to the defining conditions (policy discrepancy between core and periphery on an issue that is salient to the periphery), two additional contextual conditions arise: (1) the case involves an issue area in which the core is able and willing to punish the periphery, and (2) the case involves an issue area in which the periphery cannot afford such punishment. Ecuador's appeasement of its creditors on the CEL conforms with each of these conditions. The conditions' strength is bolstered by evidence in table 17 which demonstrates that these contextual conditions did not hold for any other case.

B. Consensus

Consensus explains three of the cases, performing significantly better than compliance. This lends credence to Moon's (1985) assertion that consensus is a better description than compliance of the process through which pro-core foreign policies develop. Although it performs better than compliance, consensus still accounts for only 24 percent of the cases, suggesting that pro-core foreign policies do not emerge with the frequency that most dependent foreign policy scholars expect.

Recall that the principal defining condition of consensus is agreement between core and periphery leaders on the policy matter at hand. As table 18 demonstrates, five of the twelve cases display that defining condition. In Ecuador during the 1980s, such agreement was more likely to occur under Febres Cordero than under Hurtado. This challenges dependency theory's expectation that Latin American leaders conspire with their US counterparts to develop policy favoring their particular economic interests (Moon 1985:306, 308). While Febres Cordero provides perhaps one of the best modern examples of this phenomenon, Osvaldo Hurtado clearly does not fit the pattern dependency theorists expect. Hurtado was not educated in the US, does not speak English, and does not maintain business contacts with North Americans. That he arrived to Ecuador's top office counters the contention that pro-US economic elites always or even usually gain control over the policy process.

As table 18 also demonstrates, the existence of the defining condition does not necessarily lead to either a pro-core policy or to consensus theory's explaining the case. Other contextual conditions can be identified that further specify when consensus will explain. First is that consensus tends to emerge when the leader is in command of the policy. Hurtado's personal animosity towards Daniel Ortega and his belief that the Sandinistas were undemocratic were reflected in his Nicaragua policy. With no domestic opposition on this low-profile issue, the president could direct policy unhindered. Similarly, in the OPIC case, Febres Cordero and his economic team assumed command of the policy and saw it through to the end. In Blazing Trails, Febres Cordero and his defense minister launched the initiative before domestic opponents learned of their plans and could react. In all three cases, control over policy remained largely within the executive branch. A contrasting example is the Febres Cordero administration's joining the Contadora Support Group. There was ideological agreement between the executive and the US government, but Febres Cordero did not assume command of that policy, leaving it instead to his Foreign Ministry.

Does consensus develop within a particular issue area? Hurtado's one example of consensus emerged in the diplomatic realm while both of Febres Cordero's consensus policies were in the economic/development area. Few generalizable conclusions derive from Hurtado's failure to support the Sandinistas diplomatically. It is important to remember that this non-policy coincided with an anti-US policy that blatantly rejected US methods in Central America. Hurtado's failure to proceed with support for the Nicaraguan government, while motivated by concerns about the Sandinistas similar to the Reagan administration's, is more a product of the Ecuadoran president's personal views on this specific issue than of ideological alignment between Hurtado and Reagan. The overall policy remained anti-US.

Febres Cordero's consensus policies are more fruitful for issue-area conclusions, if only tentative ones. That both of Febres Cordero's consensus cases emerged in the economic realm signifies that a generally pro-US leader can implement pro-US policies in the economic realm. Nationalistically-minded political actors in Ecuador regularly oppose pro-US economic policies, arguing that they undermine Ecuadoran sovereignty and increase economic misery among the majority of the population. Pro-US economic policies are politically very difficult. Under consensus, the leader's pro-US tendencies combine with the support of external forces to overcome the domestic opposition that arises towards pro-core policies. Core support may be overt, as was the case in Blazing Trails and OPIC, or implicit. This support helped shield Febres Cordero from domestic opponents. This was particularly true under OPIC, where domestic opponents were entirely unable to prevent or modify the administration's policy. In the Blazing Trails example, domestic opposition emerged only after the administration had invited and prepared the site for US troops. External support gave Febres Cordero maneuvering room to develop Blazing Trails outside of normal domestic political channels. Furthermore, the administration was able to keep the troops in Ecuador until November despite tremendous domestic opposition. Support from the Pentagon, the Reagan administration, and the US ambassador in Quito helped Febres Cordero to disregard domestic opponents for a significant period of time. These types of policies are further facilitated by the support, albeit often implicit, of the domestic economic elites. The Chambers of Production failed to join the opposition to Blazing Trails, lending tacit support to the development project. In OPIC, the Chambers' support was overt. Outside the administration, they acted as OPIC's primary domestic champion.

This coalition of supporting forces, consisting of the administration, the US government and other core actors, and the local economic leaders, provides a pro-US administration with the backing needed to implement often unpopular pro-US economic policies. A leader lacking in this alliance would find the implementation of such policies much more difficult.

In summary, in addition to the defining condition (policy agreement between core and periphery), consensus tends to emerge under two additional contextual conditions: (1) when the leader is in command of the policy, and (2) when the leader receives explicit or implicit support from the core and domestic economic elites. Core-peripheral elite consensus lends the dependent state leader enough support to withstand domestic opposition to pro-US economic policies. In 1980s Ecuador, these conditions were more likely to develop in economic, rather than diplomatic, issue areas. These conditions are further verified by the fact they do not hold for those cases that were not explained by consensus (table 18).

Table 18: Conditions of Consensus

	Defining condition	Contextual Conditions	
Case	Ideological agreement among core & periphery leaders	Periphery leader in command of policy	Implicit or explicit core & domestic economic elite support for the policy
Osvaldo Hurtado			
1a. Rejection of US intervention in Nicaragua	no	yes	no
1b. Failure to support Sandinistas[a]	yes	yes	yes
2a. Invite foreign investment to oil industry	no	yes	yes
2b. Investment reform law	no	no	yes
3a. Initiate debt summit	no	yes	no
3b. Summit document generation	no	yes	no
3c. Appease USG and creditors	no	no	yes
León Febres Cordero			
1. Join Contadora Support Group	yes	no	?[b]
2. Break relations with Nicaragua	yes	yes	?[b]
3a. Invite Blazing Trails[a]	yes	yes	yes
3b. Dismiss troops	no	no	no
4. Sign OPIC agreement with United States[a]	yes	yes	yes

[a] Insufficient data to determine.
[b] These cases were explained by consensus.

C. Counterdependence

As table 16 illustrates, counterdependence accounts for four cases. This alone is significant in that counterdependence performs better than either compliance or consensus, the predominant theoretical approaches that expect dependent states to develop pro-core foreign policies. This study has found that counterdependence, which expects anti-core policies, alone explains the same number (four) of cases that compliance and consensus explain together. At least for the foreign policy cases examined here, the supposition that dependent states will usually follow the foreign policy guidance of the core is inaccurate.

Counterdependence's defining condition, that the policy be designed to reduce dependence, holds for four of the case studies. Interestingly, in every case in which the defining condition was present, counterdependence went on to explain the case. This suggests that perhaps that single defining condition is sufficient to predict counterdependence's ability to explain. However, such a strong conclusion cannot be based on the small number of cases in this study. It is therefore useful to identify what other contextual conditions emerged in the counterdependence cases.

There are three other identifiable conditions under which counterdependence emerges. First, the actor in control of the policy tends to oppose US interests and preferences. Under Osvaldo Hurtado (in whose administration three of the four counterdependence cases are found), that actor was the president himself. Hurtado expressed primarily economic nationalist and anti-imperialist convictions, views that were difficult to implement during a time of severe economic crisis. Nonetheless, three out of the five times that Hurtado was able to implement his preferences, he developed a counterdependent policy. This behavior is consistent with his ideological orientation advocating Ecuador's political and economic autonomy from the United States. Under Febres Cordero, the actor in control of the single example of counterdependence was the Congress, whose members severely opposed Febres Cordero's foreign policy of strong alignment with the Reagan administration. Congress, together with other political actors in Ecuador, pressured the Febres Cordero administration so strongly on Blazing Trails that the president defied his own wishes and ousted the troops. The driving force behind the policy was the reattainment of Ecuador's sovereignty, a highly counterdependent motivation. Counterdependence, then, will develop when the policy leader within Ecuador or other dependent state opposes US economic and/or political domination.

The second condition of counterdependence is that the policy leader confront little opposition from domestic political groups. It is important to remember that a counterdependent policy challenges the core and thus is expected to meet opposition from core leaders. However, there is only one example in this study of a successful counterdependent policy that received significant opposition from *domestic* actors. The Febres Cordero administration strongly opposed the dismissal of the troops but was unable to extend their stay. The troops' dismissal is the single case in which an actor other than the president implemented a counterdependent policy. When the executive is in command of a counterdependent policy, domestic opposition is inactive. For example, Osvaldo Hurtado's rejection of US policy in Central America and his initiation of the CEL did not appear to upset potential opponents within Ecuador.

A third condition is the core's willingness to tolerate counterdependence in the policy. In all four examples of counterdependence, the US demonstrated that the policy was of little importance. In the CEL, for example, US and other core leaders indicated that debt conferences could be held so long as no debtors' club that might threaten payments was established. Hurtado had complied on that point and was free to proceed with the CEL. Hurtado's rejection of US interventionism in Nicaragua was similarly unimportant to the Reagan administration, which pursued its policy in the region despite harsh criticism from Latin American neighbors. A lack of US opposition is slightly less true for Febres Cordero's dismissal of the troops. US ambassador Rondón advocated the Blazing Trails troops' staying in Ecuador. However, he advanced no effort beyond talks with congressional leaders in order to achieve that goal. Because the operation was going poorly, the US did not prioritize the operation's continuance. Furthermore, domestic opposition to Blazing Trails was powerful enough to withstand Rondón's pressure. These examples appear to indicate that counterdependence will succeed on those issues where potential opponents remain relatively weak or disinterested.

Issue area is also important. As the final two rows of table 16 illustrate, each time that counterdependence emerged in this study, it did so in the diplomatic issue area. This is consistent with the above findings that compliance and consensus, in many ways the antitheses of counterdependence, developed primarily in economic issue areas. The finding suggests that policy-makers perceive that counterdependent, or anti-US, policies will be tolerated more in the diplomatic arena than in the economic. They therefore sense more maneuvering room to oppose the US in diplomatic matters. Indeed, there is significant evidence suggesting that the US and other actors in the North allow counterdependence in diplomatic areas more often than they do in economic areas. The US was willing to permit Latin American neighbors to participate in a multitude of regional multilateral initiatives aimed at rejecting US policy in Central America, restructuring the region's debt, and other noble causes. US policy-makers reacted mildly to these types of policies, providing only rhetorical support or merely ignoring them. However, the US, the IMF, and the World Bank did not allow Latin Americans such maneuvering room on economic policy, where new loans were directly tied to the willingness of dependent states to adopt the policies preferred by the lenders.

The emergence of counterdependence in solely diplomatic issue areas supports the notion that anti-core behavior can occur only in those matters about which the core cares little. It also contrasts sharply with a series of studies that predicted dependent states to comply most frequently on Cold War issues, defined as those most salient to the US (Richardson and Kegley 1980; Armstrong 1981; Ray 1981). This study finds that the Cold War issue of the decade, Central America, was twice the object of anti-US behavior on Ecuador's part (Hurtado's rejection of US policy and Febres Cordero's joining the Support Group). Dependence on the US failed to produce compliance from Ecuador in one of the Reagan administration's most important policy areas.

What accounts for the failure of the United States to sanction counterdependence in diplomatic areas? The answers are too complex to examine closely in a study that does not focus on US foreign policy behavior. However, a preliminary explanation is merited. It appears that the Reagan administration understood that its Central America policies depended very little on regional support. Even in the face of significant Latin American opposition, the US was able to proceed with its policy. Opposition to Latin American counterdependence in this area was therefore unnecessary. Furthermore, policy instruments would have been difficult to identify. Any direct sanctions against Ecuador for counterdependence in the diplomatic area would have been met with cries of neocolonialism and intervention in other states' affairs. The US had little reason to risk such an outcry, particularly because Ecuador's counterdependent behavior had very little impact on US policy success in Central America and elsewhere.

In the economic realm, the situation is quite different. The stakes for the US were much higher. Latin Americans owed Northern banks large sums of money. That alone justified and necessitated the North's intervention into Latin American economic decision-making. Furthermore, the policy instruments available to Northern actors are more easily identified and used in the economic arena. The primary instrument, new loans, can be used as a carrot to encourage pro-core behavior or as a stick (when denied) as punishment for incorrect economic policy. Because the economic well-being of the region and the financial stability of the banks depended on particular actions by Latin America, Northern actors were much more likely to intervene in Latin America's decisions.

In sum, counterdependence explains dependent foreign policy under four conditions. First is the defining condition that the policy be designed to reduce dependence. In addition, there are three contextual conditions: (1) the periphery's policy-maker opposes core preferences on this issue, (2) the relevant domestic opposition is inactive, and (3) the core is willing to tolerate counterdependence on this matter. As this section has shown, these conditions, particularly the third, are more likely to emerge with regard to diplomatic than economic issues in US-Latin American relations. However, they could develop in different issue areas under another core-periphery relationship. Table 19 reveals that all four conditions do not hold for any cases not explained by counterdependence. One case, Ecuador's joining the Contadora Support Group, comes close to meeting the criteria. The first two conditions, that the policy be designed to reduce dependence and that the periphery policy-maker oppose core preferences, are difficult to determine in this case. The Foreign Ministry may have wanted to reduce its dependence on the US by joining Contadora. However, the desire to counterbalance Peru's power was stronger. The preferences of both the Reagan administration and Ecuadoran Foreign Ministry officials are ambiguous. Had the US clearly opposed Ecuador's entry into the Support Group, its doing so would have been explained by counterdependence.

Table 19: Conditions of Counterdependence

| Case | Defining Condition | Contextual Conditions | | |
	Policy designed to reduce dependence	Periphery policymaker opposes core preferences	Relevant opposition is inactive	Core willing to tolerate periphery's dissent on this policy
Osvaldo Hurtado				
1a. Rejection of US intervention in Nicaragua[a]	yes	yes	yes	yes
1b. Failure to support Sandinistas	no	no	yes	yes
2a. Invite foreign investment to oil industry	no	no	no	?[b]
2b. Investment reform law	no	no	no	?[b]
3a. Initiate debt summit[a]	yes	yes	yes	yes
3b. Summit document generation[a]	yes	yes	yes	yes
3c. Appease USG and creditors	no	yes	yes	no
León Febres Cordero				
1. Join Contadora Support Group	?[b]	?[b]	yes	yes
2. Break relations with Nicaragua	no	no	yes	yes
3a. Invite Blazing Trails	no	no	yes	yes
3b. Dismiss troops[b]	yes	yes	yes	yes
4. Sign OPIC agreement with United States	no	no	yes	yes

[a] Insufficient data to determine.
[b] These cases were explained by counterdependence.

Table 20: Conditions of Realism

	Defining Conditions		Contextual Condition	
Case	Policy pursues development or prestige	Periphery has resources needed to achieve policy	policy is salient to core (if pro-core outcome)	policy is not salient to core (if anti-core outcome)
Osvaldo Hurtado				
1a. Rejection of US intervention in Nicaragua	no	yes	*a	yes
1b. Failure to support Sandinistas	no	yes	no	*a
2a. Invite foreign investment to oil industry[b]	yes	yes	yes	*a
2b. Investment reform law[b]	yes	yes	yes	*a
3a. Initiate debt summit	no	yes	*a	yes
3b. Summit document generation	no	yes	*a	yes
3c. Appease USG and creditors	no	yes	yes	*a
León Febres Cordero				
1. Join Contadora Support Group[b]	yes	yes	*a	yes
2. Break relations with Nicaragua	no	yes	no	*a
3a. Invite Blazing Trails[b]	yes	yes	?c	*a
3b. Dismiss troops	no	yes	*a	?c
4. Sign OPIC agreement with United States[b]	yes	yes	yes	yes

[a] Not applicable.
[b] These cases were explained by realism.
[c] Insufficient data to determine.

D. Realism

Table 16 reveals that realism explained better than counterdependence, accounting for just under half (five) of the cases examined. Recall that realism's defining conditions were very broadly defined as (1) a policy seeking regional prestige or national development and (2) a policy to which a government had sufficient resources to commit. As table 20 reveals, this second criterion held true for every case examined in the entire study. There was no example of Ecuador's overcommitting its resources and meeting a failed policy as a result. This alone is significant. The vast majority of foreign policies reviewed here required only diplomatic resources. During economic crisis, Ecuador avoided pursuing ambitious or risky foreign policy goals that required financial or military resources. Dependence appears to have curtailed significantly Ecuador's willingness to commit resources to foreign policy. Examples of economically weak states' implementing costly foreign policies do exist. Argentina's invasion of the Malvinas Islands during a severe economic crisis is perhaps the most impressive modern example. Facing popular opposition and pursuing a failing economic strategy, Argentine president General Leopoldo Galtieri opted for a military occupation of the Malvinas. The regime had sufficient resources to overtake the islands, but did not anticipate that the British would respond. In a war with the British, the Argentines were woefully underequipped (Pion-Berlin 1985:68-70).

Such acts of desperation are probably more the exception than the rule in Latin American foreign policy. Ecuador's record during the 1980s shows two regimes that were cautious in committing financial or military resources to foreign policy goals. They dedicated expensive resources to domestic development projects while foreign policy earned the administrations' diplomatic energy. Realism's expectation that regimes are unlikely to commit themselves to foreign policy goals for which they have insufficient resources held true for every case in this study. This is both a pro and a con of the theory. It demonstrates that realism's concept of power is useful for understanding Ecuador's foreign policy. The country did not commit resources it did not have. However, this criterion cannot indicate when realism, or any other theory, will explain a case. Since it universally applied, it does not aid in determining when other critical conditions may also hold.

Realism's other defining condition, that a policy aim to enhance development or regional prestige, also demonstrates strengths and weaknesses. These indicators of the national interest are sufficiently vague that one might expect realism to explain more than five of the twelve cases of Ecuador's foreign policy. Policy-makers in Ecuador frequently develop policy aimed to improve the country's development levels and, less often, its regional prestige. Hence, realism accounts for five cases, most of which are directed at improving Ecuador's development. Realism could apply to these cases without their displaying a specific content, as was a criterion for compliance, consensus, and counterdependence. In other words, a realist policy designed to enhance Ecuador's development or prestige can be pro-core or anti-core, whereas the other theories thus far evaluated require that the policy be one or the other. For this reason realism accounted for development-related policies ranging from Hurtado's investment reform law to Febres Cordero's inviting US troops to build roads in Ecuador's Oriente region.

Realism's failure to explain more cases is also a function of its very broad use of national interests as the motivation behind dependent foreign policy. Realism eschews domestic political sources of foreign policy in favor of national interests that can presumably be identified from afar and without an examination of the specific political circumstances of the country under study. For example, realism could not account for Ecuador's dismissal of the Blazing Trails troops from Ecuador. Expecting Ecuador to serve its national interest, realism would have anticipated the troops to remain and help in road construction and other development projects. Only an understanding of the intense domestic opposition to US troops on Ecuadoran soil can explain Congress' success in ousting the soldiers. Realism similarly ignores the sometimes parochial or idiosyncratic preferences of leaders in command of the foreign policy process. For this reason realism does not account for a number of critical policies such as the entirety of Hurtado's debt summit and Febres Cordero's breaking relations with Nicaragua. Both of these policies depended largely on executive preferences. Hence, an understanding of these presidents' peculiar perceptions of the situation at hand is needed to explain the policy outcomes.

Under what conditions does realism explain? Realism accounts for those cases containing the defining elements of the theory. In this study, a policy was said to be explained by realism if it was designed with development or prestige in mind. However, a number of policies with potential benefits to Ecuador's prestige and development were not explained by realism. The CEL is perhaps the best example. The conference could have led to a reduction in Ecuador's debt and to improved development levels as a result. However, that conference was more the product of Hurtado's personal desires than of a sense of the country's national interest. Similarly, it could be argued that Ecuador's dismissing the Blazing Trails troops was designed to impress regional leaders and to increase Ecuador's regional status. Congressional leaders who forced the dismissal concerned themselves almost exclusively with domestic political considerations and never sought to portray the policy as one that would gain them regional praise. These examples lead to a tentative conclusion that a policy-based condition for realism is difficult to identify. Realist policies pursue development and prestige, but all policies that achieve these goals do not conform with realism.

Nor can it be said that realism develops under a particular type of leader. Both Hurtado and Febres Cordero implemented policies explained by realism. Similarly, the role of domestic politics varies under realism. In some cases, domestic political actors were important (the investment reform initiative and law and joining the Contadora Support Group) while in others domestic actors played a very minor role (Blazing Trails initiative and OPIC).

Realism cannot alone determine whether domestic political actors will overcome the influence of the leader or of outside actors. It is important to remember here that realism claims that information on these internal political dynamics is not necessary to predict or explain policy. This study undermines this claim. Saying that dependent states will seek regional prestige and development is essentially meaningless if the content of those policies cannot be determined. It is necessary to obtain additional information identifying the actors in charge of policy and the manner in which they define the country's national interests. For example, we may need to know the leader's ideological preference or the opposition's prescriptions for development to explain policy content. This need is evidenced in table 16, which demonstrates that in all but one of the cases, realism co-occurs with another theory that provides some understanding of the policy content. Joining the Contadora Support Group is the only example of a case explained by realism for which another theory does not also apply. Recalling the discussion in chapter 6, a theory of bureaucratic politics focusing on the role of the Foreign Ministry would have explained Ecuador's decision to enter the Support Group well. However, bureaucratic politics is an approach very rarely applied to dependent foreign policy and for this reason was not included in this study (Van Klaveren 1984:14; Ferguson 1987:150-51).[2] The point is that realism alone rarely adequately explains a policy's content and must therefore be supplemented with other theoretical approaches.

A related problem is that those cases explained by realism did not necessarily exhibit the types of behavior realists expect, namely that a "unitary actor" exhibits "rational behavior." In many of the cases explained by realism, such as the oil investment reforms, joining Contadora, Blazing Trails, and OPIC, Ecuador did not act as a unified body. Domestic disagreement characterized all these cases. The notion that the nation-state acts as a single and united entity in foreign policy is not supported by this study's empirical evidence. It could be said that Ecuador acted "rationally" in these examples. That is to say that its leaders did not embark on policies for which they had insufficient resources. However, this criterion holds for every case examined, even those not explained by realism.

Despite these problems, realism does demonstrate consistency regarding issue area. Table 16 provides information with which to salvage some conclusions about the theory. Four out of the five examples of realism emerge in the economic/development issue area. In general, realism argues that Ecuador will implement policies that maximize Ecuador's utility. In other words, Ecuador's leaders will make rational choices regarding their country's economic and diplomatic interests. These are choices that outside

---

2. Ferguson (1987:150-51) explains the literature's failure to apply bureaucratic politics to studies of Latin American foreign policy. First, foreign policy-making power is ordinarily concentrated at high levels of government. Second, it is difficult to identify which of the multitude of bureaucratic agencies require attention in the often fragmented foreign policy-making process. Finally, agencies frequently appear and disappear under Latin American political systems, making it difficult to focus on this unit of analysis.

observers can anticipate with little knowledge about Ecuador's political leaders. These types of policies occurred more frequently in the economic realm, where Ecuador's options were more limited. Similarly, the economic arena is one in which Ecuador's interests, the prevention of financial collapse, are more objective in nature. Ecuador's economic objectives during the 1980s were less tied to the idiosyncracies of the policy-makers in power at any particular time. Despite differing ideologies, both Hurtado and Febres Cordero felt the need to increase revenues to stave off bankruptcy. For example, both sought increased foreign investment. Hurtado developed new laws for foreign investment in the oil industry and Febres Cordero signed an agreement with OPIC. This contrasts sharply with their diplomatic goals, which varied significantly with their ideological orientations. In essence, there is *less* policy variation on the economic issues than on diplomatic issues, providing evidence for realism's claim that an understanding of local political and personal dynamics is relatively unimportant.

This point coincides with the above discussions on compliance and counterdependence. It was argued that the US and other Northern financial actors had more power and interest in modifying Ecuador's economic policy than its diplomatic behavior. Also, Ecuador's economic vulnerability made it extremely difficult for its leaders to defy the North on economic issues. Since the hegemon's position throughout the period under study remained relatively constant, we would expect less variation in Ecuador's economic policy behavior than in the diplomatic realm. This conforms with realism, which considers the global distribution of power as a primary source of dependent states' foreign policy behavior. So while realism remains a rather poor predictor of specific policies, it does lend some explanation to Ecuador's limited ability to develop economic policy autonomously.

Looking solely at those cases which realism explains, two conditions beyond the defining conditions appear: (1) When a realist policy exhibits pro-core content, it does so in an issue area of high salience to the core. The reverse also appears to be true. (2) When a realist policy exhibits anti-core content, it does so in issues not salient to the core. This holds true for all of the cases explained by realism except the Blazing Trails initiative, in which the salience of the issue to the core is not clear. However, as table 20 indicates, these conditions do not hold up for the other cases. There are five examples of cases in which these conditions hold and realism could *not* explain the policy. Therefore, while there is evidence that pro-core realist policies will develop in areas salient to the core and anti-core realist policies will develop in areas not salient to the core, there is no evidence to conclude that realism usually explains when these conditions hold.

Realism's highly general defining conditions help it to explain a significant number of cases. However, its explanatory ability appears to be randomly distributed. Its central tenets, that countries are unitary actors implementing rational choices, also do not hold in these cases.

E. Leader preferences

Leader preferences performs better than any other theory examined, explaining eight, or two-thirds, of the cases. The first point to be made relates to the significance of this performance. Leader preferences is in many ways the opposite of compliance, the prevailing theory. Recall that compliance theorists argue that dependent leaders would implement pro-core foreign policies *against their wishes*. This study has found that quite the reverse is true. In most cases, leaders were able to do what they wanted and in many instances their objectives opposed US interests. That during the severe economic crisis of the 1980s Ecuador's leaders were still able to implement their preferences is evidence that the dependence/compliance relationship is at the very least more complex than has often been described.

The principal defining condition for leader preferences is that the leader is interested in or actively involved in the policy matter. Table 21 indicates that in all but one of the cases, this condition held true. Only in joining the Contadora Support Group was the executive essentially uninterested in and removed from the policy process. However, leader commitment was insufficient to predict whether the policy output would conform with the leader's preferences. What additional contextual conditions, then, determine when this theory will prevail?

Table 21: Conditions of Leader Preferences

	Defining Conditions		Contextual Conditions		
Case	Leader active in the policy process	Domestic opposition inactive or preempted	Core supports or does not oppose	if pro-core outcome, issue is salient to core	if anti-core outcome, issue is not salient to core
Osvaldo Hurtado					
1a. Rejection of US intervention in Nicaragua[a]	yes	yes	yes	*b	yes
1b. Failure to support Sandinistas[a]	yes	yes	yes	no	*b
2a. Invite foreign investment to oil industry[a]	yes	yes	yes	yes	*b
2b. Investment reform law	yes	no	yes	yes	*b
3a. Initiate debt summit[a]	yes	yes	yes	*b	yes
3b. Summit document generation[a]	yes	yes	yes	*b	yes
3c. Appease USG and creditors	yes	yes	no	yes	*b
León Febres Cordero					
1. Join Contadora Support Group	no	no	?c	*b	*b
2. Break relations with Nicaragua[a]	yes	yes	yes	no	*b
3a. Invite Blazing Trails[a]	yes	yes	yes	?c	*b
3b. Dismiss troops	yes	no	no	*b	?c
4. Sign OPIC agreement with United States[a]	yes	yes	yes	yes	*b

[a] These cases were explained by leader preferences.
[b] Not applicable.
[c] Insufficient data to determine.

Based on these cases, two contextual conditions under which leader preferences emerges can be identified. First, domestic opposition to the leader is absent, weak, or preempted. In all the examples of leader preferences under President Hurtado, domestic opposition was very slight. It is important to remember that Hurtado did confront intense general opposition to his administration, both from Ecuador's popular sectors angry at austerity programs and from the country's economic elites who labeled him a statist hostile to entrepreneurial interests. However, the opposition did not mobilize on most foreign policy issues, enabling him to implement his personal choices. Similarly, President Febres Cordero met little domestic opposition to his OPIC policy. In the other two examples of leader preferences under Febres Cordero, conditions were slightly different. Febres Cordero faced potentially significant opposition to both his Blazing Trails initiative and to breaking relations with Nicaragua. The executive successfully preempted the opposition in both of these cases, implementing the policies before opponents were able to voice their outrage.

A second and related condition appears to be the absence of core opposition to the policy. For Febres Cordero, this was commonplace. The US agreed with the majority of Febres Cordero's foreign policy proposals. Under Hurtado, US support was not so automatic. In all of the cases in which Hurtado implemented his preferences, the US government, the IMF, World Bank, and other core actors either cared little about the policy or agreed with it. For example, the core supported Hurtado's foreign investment reforms and his failure to back the Sandinistas. On the diplomatic components of the CEL, the US and other creditors demonstrated little concern, confident that Latin American payments would not cease.

These conditions signify that, at least in the cases reviewed here, the leader was able to implement his own preferences when domestic and international actors did not strongly oppose him. When the leader was vulnerable, he tended to give in to opponents. Leader preferences thus emerges as weaker than table 16 would indicate. While leader preferences did explain more cases than any other theory, it only explained in those instances when the leader went essentially unchallenged. Two factors combine to explain why potential opponents rarely challenged Ecuador's leaders on foreign policy matters during the 1980s. First, during this era of economic austerity, Ecuador rarely embarked on risky or ambitious foreign policy initiatives that would threaten potential opponents. Second, in many instances, the leader's preference conformed with that of important domestic or international actors, largely eliminating conflict. Under Hurtado that agreement existed mostly with domestic political actors. Congress rarely challenged Hurtado's foreign policy, particularly in the diplomatic sphere, because it conformed with Ecuador's foreign policy traditions and was not viewed as a threat. Under Febres Cordero, the agreement existed with core actors, who were happy to have a pro-US administration in Ecuador and were unlikely to challenge his foreign policy decisions.

An interesting pattern relating to issue area also surfaces under leader preferences. Four-fifths of Hurtado's examples of this theory emerge in the diplomatic arena while two-thirds of Febres Cordero's leader preference examples are in economic/development matters. This suggests that a leader who tends towards counterdependence (Hurtado) will be able to implement his preferences in diplomatic arenas. His anti-core proclivities will be less tolerated and therefore more difficult to implement in the economic realm. In contrast, a pro-core leader (Febres Cordero) will not experience these same restraints and will be able to develop economic policies that favor the US. However, he will be less able to do so in the diplomatic area, where domestic actors pressure him to soften his pro-US tendencies.

In sum, the conditions under which leader preferences explains include (1) that domestic opponents are inactive or preempted, and (2) that the core either supports the policy or does not oppose it. Furthermore, (3) pro-core policies tend to emerge in issue areas salient to the core, while (4) anti-core policies tend to emerge in issues not salient to the core. These conditions are listed in table 20, which reveals that the first two contextual conditions hold for all the cases explained by leader preferences. The third and fourth conditions are more problematic. Two pro-core policies towards Nicaragua, Hurtado's failure to support the Sandinistas and Febres Cordero's breaking relations with Nicaragua, did not occur in an area salient to the US. However, no anti-core policies explained by leader preferences occurred in an area salient to the core. It therefore appears that salience becomes important only when a peripheral state attempts counterdependence. If the issue is salient to the core, the leader is unlikely to implement an anti-core policy.

An additional point requires attention here. This study has not addressed leaders' agendas and the constraints that affect their ambitions. To what extent are dependent leaders' preferences developed and pursued within a limited number of choices, constrained by dependence or other factors? Recalling the above discussion on realism, in no case did a leader embark on a policy for which resources were not clearly available. This suggests that indeed dependence does limit leaders' foreign policy ambitions. For example, it has been determined that Hurtado's initiating the CEL conformed with his preferences. What is not known is whether in the absence of an economic crisis Hurtado's regional diplomatic ambitions would have been more lofty. Similarly, Febres Cordero certainly agreed with the signing of the OPIC agreement with the US. Recalling his antipathy towards multilateral regional organizations, it is worthwhile to consider that he might have preferred to abandon the Andean Pact altogether. It is possible that the domestic political environment nullified that possibility. The signing of OPIC and the violation of the Andean Pact, which the agreement entailed, would under this scenario conform with his preferences only mildly. Understanding a leader's preference is difficult enough. Investigating the degree to which his agenda truly corresponds to his preferences requires additional study. However, it is important to remember when evaluating this theory's performance that leader preferences are subject to external constraints. The extent to which dependence, for example, constrains agenda setting may be as important as its effect on a leader's stated preferences within a dependent environment.

F. Domestic politics

Domestic political dynamics explain only two of the twelve cases examined, a finding that conforms with the dependent foreign policy literature which generally does not stress the role of domestic political forces in foreign policy. But the two cases in which domestic politics did explain, the investment reform laws and the dismissal of the Blazing Trails troops, involved policy matters highly salient to the president and external actors. In other words, domestic political actors did not influence policy only in relatively unimportant or inconsequential cases. The ouster of Blazing Trails troops and the details of the investment reform had significant impacts on Ecuador's economic and political situation.

The defining condition of this theory, that a relevant domestic opposition group express a preference, holds true for five of the cases examined. In only two of those five cases did the opposition proceed to have its preferences implemented. It is therefore necessary to consider what other conditions explain the opposition's success.

It is difficult to extract generalizations from two examples. However, these two cases share conditions that are important to recognize. First, in both of the domestic politics examples, the relevant opposition was united. During consideration of the oil investment reforms, the majority in Congress, led by Hugo Caicedo, remained committed to Ecuadoran autonomy over the oil industry. The absence of congressional ambiguity over this issue aided Congress in achieving the legislative reforms it sought. Blazing Trails provides perhaps the strongest example of a nationwide united opposition to President Febres Cordero. Congress joined with a variety of non-governmental political groups to oppose fiercely the presence of US troops on Ecuador's soil. The strength of the opposing front was too great for Febres Cordero to resist, even though he was personally committed to the operation and was backed by the US. Had the opposition been weaker or more diffuse, the president would most likely have continued the Blazing Trails operation.

Second, the opposition perceives a threat or opportunity in this policy area. In the oil legislation case, the Congress perceived a threat to Ecuador's control over its highly valued oil industry. The reform bills as advanced by the administration strongly favored foreign interests. Hugo Caicedo and other Congress members worked to maintain significant decision-making power and profit opportunities in Ecuador. Congress also perceived a political opportunity in the reform bills. They provided Congress with a chance to influence a very high-profile policy of significant national concern.

A third apparent condition for domestic politics is that the opposition operate in an area under its authority. This is most clear in the oil investment case. Hurtado's proposed reforms required congressional approval. This proviso strengthened Congress' ability to effect modifications. In other areas of economic policy, such as management of the foreign debt, Congress had no constitutional role and therefore was less likely to effect policy change. In the Blazing Trails example, Febres Cordero ostensibly had the final say as to whether the Blazing Trails troops stayed or left. However, Congress made this foreign policy issue one of its own. The Special Committee on Foreign Affairs quickly called hearings on the issue. Its members also succeeded in convening an extraordinary session of the entire Congress. Although the Committee and the Plenary constitutionally had only an advisory role, they exploited that role to its fullest. In essence, they moved Blazing Trails out of the executive arena and into the legislative realm. In so doing they succeeded in changing the executive's policy quite significantly.

A final condition is that the opposition is willing and able to commit resources to extend its influence. In both of the examples here, these resources were comprised primarily of legislative energy. The Economic, Agrarian, Industrial, and Commercial Committee studied the oil investment reform bills for over a year, making significant modifications and negotiating with administration officials. The full Congress, too, debated the bills heatedly and offered its own changes to the Committee's recommendations. This congressional commitment made it impossible for Hurtado to disregard Congress' wishes. Similarly, Congress quickly mobilized its resources to oust the Blazing Trails troops. In addition to calling an extraordinary session to discuss Blazing Trails, Congress members frequently denounced the operation in the press and successfully called for the Tribunal of Constitutional Guarantees to censure the policy. Other opposition groups also responded immediately and forcefully to the policy.

Outside of these conditions, little more can be ascertained from these two examples of domestic politics. For example, it cannot be said that domestic politics prevailed in cases where the leader was relatively uncommitted. Both Hurtado and Febres Cordero were strongly dedicated to these policy areas. Similarly, the international reaction to these policies shows no pattern. The US did not become involved in the oil investment reforms but was directly interested in the Blazing Trails outcome. Issue area also differed. The oil investment reform was economic while the ouster of the troops was diplomatic.

Nonetheless, a point about the policy content can be made. Unlike compliance, consensus, and counterdependence, under which policy content (pro-core or anti-core) is known, domestic politics entails no a priori determination of the substance of policy. Domestic political actors could conceivably pressure an administration's decision-making in either direction. It is interesting to note that in both of this study's examples of domestic opposition, policy was directed *against* the core's interests. In the investment reforms, Congress maintained constant pressure on the Hurtado administration to make sure that the policy did not provide foreign investors with too much control over Ecuador's oil industry. In Blazing Trails, the opposition fiercely rejected the intensification of dependent ties with the US that the troops signified. There is no example in this study of the opposition's exacting pro-core policy concessions from the administration. This pattern suggests that politically powerful domestic groups capable of swaying a leader away from his preferences tend to oppose pro-US policies. This also conforms with the finding that in every instance in which Febres Cordero did not implement his preferences, domestic forces directed him away from a pro-core position. Of course, not all anti-core policies are explained by domestic politics. But it is important to note that domestic groups have most influence in those areas not salient to the core.

Four conditions lead to an expectation that domestic politics will explain foreign policy: (1) the relevant opposition is united; (2) the opposition perceives a threat or opportunity in this policy area; (3) the opposition operates in an area of authority; and (4) the opposition is willing and able to commit resources to influence the policy. Table 22 reveals that all of these conditions hold for the two examples of domestic politics and do not hold for the other cases. These specific conditions do not often hold in the foreign policy realm, particularly in countries such as Ecuador, where foreign policy is largely under executive control. However, when they do hold, the opposition has achieved sufficient political legitimacy to force the foreign policy option of its choice, often with regard to critical policies.

Table 22: Conditions of Domestic Politics

Case	Defining Conditions		Contextual Conditions		
	Relevant opposition has a policy preference	Relevant opposition is united	Opposition group perceives threat or opportunity	Opposition group operates in area of authority	Opposition group commits resources
Osvaldo Hurtado					
1a. Rejection of US intervention in Nicaragua	no	no	no	no	no
1b. Failure to support Sandinistas	no	no	no	no	no
2a. Invite foreign investment to oil industry	yes	no	yes	yes	no
2b. Investment reform law[a]	yes	yes	yes	yes	yes
3a. Initiate debt summit	no	no	no	no	no
3b. Summit document generation	no	no	no	no	no
3c. Appease USG and creditors	yes	no	no	no	no
León Febres Cordero					
1. Join Contadora Support Group	no	no	no	no	no
2. Break relations with Nicaragua	no	no	no	no	no
3a. Invite Blazing Trails	no	no	no	no	no
3b. Dismiss troops[a]	yes	yes	yes	yes	yes
4. Sign OPIC agreement with United States	yes	no	no	no	no

[a] These cases were explained by domestic politics.

G. Summary

Tables 17 through 22 together summarize the conditions under which the different theories explain this study's cases. It is important to stress that these findings are tentative, in some cases based on a single or a pair of examples. Nonetheless, there is sufficient information for two important general conclusions. First, domestic political factors such as the leader's orientation and the strength of domestic opposition frequently weigh heavily in determining whether a theory applies. This indicates that the foreign policy of a dependent state like Ecuador is clearly not determined solely or even primarily through external considerations, as compliance and realism imply. Second, pro-core policies occur more frequently in the economic realm while anti-core policies develop more often in the diplomatic realm. As discussed above, this tendency appears to be a function of the United States' desire, willingness, and capacity to pressure Ecuador's policy in the economic realm. This combines with Ecuador's limited options in this area to generate pro-US economic policies with greater frequency.

This pattern may evidence a stronger relationship between economic dependence and foreign policy behavior than table 15 first appears to indicate. The United States and other core actors achieve their policy preferences and goals in Ecuador in the area most salient to them. Even when a dependent leader tends towards counterdependence (Hurtado), the core is able to exact economic policy concessions. When the dependent leader tends to consensus (Febres Cordero), the US can anticipate good behavior on economic questions. In both examples, the core largely achieved its desired economic policy results in Ecuador.

In the diplomatic realm this model works in the reverse. The proclivities of a counterdependent leader will direct him/her to enact defiant policies in the diplomatic realm. Domestic sources desirous of national autonomy will tend to support the leader in these endeavors. Since the US has found that Ecuadoran antagonism on diplomatic questions has little impact on Washington's ability to continue with its preferred regional policies and also does not endanger its capacity to achieve economic results in the region, defiant diplomatic policies will be tolerated. However, a pro-US leader will meet strong opposition from local forces attempting to counteract the administration's inclination to favor the United States.

The result is that the core generally achieves its desired policy outcomes in Ecuador. However, the process is not one described by compliance theorists. At times, pressure towards a pro-core economic policy is overt, as was somewhat the case in the CEL appeasement example. However, other channels are more common. Sometimes, the mere existence of an economic crisis was sufficient to steer Ecuador towards pro-core policies, such as increasing foreign investment. In other cases, the fact that a consensual leader, Febres Cordero, presided over the country was the primary factor.

Two important summary points should be clarified here. First, dependence does not directly lead to pro-core policies, particularly in the diplomatic realm, where dependence is in most cases correlated with anti-core policies. Second, the US need not implement the instruments of compliance, such as threats and sanctions, in order to achieve its desired economic results.

III. INTERACTIVE AND CONDITIONAL THEORIES

A. Interactive theories

The frequency with which different theories explain a single case suggests that a consideration of the interaction among theories will also prove fruitful in understanding Ecuador's foreign policy during the 1980s. While no single theory can explain dependent foreign policy, the combination of two or more theories may explain it quite well. It has been demonstrated, for example, that leader preferences and realism can alone account for eight and five cases respectively. The problem with these two theories is that alone they provide little information on the motivation behind policy, the process through which it emerged or, perhaps most importantly, its content. When combined with other theories a fuller explanation is derived.

Referring to table 16, it is clear that while leader preferences performs better than any other single theory, it co-occurs with either consensus or counterdependence in all but one case. This is not surprising since the tenets of consensus and counterdependence do not compete with those of leader preferences. Leader preferences guides the observer to the source of the policy—the leader. However, this alone provides no information on the content of the policy. Consensus explains that a leader whose ideological orientation accords with leaders in the US will develop generally pro-US policies. In contrast, a leader who espouses neocolonial explanations of Ecuadoran underdevelopment will implement counterdependent policies aimed at diminishing North-South dependent ties. Consensus and counterdependence provide the substance behind leader preferences. Leader preferences combined with consensus or counterdependence provides a fuller understanding of more policies than either of the theories can alone.

This pattern somewhat undermines the force of either consensus or counterdependence as a single explanatory theory of dependent foreign policy. For example, Moon (1985) sought to demonstrate that consensus explained policy better than compliance. Biddle and Stephens (1989) suggest that dependency will lead to counterdependence. Although sometimes implicitly, these authors attempt to capture the single most important operative force behind dependent foreign policy. This study has demonstrated, in contrast, that both consensus and counterdependence can explain dependent foreign policy, but that leader preferences is needed to predict which of the two will apply.

Ecuador in the 1980s illustrates this point well. During the 1980s Ecuador produced two leaders with very different ideological orientations. Hurtado, a social democrat, viewed dependent relationships as obstacles to real and redistributive development. Accordingly, he advocated a reduction in dependence and a foreign policy reflecting that view. Febres Cordero, on the other hand, conforms to the ideal of a consensus leader. He was educated in the US, maintained business ties with the North, and valued a free market system. Accordingly, he often agreed with US policy and developed foreign policy that merged with US interests. The fact that both of these leaders emerged in Ecuador during an economic crisis damages the ability of either consensus or counterdependence to act as a single theory of dependent foreign policy. A dependent economy does not generate a single type of leader, either consensual or counterdependent. Once the type of leader is known, however, consensus and counterdependence explain the process behind policy quite well.

Similarly, if domestic actors other than the executive generate the policy, they too may reflect either consensus or counterdependence. The best example from this study is the dismissal of the Blazing Trails troops. Congress took control of that policy, indicating that domestic politics was at work. However, the essence of that policy was counterdependent. Congress, like Hurtado in other cases, was frustrated with Ecuador's heavy reliance on the United States and sought a foreign policy to weaken dependent ties. Equally possible is that domestic actors favorable to the US, such as local industrial elites, would assume command of a policy reflecting consensus between them and economic and political leaders in the US. Domestic politics, then, can also coincide with consensus and counterdependence.

A similar point can be made regarding realism's occurrence in table 16. In four of the five cases realism explained, it co-occurred with another theory. In three of those instances, realism emerged with a theory other than leader preferences (two examples of consensus and one of domestic politics). Like leader preferences, the tenets of realism do not exclude the applicability of other theoretical approaches. The search for development and prestige (realism) can follow the processes outlined by consensus or counterdependence. Also, realism could be implemented by a leader whose preferences are being served or by domestic political actors. Realism and these other theories are not mutually exclusive and need not compete. As has been argued throughout this study, theories other than realism generally provide more specific information on the policy's content.

The fact that leader preferences and realism co-occur with other theories provides evidence that interactive theorizing is a useful way to approach dependent foreign policy. No single theory has obviously captured the essence of Ecuador's foreign policy during the period under study, but combinations of theories provide a rather satisfactory account of the cases. However, no single combination of two theories explains a majority of the cases. Three combinations, leader preferences and counterdependence, leader preferences and consensus, and realism and leader preferences, each explain three cases. So while there is evidence that interactive theories explain Ecuador's foreign policy better, there is no set of theories which clearly performs best.

B. Conditional theories

This identifies a need to consider a different, or additional, approach. Thus far it has been demonstrated that leader preferences and realism account for many of the cases, but that these theories alone provide only a partial account of the policy under question. When combined with others, such as consensus or counterdependence, a fuller account of the policy's content and the process through which it develops emerges. However, the failure of any pair of theories to explain a majority of the cases suggests that interactive theorizing alone does a rather poor job of explaining dependent foreign policy. Interactive theories provide an ample explanation of different cases, but do not develop with sufficient frequency to generalize their applicability. This indicates that middle-range theories, explanations that emerge under specific conditions, may be more helpful.

Consider the theories, other than leader preferences and realism, which together can account for ten of the twelve cases. Nine of these ten cases are also explained by theories other than the predominant two. In each of these examples, there is only one theory other than leader preferences and/or realism accounting for the case. There is no obvious winner among these extra theories. Counterdependence accounts for three cases, consensus for three, and domestic politics for one. If we accept that leader preferences and realism benefit from combining with other theoretical approaches that help to explain the content and process behind policy, there is evidence to support a conditional or middle-range theoretical approach to explaining the entire set of cases. In other words, under certain conditions, consensus, counterdependence and domestic politics will combine with realism or leader preferences to explain.

Those conditions are outlined in section II and summarized in tables 17 through 22 of this chapter. The conditions for the interactive theories can be derived by combining the conditions under which individual theories develop. For example, leader preferences combines with consensus to explain policy when a pro-US leader is in command of policy and meets little opposition. This combination also tends to explain policy more often in policy areas salient to the core. Leader preferences combines with counterdependence when an anti-core leader meets little opposition, usually in realms less salient to the core. Realism will combine with consensus and counterdependence in those policy areas dealing with development or prestige under the conditions of consensus and counterdependence respectively. Realism, it is important to note, explains more frequently consensus policies than counterdependent ones.

IV. WITHIN-POLICY PATTERNS

A. Pro-core and anti-core elements

An important observation of cross-theoretical analysis then is that theories co-occur and that leader preferences and realism tend to combine with a variety of other theories under distinct conditions. A second way to analyze table 16 is to consider the theoretical application to whole policies. An analysis of which theories explain individual policy components, such as the appeasement component of the CEL or the dismissal of the troops, has already been performed. It is also fruitful to consider what patterns emerge when examining the entire CEL, Febres Cordero's policy towards Nicaragua in general, the oil investment reform from start to finish, and so forth.

An examination of whole policies (each presented in a case study chapter) reveals tendencies, one pro-core, the other anti-core, occurring simultaneously within a single policy area. Most of the policies contain different components representing these two dis-

tinct interests. Perhaps the most obvious illustration of this interplay of pro-core and anti-core forces is Hurtado's Conferencia
Económica Latinoamericana. The anti-core interest originated
largely in the executive office. President Hurtado called a regional
debt meeting with the goal of lessening Latin America's dependence
on foreign creditors. The pro-core component of the policy was
born largely in Hurtado's understanding of Ecuador's economic
crisis and its vulnerability to potential sanctions from the North. In
order to avoid this possible punishment, Hurtado promised creditors that Ecuador would not cease its loans and that the Conference
would not institute a debtors' club. These conditions severely
undermined the potential and real impact of the CEL. Because
creditors understood the CEL would not damage their vital economic interests, they had little incentive to modify their behavior.
Hurtado's dual approach produced an essentially self-annulling
policy.

A similar pattern emerges in the oil investment reform case. The
counterdependent component of this policy developed at two
different points. First, early in his career Hurtado advocated
national control over petroleum, claiming that multinational participation in the industry damaged Ecuadoran development potential. This same view, though in a somewhat diluted form, was
expressed in Congress during the debates over the proposed investment reforms in 1982. Once president, Hurtado advocated the pro-
core position. Responsible for Ecuador's financial survival under
economic crisis, he sought foreign investment as an important and
relatively short-term method to increase revenues. Unlike in the
CEL, the pro-core and anti-core forces did not necessarily cancel
each other out. The resulting reforms represented a compromise
between those who sought a tremendous increase in incentives for
foreign investors and those who wanted to maintain significant
local control. The compromise legislation generally pleased most of
the actors participating in its development.

A third example of this pattern under the Hurtado administration is the policy towards revolutionary Nicaragua. In this case, the
anti-US component was the administration's rejection of US policy towards Nicaragua. Pressures came from a variety of sources:

Hurtado's personal antipathy towards US interventionism, Ecuador's foreign policy tradition opposing intervention, the political expediency of continuing Roldós's rejection of US methods, and insistence from a variety of domestic political groups that Ecuador not support US regional policy. The pro-US element of the Nicaragua policy was Hurtado's quiet failure to support the Sandinistas. This policy was partly born in the president's own distaste for Daniel Ortega and the Sandinistas, whom he considered non-democratic. However, his failure to be more active in Nicaragua in general is also explained as a function of Hurtado's being overwhelmed with economic and political problems at home.

These same conflicting tendencies are evident under the Febres Cordero administration and are most pronounced in the Blazing Trails case, where the president and his close advisers agreed with Pentagon officials to a US military operation in Ecuador. Febres Cordero arranged Blazing Trails seemingly without considering the intense domestic opposition it promised to incite. The efficiency and potency with which opponents responded to Blazing Trails forced the Febres Cordero administration to call for a withdrawal. Again, the interplay of pro-US and anti-US forces caused the policy to cancel itself.

A similar situation occurred in Ecuador's approach to revolutionary Nicaragua under Febres Cordero. The anti-core element of this policy was the Foreign Ministry's decision to join the Contadora Support Group, a body that overtly supported the Sandinistas in their battle against the Reagan administration. Febres Cordero immediately annulled that act with his unilateral decision to break relations with Nicaragua. While Febres Cordero may not have taken this action in order to please the US, the policy had a distinctly pro-Reagan flavor.

Five of the six case study chapters demonstrate a mix of counteracting forces. Table 23 summarizes the pro-core and anti-core components of these five examples and indicates the issue area of each. Consistent with conclusions discussed in sections II and III above, table 23 demonstrates that most (four of five) anti-core policies emerged in the diplomatic realm while most (three of five) pro-core elements emerged in the economic realm. The point to be made here is that these disparate policy forces will occur simultaneously within a single policy area. In some instances, such as the oil investment reforms, this resulted in a compromise reasonably attractive to most participants. More frequently, this interplay generated a contradictory and self-annulling policy.

Table 23: Pro-Core and Anti-Core Elements of Five Policy Areas

Case	Pro-core component	Anti-core component
CEL (Hurtado)	Appeasement of creditors (E)	CEL initiative and language (D)
Nicaragua (Hurtado)	Failure to support Sandinistas (D)	Rejection of US methods in Nicaragua (D)
Oil investment reform (Hurtado)	Increase foreign investment (E)	Limit loss of national control over oil industry (E)
Blazing Trails (Febres Cordero)	Invite US troops (E)	Dismiss US troops (D)
Nicaragua (Febres Cordero)	Break relations with Nicaragua (D)	Join Contadora Support Group (D)

Note: (D) indicates diplomatic issue area, (E) indicates economic/development issue area.

An additional point conforming with the above discussion relates to the source of these different policy thrusts. All of the anti-core behavior in table 23 served a domestic audience or resulted from domestic pressure. The CEL, for example, was born principally in President Hurtado's own ambitions. Rejection of US methods in Nicaragua not only served Hurtado's personal interests but also conformed with Ecuador's foreign policy traditions. Congress clearly was the principal actor forcing changes in the oil investment laws and the ouster of the Blazing Trails troops. Finally, Ecuador's Foreign Ministry generated the Contadora Support Group policy. This pattern provides strong evidence that domestic actors, within or without the executive office, will pressure for anti-core foreign policies.

The reverse of this point, that pro-core policies originated in the exterior, cannot necessarily be made. An examination of the pro-core policies in table 23 reveals that two under Febres Cordero were essentially administration initiatives. Neither Blazing Trails nor the break in relations with Nicaragua can be described as externally imposed policies, though they did serve US interests to some degree. However, external interests did have a greater impact in generating Hurtado's examples of pro-core policies. The appeasement of creditors under the CEL was a direct response to external pressure and fear of retribution. Similarly, Hurtado's commitment to increasing investment in the petroleum industry developed largely as a response to an intense economic crisis. This crisis is external in that it was not unique to Ecuador and was caused in large part by a global economic recession. Finally, Hurtado's failure to support the Sandinistas was at least partially a function of the president's inability to extend himself diplomatically during an intense financial emergency. Hence, it appears that the pro-core components of a policy will develop externally when the leader tends to be counterdependent.

Though the pattern is less clear for the pro-core than the anti-core policies, it can be said that pro-core policies more frequently respond to external pressures while anti-core policies more frequently develop from domestic pressures. The tentative conclusion emerging from this discussion is that, contrary to what both compliance and counterdependence theorists expect, dependence does not lead to a single type of foreign policy. Rather, dependence produces *both* anti-core and pro-core tendencies. Domestic groups frustrated with dependence will pressure leaders to adopt anti-core policies while external actors and conditions direct dependent leaders to implement policies favorable to the core.

B. Leaders and internal or external opposition

A second pattern evident in within-case analysis concerns policy battles between the executive and either internal opponents or core actors. In four of the six case studies the executive was able to implement his preference in one or two components of the policy, while an opponent within or without Ecuador had control over the remaining components. For example, in the oil investment case, Hurtado achieved significant influence at the initiative level, but had to compromise with Congress at the legislative stage. The CEL case demonstrates the same pattern, but with external actors. While Hurtado was very powerful in initiating the conference and drafting its documents, core actors prevailed in the appeasement component of the policy.

Febres Cordero's opponents were essentially domestic. His Foreign Ministry was able to join the Contadora Support Group even though the president opposed multilateral action. However, Febres Cordero had the final say when he alone broke diplomatic relations with Nicaragua. Similarly, in the Blazing Trails case, the executive implemented his preferences at the initiative stage but gave in to congressional opponents and agreed to dismiss the troops.

This demonstrates that in addition to pro-core and anti-core elements co-occurring within a single policy area, both the executive and his opponents may prove victorious over different elements of the same policy. As was the case with the interplay of pro-core and anti-core forces, this interaction may lead to contradictory and self-annulling policies. However, it may also result in working compromises.

V. SUMMARY AND CONCLUSION

This final section condenses this chapter's discussion into three principal conclusions. The first is directly theoretical while the remainder are substantive. The substantive conclusions, however, will contribute to better theorizing on dependent foreign policy. These conclusions, though based on the Ecuadoran case, are expected to generalize to other cases within Latin America, and with some modifications, to dependent foreign policy in general. At the very least, future studies can examine their applicability to other dependent states' foreign policy behavior.

A. The ability of interactive theories to explain dependent foreign policy

This study has found that both interactive and conditional theories explain Ecuador's foreign policy. The most successful theory was leader preferences, which combined with either consensus or counterdependence to explain half of the cases. Realism, and less frequently domestic politics, also combined with consensus and counterdependence under certain conditions to explain dependent foreign policy.

I have found that no single theory can fully explain the content and process behind policy. Consensus and counterdependence each have the theoretical capacity to provide this service. However, neither emerges by itself with reliable frequency. Instead, leader preferences, and to a lesser extent realism and domestic politics, co-occur with the other theories. No combination of theories develops with sufficient regularity to identify it as the best explanation. Instead, interactive theories, emergent under specific conditions, best account for the set of cases examined here. Contrary to what much of the previous literature on dependent foreign policy suggests, this study proposes that dependent foreign policy is highly complex and impossible to predict with any single set of variables.

That different and conditional theories are needed to explain dependent foreign policy should not dampen dependent foreign policy analysts' spirits. This finding parallels conclusions stated by Alker (1966) and reiterated by Russett in his examination of dependency and arms races. "To be sure, we find patterns of behavior that are complex, interactive and heavily conditioned. A good theorist does not expect most relationships to be simple" (Russett 1983:561). Nor should the theoretical complexity that explains the Ecuadoran cases generate fears that these findings are not generalizable. Complex explanation can be replicated and is demanded of complex phenomena. This study has begun to identify the conditions under which those variables combine to produce patterned foreign policy outcomes. Additional studies will contribute to specifying these patterns further.

B. The development of pro-core behavior
   in the economic realm and anti-core
   behavior in the diplomatic realm.

This conclusion relates not only to dependent states' foreign policy, but to core foreign policy as well. It has been argued that two related forces combine to produce pro-core policies in the economic realm. First, the core (in this case the US and creditor institutions) was interested in modifying the economic policy of its dependencies. It also held the policy instruments with which to exercise that influence. Second, Ecuador was particularly weak and vulnerable economically during the financial crisis of the 1980s. This severely limited its policy options. Desperately in need of cash, the country's leaders had few alternatives to policies that would facilitate new loans and investment. The combination of these forces led to pro-core policies in all but one of the economic policies examined in this study.

This point is theoretically important. It suggests that in the economic realm, analysts need little specific information on the country at hand to predict policy. Recalling the discussion above, those theories that require little or no information on Ecuador's domestic situation, compliance and realism, pertained almost exclusively to policies in the economic realm. In other words, the distribution of global resources can predict this dependent state's foreign policy behavior in general terms. Regardless of the leader and domestic political situations, Ecuador usually implemented pro-core economic policies.

The reverse holds for the diplomatic arena. While the core may be little interested in Ecuador's diplomatic behavior, domestic actors are. Ecuador's national political groups paid strong attention to the administrations' diplomatic behavior. Because Hurtado's diplomatic proclivities generally adhered to Ecuador's foreign policy traditions and to the Congress' diplomatic preferences, domestic groups allowed him to develop diplomatic policy as he saw fit. Febres Cordero, on the other hand, met significant opposition in the two instances in which he tried to implement his own pro-core preferences (keeping the Blazing Trails troops in Ecuador and breaking relations with Nicaragua). The point is that domestic groups do consider diplomatic concerns salient and are therefore likely to try to influence government behavior on them.

Similarly, domestic groups have some instruments of policy influence available to them. Certainly, the constitutional provision that the executive has control over foreign policy can prevent Congress and other groups from modifying policy, as was the case when Febres Cordero broke relations with Nicaragua. However, the Foreign Ministry did mobilize its bureaucracy to join the Contadora Support Group even though the executive was not particularly interested in such an action. Similarly, Congress and other groups used all the available means to void Febres Cordero's Blazing Trails operation.

A very critical issue is the core's role in diplomatic questions. It appears that domestic groups are able to influence diplomatic policy largely *because* the core is content to disregard the diplomatic arena. Remember that domestic groups are arguably more interested in economic policy than in diplomatic policy, particularly during a financial crisis. Even though domestic actors were highly concerned with economics, they were less able to influence decisions in that area. Core interest, then, appears to determine what was left over for domestic actors to influence. Nothing indicates, for instance, that had the United States prioritized the diplomatic arena it would not have succeeded in modifying Ecuador's diplomatic policy. Thus, it appears that Ecuadoran domestic leaders are able to influence policy largely on those issues the core has not deemed salient. While this finding is by no means without variation, it has significant implications concerning core power over dependent foreign policy behavior.

This pattern is also important for an understanding of leader preferences. A trend has developed by which pro-core leaders will be able to implement their preferences in economic areas while anti-core leaders will be able to do so in the diplomatic arena. In both instances, the core has achieved its desired results. A leader such as Febres Cordero has the good fortune that the core condones his economic policies, while a leader like Hurtado must bend his economic policies to conform with core preferences. Again, it is important to remember that these policies do not necessarily develop through a process of coercion. The mere existence of the economic crisis steered leaders towards pro-core economic behavior.

This discussion also helps to specify the conditions under which leader preferences will prevail. Knowledge of a leader's orientation can help to predict his policies. If the leader tends to counterdependence, we can expect that he will develop generally successful policies in the diplomatic realm. Most domestic forces, frustrated with pro-US economic policies and other aspects of dependence, will support his counterdependent diplomatic policies. On the other hand, a pro-core leader can be expected to implement successful economic policies with the support of the core. However, domestic groups will be doubly committed to counteracting that behavior in the diplomatic realm, where the core provides little or no support.

Finally, it is important to remember that economic and diplomatic issue areas assumed particular roles in the relationship between Latin America and the United States during the 1980s. In different historical circumstances or in a different geographical context, another set of issue areas could take on these roles. Core salience appears to be the critical variable determining which issue areas will experience a high degree of pro-core foreign policy by the peripheral country.

C. The development of pro-core and anti-core elements within individual policy areas

A final and related conclusion is that the interaction of externally and internally-derived policy pressures often occur within a single policy area. Dependence subjects Ecuador to pressures that direct its foreign policy in both pro-core and anti-core directions. Dependent foreign policy can be viewed as a balancing act in which policy-makers attempt to respond to these divergent forces. The sometimes unfortunate response is a contradictory policy the components of which cancel themselves out. This was evident in the CEL and Blazing Trails cases. The interplay of pro-core and anti-core forces can also result in an acceptable and working compromise, as was the case in the oil investment reform example.

This is certainly not the first study to reveal contradictory foreign policies. Graham Allison (1969, 1971) demonstrated over two decades ago that the United States, at the height of its global power, generated a sometimes confused and disjointed policy during the Cuban Missile Crisis. This study's contribution is not so much to point out that dependent states at times will produce self-annulling foreign policies, but instead to identify the source of that phenomenon. In developed countries, contradictory policies may develop in large bureaucracies whose units compete and employ standard operating procedures (Allison 1969, 1971). The origin of policy contradictions are inherent to the foreign policy-making body. In dependent states, the source of policy confusion is more structural. It is born in the economic relationship between periphery and core and is therefore largely beyond the control of dependent states' leaders. This is not to say that dependent states may not have bureaucracy-related policy confusion as well, though they will be less likely to as their foreign policy decision-making tends to be concentrated at high levels of government. But the bureaucracy will not be the sole source of confusion. Ecuadoran leaders cannot single-handedly alter their country's dependent status. They therefore cannot eliminate a principal source of their contradictory foreign policy behavior. This differs significantly from the United States and other core states whose leaders could conceivably make more efficient their foreign policy bureaucracy. The means to eliminating their policy confusion lie within the bounds of their own jurisdiction.

Dependent policy-makers' need to respond to anti-core domestic forces and well as pro-core forces emanating from the exterior perhaps points to the essential element of dependent foreign policy. It is as much (or more) reactive as it is creative. The condition of dependence generates economic vulnerability directing policy towards the core. However, that same dependence also creates a foreign policy pressure to overcome itself. Leaders find themselves simultaneously developing foreign policy to please the core on whom they rely or to sever the dependent ties they or their constituencies find so distasteful. Developing policy to achieve this balance may leave little room for dependent leaders to design policy in other areas or to pursue the national interest as they wish to define it. This necessity of responding to dependence severely limits what dependent leaders may add to their foreign policy agendas. They are restricted in the range of foreign policy questions they may address.

D. Implications for dependency theory

A final issue to be addressed is to what degree do this study's conclusions conform with dependency theory? Although it has many harsh critics, dependency remains a leading competitor to neo-classical economics in the study of core-periphery relations. Given dependency's fragile status in social science, it is worthwhile to examine explicitly whether this study substantiates the theory's central tenets.

Dependency theory was not developed to explain the foreign policy of dependent states. Rather, its main purpose is to explain development, or its absence, in the less developed world. In what Biersteker (1987) labels the "vulgar dependista" tradition, true development in the periphery is impossible within the modern capitalist system, which favors core-based multinational corporations in their extraction of profits from the periphery. Independent decision-making to foster development within peripheral societies is impossible because peripheral economies are inextricably tied to the core and to decisions made there. Critics claim that dependency is empirically weak and overly deterministic in its expectation that Latin American countries tied to the capitalist world can under no circumstances achieve industrial development (Moran 1974; Kaufman, Chernotsky, and Geller 1975; Evans 1979; Muñoz 1981; Becker 1983; Kay 1989:174-75).

Foreign policy's analog to the vulgar dependista in development theory is the "vulgar" compliance theorist, who might claim that Latin American foreign-policy makers can under no circumstances develop foreign policy independently or in their countries' true national interests. While even the most strict compliance theorists do not make such broad statements, they can be criticized for over-generalizing and failing to substantiate their views with rigorous empirical analysis. This study provides evidence to criticize an overly deterministic analysis of the relationship between dependence and foreign policy compliance. In many cases, Ecuador operated independently of the United States and even developed policies directly contrasting the core's interest. The direct links between dependence and foreign policy compliance that a vulgar dependista might expect have not been found.

Few development scholars or foreign policy analysts cling to such deterministic views. As dependency theory's universalism has been discredited (and often exaggerated), so too have the simplistic compliance models developed in the late 1960s and early 1970s (Kay 1989:174). Dependency critics too frequently ignore the more sophisticated versions of dependency, particularly those allowing for industrial development within dependency and those expecting significant cross-case variation. In their classic study, *Dependency and Development in Latin America*, Cardoso and Faletto (1979:173) explicitly reject the notion that a dependent relationship will always produce the same outcome. They accordingly call for an examination of variation across dependent states. Others have outlined the conditions under which some types of development can occur within a situation of dependency (see, e.g., Cardoso 1973; Gereffi 1978; Evans 1979; Muñoz 1981; Russett 1983). As Duvall (1978:56-57) explains, dependence for many sophisticated dependency theorists is less a variable than it is a situation or a context within which particular variables become important. Sophisticated dependistas do not abandon the relationship between core and periphery. They in fact emphasize the vulnerability of dependent states to external economies (Biersteker 1987:36). However, they agree that historical and structural differences will lead to varied degrees and forms of development (Biersteker 1987:33-34).

This study reaches similar conclusions about dependent foreign policy. Researchers of the foreign policy process in Ecuador cannot abandon the impact of dependence. However, a wide range of possible foreign policy behaviors emerges within that context. Dependence serves to constrain the options available to Ecuador's policy makers, to circumscribe their foreign policy ambitions, and at times to determine what behavior they follow. Indeed, it has been discovered that on those issues most critical to core actors, Ecuador's foreign policy decision-making was most constrained. Overall, this study provides empirical evidence to support the more sophisticated versions of dependency theory. The dependent relationship proved critical to Ecuador's foreign policy process, but did not lead to a single set of foreign policy outcomes. Dependence is a critical variable, but not the exclusive one needed to understand Ecuador's foreign policy outcomes.

Bibliography

Acosta, Alberto. 1990a. "Democracia vs. Políticas de Ajuste: El Dilema de los Ochenta," unpublished paper.

——— 1990b. *La Deuda Eterna*. Quito: El Duende.

Agee, Philip. 1975. *Inside the Company: CIA Diary*. Harmondsworth, England: Penguin Books.

Aguirre Asanza, Carlos. 1991. Personal interview with author, 2 July, Quito.

Alker, Hayward R., Jr. 1966. "The Long Road to International Relations Theory: Problems of Statistical Nonadditivity." *World Politics* 18: 623-55.

Allison, Graham T. 1969. "Conceptual Models and the Cuban Missile Crisis." *American Political Science Review* 63: 689-718.

———. 1971. *Essence of Decision: Explaining the Cuban Missile Crisis*. Boston: Little, Brown.

Ames, Barry. 1987. *Political Survival: Politicians and Public Policy in Latin America*. Berkeley: University of California Press.

Appleton, Sheldon. 1975. "The Role of the Opposition in Foreign Policymaking." In Richard Merrit, ed., *Foreign Policy Analysis*, 55-59. Lexington, MA: Lexington Books.

Aráuz, Luis. 1990. *Frente a Nuestra Realidad Petrolera*. Quito: INSOTEC.

Armstrong, Adrienne. 1981. "The Political Consequences of Economic Dependence." *Journal of Conflict Resolution* 25: 401-28.

Aspiazu, Fernando. 1991. Personal interview with author, 30 May, Guayaquil.

Atkins, G. Pope. 1989. *Latin America in the International Political System*. 2d. ed. Boulder, CO: Westview Press.

Ayala Mora, Enrique. 1989. *Los Partidos Políticos en el Ecuador: Síntesis Histórica*. Quito: Ediciones La Tierra.

Bagley, Bruce. 1987. "The Failure of Diplomacy." In Bruce Bagley, ed., *Contadora and the Diplomacy of Peace in Central America. Volume I: The United States, Central America, and Contadora*, 181-211. Boulder, CO: Westview Press.

Bagley, Bruce, and Juan Gabriel Tokatlian. 1987. *Contadora: The Limits of Negotiation*, Case #309 in Pew program in case teaching and writing in international affairs. Pittsburgh: The Pew Charitable Trusts.

Banco Central. 1989a. *Boletín Anuario*, no. 11 (1988). Quito: Banco Central del Ecuador.

————. 1989b. *Memoria Anual* (1988). Quito: Banco Central del Ecuador.

Banco Central (División Técnica). 1990a. *La Actividad Petrolera en el Ecuador en la Década de los 80*. Quito: Banco Central del Ecuador.

————. 1990b. *Ecuador en Cifras*. Pamphlet. Quito: Banco Central del Ecuador.

Becker, David G. 1983. *The New Bourgeoisie and the Limits of Dependency: Mining, Class, and Power in "Revolutionary" Peru*. Princeton: Princeton University Press.

Benalcázar, René R. 1989. *Análisis del Desarrollo Económico del Ecuador*. Quito: Ediciones Banco Central del Ecuador.

Biddle, William Jesse, and John D. Stephens. 1989. "Dependent Development and Foreign Policy: The Case of Jamaica." *International Studies Quarterly* 33: 411-34.

Biersteker, Thomas J. 1987. *Multinational Corporations, the State, and Control of the Nigerian Economy*. Princeton: Princeton University Press.

————. 1990. "Reducing the Role of the State in the Economy: A Conceptual Exploration of IMF and World Bank Prescriptions." *International Studies Quarterly* 34: 477-92.

Bitar, Sergio. 1988. "Comments." In Richard E. Feinberg and Ricardo Ffrench-Davis, eds., *Development and External Debt in Latin America: Bases for a New Consensus*, 175-80. Notre Dame, IN: University of Notre Dame Press.

Blum, William. 1986. *The CIA: A Forgotten History*. London: Zed Books.

Borge, Tomás. 1991. "An Anguished, Frustrated World." *Latin America News Update* 7: 19-21.

Bradshaw, York W., and Ana-Maria Wahl. 1991. "Foreign Debt Expansion, the International Monetary Fund, and Regional Variation in Third World Poverty." *International Studies Quarterly* 35: 251-72.

Brock, Philip L., Michael B. Connally, and Claudio González-Vega, eds. 1989. *Latin American Debt and Adjustment: External Shocks and Macroeconomic Policies*. New York: Praeger.

Bustamante, Fernando. 1987. "El Desarrollo de las FFAA de Ecuador y Colombia. Una Revisión Comparativa." Working Paper no. 346, FLAC-SO—Santiago de Chile.

Canak, William. 1989a. "Debt, Austerity, and Latin America in the New International Division of Labor." In William Canak, ed., *Lost Promises: Debt, Austerity, and Development in Latin America*, 9-27. Boulder, CO: Westview Press.

————, ed. 1989b. *Lost Promises: Debt, Austerity, and Development in Latin America*. Boulder, CO: Westview Press.

Caporaso, James A. 1978. "Dependence, Dependency, and Power in the Global System: A Structural and Behavioral Analysis." *International Organization* 32: 13-42.

Cardoso, Fernando Henrique. 1973. "Associated-Dependent Development: Theoretical and Practical Implications," In Alfred Stepan, ed., *Authoritarian Brazil: Origins, Policies, and Future*, 142-76. New Haven: Yale University Press.

Cardoso, Fernando Henrique, and Enzo Faletto. 1979. *Dependency and Development in Latin America*. Translated by Marjory Mattingly Urquidi. Berkeley: University of California Press.

Carrera, Raúl A. 1990. "Ecuador and the Diplomacy of Dependence in Hemispheric Relations." Master's thesis, University of Miami.

————. 1991. Personal correspondence with the author.

Carrión, Alejandro. 1985. "Nuestro Apoyo a Contadora." *El Comercio* (9 October): a4.

Carrión, Leonardo. 1990. Personal interview with author, 17 July, Quito.

————. 1991. Personal interview with author, 3 May, Quito.

Carrión Mena, Francisco. 1989. *Política Exterior del Ecuador: Evolución, Teoría, Práctica*. 2d ed. Quito: Editorial Universitaria.

————. 1991. Personal interview with author, 9 May, Quito.

CCQ (Cámara de Comercio de Quito). 1985. *Informe Anual, 1984-1985*. Quito: Cámara de Comercio de Quito.

————. 1986. *Informe Anual, 1985–1986*. Quito: Cámara de Comercio de Quito.

Cherol, Rachelle L., and José Nuñez del Arco. 1983. "Andean Multinational Enterprises: A New Approach to Multinational Investment in the Andean Group." *Journal of Common Market Studies* 21: 409-28.

Chicago Tribune. 1985. "Latin Nations Ask Debt Curbs," 22 December.

Chomsky, Noam. 1985. *Turning the Tide: U.S. Intervention in Central America and the Struggle for Peace*. Boston: South End Press.

Christian Science Monitor. 1994. "U.S. Soldiers Spark Controversy" (18 February): 24.

CIG (Cámara de Industrias de Guayaquil). 1985. "Bienvenido Capital Extranjero." Unpublished bulletin of the Guayaquil Chamber of Industry.

CIP (Cámara de Industriales de Pichincha). 1982. *Informe Anual 1981-1982*. Quito: Cámara de Industriales de Pichincha.

————. 1984. *Informe Anual 1983–1984*. Quito: Cámara de Industriales de Pichincha.

————. 1987. *Informe Anual 1986–1987*. Quito: Cámara de Industriales de Pichincha.

Cochrane, James D. 1978. "Characteristics of Contemporary Latin American International Relations." *Journal of Interamerican Studies and World Affairs* 20: 456-67.

Coleman, Kenneth M., and Luis Quiros-Varela 1981. "Determinants of Latin American Foreign Policies: Bureaucratic Organizations and Development Strategies." In Elizabeth G. Ferris and Jennie K. Lincoln, eds., *Latin*

American Foreign Policies: Global and Regional Dimensions, 39-59. Boulder, CO: Westview Press.

El Comercio. 1982a. "Demora en Comisión Aprobación de Reformas Hidrocarburíferas." (1 June): a3.

————. 1982b. "Aprobado en Segunda Proyecto de Reformas a Ley de Hidrocarburos." (4 June): a1.

————. 1982c. "Reformas a Ley de Hidrocarburos Serán Analizadas en el Plenario." (8 June): a3.

————. 1982d. "Varias Observaciones se Hicieron a Reformas a Ley de Hidrocarburos." (12 June): a3.

————. 1982e. "El Petróleo en al Encrucijada." (13 July): a1.

————. 1982f. "Listas Reformas Hidrocarburíferas para Segundo Debate en Plenario." (16 July): a3.

————. 1982g. "Entregan Proyecto de Impuesto a la Renta en Contratos Hidrocarburíferas." (21 July): a3.

————. 1982h. "Plenario Continuará Hoy Debate de Reformas Hidrocarburíferas." (26 July): a3.

————. 1982i. "Cámara de Comercio Observa Política Hidrocarburífera." (19 August): a6.

————. 1982j. "Cefepistas Votarán Según su Conciencia." (2 September): a1.

————. 1982k. "Borrascosa Sesión de la Cámara Ayer." (3 September): a1.

————. 1983a. "Deuda Externa Debe Negociar Cada País." (3 November): a6.

————. 1983b. "Cancilleres Americanos Reiteran Decisión de Estar en Conferencia de Quito." (21 November): a2.

————. 1983c. "Estados Unidos Mayor Comprador de Nuestro Crudo." (24 November): a8.

————. 1983d. "Se Acelera Trámites para la Conferencia Económica." (1 December): a6.

————. 1983e. "SELA Intensifica Consultas para Reunion de Quito." (3 December): a1+.

————. 1983f. "La Conferencia Económica." (11 December): a4.

————. 1983g. "El País ha Sobrepasado los Límites de Endeudamiento." (14 December): a1.

————. 1983h. "Se Pedirá Plazos e Intereses Blandos para Deuda de 1984." (15 December): a1.

————. 1983i. "Deuda Externa Será Tema Central de Reunión Económica de Quito." (20 December): a1+.

————. 1983j. "Está Refinanciado a Medias Tramo de la Deuda de 1984." (20 December): a1+.

————. 1983k. "El Peor Año en Medio Siglo para la Región." (21 December): a1+.

―――. 1984a. "Hay Falta de Honradez en la Etica Política Nacional." (3 January): a1+.

―――. 1984b. "No se Podrá Pagar Deuda si Siguen Condiciones Duras." (9 January): a1+.

―――. 1984c. "Paises Ricos Tienen que Dar una Solución." (12 January): a1+.

―――. 1985a. "Grupo Contadora se Ampliaría con Ecuador." (2 October): a1.

―――. 1985b. "En Próximas Horas Entraría Ecuador." (3 October): a1.

―――. 1985c. "Ecuador se Retiró de Reunión de OPEC." (4 October): a1.

―――. 1985d. "El País se Incorporá al Grupo Contadora." (4 October): a1.

―――. 1985e. "Ecuador Busca Solución a Crisis Centroamericana." (5 October): a1.

―――. 1985f. "Vínculos Internacionales." (5 October): a4.

―――. 1985g. "Hurtado Electo Presidente de Democracia Cristiana de América." (9 October): a3.

―――. 1985h. "Ecuador Rompería con Nicaragua." (11 October): a1.

―――. 1985i. "Ortega Acusa a Febres Cordero de Ser un Instrumento de E.U." (11 October): a3.

―――. 1985j. "Dan Importancia a la Inversión Extranjera." (11 October): a16.

―――. 1985k. "Rotas Relaciones con Nicaragua." (12 October): a1.

―――. 1985l. "Relaciones con Nicaragua." (12 October): a4.

―――. 1985m. "Con Nicaragua; Reacciones sobre Ruptura de Relaciones." (13 October): a8.

―――. 1985n. "Ecuador Saldrá del Grupo de Apoyo a Contadora." (13 October): a1.

―――. 1985o. "Rompimiento era 'Inevitable': E.U." (13 October): a2.

―――. 1985p. "Exhortan al Ecuador y a Nicaragua a Reanudar Nexos." (13 October): a3.

―――. 1985q. "Nicaragua Juzga Lamentable y Precipitada la Ruptura." (13 October): a3.

―――. 1985r. "Analizan Consecuencias de Ruptura con Managua." (14 October): a1.

―――. 1985s. "Febres Cordero Estudia Beneficios de Ruptura con Nicaragua." (14 October): a2.

―――. 1985t. "Estiman que Proceso de Grupo Contadora no Sufrirá Alteración." (14 October): a8.

―――. 1985u. "Pedro Chamorro: Gobierno de Nicaragua Cree que Puede Injuriar o Insultar a Cualquier País." (15 October): a1.

―――. 1985v. "Aclara Terán: Ecuador no ha Pedido que Nicaragua dé Disculpas." (15 October): a1.

―――. 1985w. "Edgar Terán: Inalterada la Solidaridad con el Pueblo Nicaragüense." (15 October): a2.

————. 1985x. "Gobierno: `Grupillo de Traidores se Opone a la Ruptura.'" (15 October): a2.

————. 1985y. "Balcón Político." (17 October): a3.

————. 1985z. "Ecuador Explica a Delegados de ONU Razones de Ruptura." (17 October): a17.

————. 1985aa. "Universidad Pide Plebiscito para el Caso de Nicaragua." (18 October): a13.

————. 1985bb. "Febres Cordero: `Estamos Contra Quienes Atropellan la Libertad.'" (19 October): a1.

————. 1985cc. "Febres Cordero: `No Prevaricaré Respecto al Proyecto de Reformas.'" (19 October): a2.

————. 1985dd. "Elliot Abrams: 'Preocupa a E.U. Estabilidad Económica de América Latina.'" (25 October): a8.

————. 1987a. "Insisten en Período Extraordinario." (1 July): a2.

————. 1987b. "Canciller Pide que TGC Deseche Demanda Contra Reservistas." (9 July): a2.

————. 1987c. "Ayala: `Actual Régimen es el Más Corrupto de la Historia.'" (9 July): a3.

————. 1987d. "Reservistas se Irán el 16 de Noviembre." (11 July): a1.

————. 1987e. "Reservistas se Irán Este Año." (11 July): a2.

————. 1987f. "Congreso Extraordinario." (13 July): a4.

————. 1987g. "No es Acto Hostil Contra el Pueblo y Gobierno de E.U." (15 July): a2.

————. 1987h. "Amplio Debate en Congreso." (16 July): a2.

————. 1987i. "Ejecutivo no Acata Demanda." (17 July): a1.

————. 1987j. "Presidente y Canciller Censurados por TGC." (17 July): a1.

————. 1987k. "Vallejo Pide al Gobierno de E.U. el Retiro de los Reservistas." (18 July): a1.

————. 1987l. "Existen las Pruebas." (18 July): a2.

————. 1987m. "Presencia de Reservistas es Asunto Concluído." (23 July): a2.

Conaghan, Catherine M. 1987. "Party Politics and Democratization in Ecuador." In James M. Malloy and Mitchell A. Seligson eds., *Authoritarians and Democrats: Regime Transition in Latin America,* 145-63. Pittsburgh: University of Pittsburgh Press.

————. 1988. *Restructuring Domination: Industrialists and the State in Ecuador.* Pittsburgh: University of Pittsburgh Press.

————. 1989. "Dreams of Orthodoxy, Tales of Heterodoxy: León Febres Cordero and Economic Policymaking in Ecuador, 1984–88." Paper presented at the International Congress of the Latin American Studies Association, 4-6 December, Miami.

————. 1990. "Ecuador." In James M. Malloy and Eduardo A. Gamarra, eds., *Latin American and Caribbean Contemporary Record*, B116-1337. New York: Holmes and Meier.

Conaghan, Catherine M., James M. Malloy, and Luis A. Abugattas. 1990. "Business and the 'Boys': The Politics of Neoliberalism in the Central Andes." *Latin American Research Review* 25 (2): 3-30.

Connell-Smith, Gordon. 1974. *The United States and Latin America: An Historical Analysis of Inter-American Relations*. London: Heinemann Educational Books.

Corkill, David, and David Cubitt. 1988. *Ecuador: Fragile Democracy*. London: Latin American Bureau.

Cox, Robert. 1987. *Production, Power, and World Order*. New York: Columbia University Press.

Cypher, James M. 1989. "The Debt Crisis as 'Opportunity': Strategies to Revive U.S. Hegemony." *Latin American Perspectives* 16(1): 52-78.

Dahik, Alberto. 1991. Personal interview with author, 5 June, Quito.

Dahl, Robert A. 1971. *Polyarchy: Participation and Opposition*. New Haven: Yale University Press.

Davis, Harold Eugene. 1975. "The Analysis of Latin American Foreign Policies." In Harold Eugene Davis and Larman C. Wilson, eds., *Latin American Foreign Policies: An Analysis*, 3-22. Baltimore: Johns Hopkins University Press.

DeRouen, Karl and Alex Mintz. 1991. "Economic Dependence and Foreign Policy Compliance: A Survey of Problems and Evidence." Paper presented at the annual meeting of the Midwest Political Science Association, Chicago.

De S. C. Barros, Alexandre. 1985. "Política Internacional en América Latina: Seguridad en los Primeros Años del Decenio de 1980 y Después." *Estudios Internacionales* 18: 32-50.

Dougherty, James E., and Robert L. Pfaltzgraff, eds. 1990. *Contending Theories of International Relations: A Comprehensive Survey*. 3d ed. New York: Harper and Row.

Duff, Ernest A. 1985. *Leader and Party in Latin America*. Boulder, CO: Westview Press.

Duvall, Raymond D. 1978. "Dependence and Dependencia Theory: Notes toward Precision of Concept and Argument." *International Organization* 32: 51-78.

Eckstein, Harry. 1975. "Case Study and Theory in Political Science," 79-137. In Fred I. Greenstein and Nelson W. Polsby, eds., *Handbook of Political Science Volume 7: Strategies of Inquiry*. Reading, MA: Addison-Wesley Publishing Company.

ECLAC (Economic Commission for Latin America and the Caribbean). 1985.

External Debt in Latin America: Adjustment Policies and Renegotiation. Boulder, CO: Lynne Rienner Publishers, Inc.

―――. 1989. *El Ecuador y los Problemas Internacionales.* Quito: Universidad Central del Ecuador, Escuela de Ciencias Internacionales.

EIU (The Economist Intelligence Unit). 1985a. *Quarterly Economic Review of Ecuador, No. 1.* London: The Economist Intelligence Unit Limited.

―――. 1985b. *Quarterly Economic Review of Ecuador, No. 2.* London: The Economist Intelligence Unit Limited.

―――. 1985c. *Quarterly Economic Review of Ecuador, No. 3.* London: The Economist Intelligence Unit Limited.

―――. 1986. *Quarterly Economic Review of Ecuador, No. 1.* London: The Economist Intelligence Unit Limited.

―――. 1987. *Quarterly Economic Review of Ecuador, No. 4.* London: The Economist Intelligence Unit Limited.

―――. 1988. *Country Profile, Ecuador 1988–89.* London: The Economist Intelligence Unit Limited.

Emanuel, Carlos Julio. 1991. Personal interview with author, 29 May, Guayaquil.

Evans, Peter. 1979. *Dependent Development.* Princeton: Princeton University Press.

Febres Cordero, León. 1991. Personal interview with author, 11 June, Guayaquil.

Feinberg, Richard E. 1988. "Latin American Debt: Renegotiation the Adjustment Burden." In Richard E. Feinberg and Ricardo Ffrench-Davis, eds., *Development and External Debt in Latin America: Bases for a New Consensus,* 52-76. Notre Dame, IN: University of Notre Dame Press.

Ferguson, Yale. 1987. "Analyzing Latin American Foreign Policies." *Latin American Research Review* 22(3): 142-64.

Ferris, Elizabeth G. 1979. "Foreign Investment as an Influence on Foreign Policy Behavior: The Andean Pact." *Inter-American Economic Affairs* 3(2): 45-70.

―――. 1981. "Towards a Theory for the Comparative Analysis of Latin American Foreign Policy." In Elizabeth G. Ferris and Jennie K. Lincoln, eds., *Latin American Foreign Policies: Global and Regional Dimensions,* 239-57. Boulder, CO: Westview Press.

―――. 1984a. "Latin American Foreign Policies: Global and Regional Dimensions." In Jennie K. Lincoln and Elizabeth G. Ferris, eds., *The Dynamics of Latin American Foreign Policies: Challenges for the 1980s,* 269-284. Boulder, CO: Westview Press.

―――. 1984b. "Mexico's Foreign Policies: A Study in Contradictions." In Jennie K. Lincoln and Elizabeth G. Ferris, eds., *The Dynamics of Latin American Foreign Policies: Challenges for the 1980s,* Boulder, CO: Westview Press.

Ferris, Elizabeth G., and Jennie K. Lincoln. 1984. "Introduction to Latin American Foreign Policy: Latin American Governments as Actors in the International System." In Jennie K. Lincoln and Elizabeth G. Ferris, eds., *The Dynamics of Latin American Foreign Policies: Challenges for the 1980s*, 3-19. Boulder, CO: Westview Press.

————, eds. 1981. *Latin American Foreign Policies: Global and Regional Dimensions*. Boulder, CO: Westview Press.

Fishlow, Albert. 1985. "Coping with the Creeping Crisis of Debt." In Miguel S. Wionczek, ed., *Politics and Economics of External Debt Crisis: The Latin American Experience*, 97-144. Boulder, CO: Westview Press.

Fitch, J. Samuel, and Andrés Fontana. 1991. "Military Policy and Democratic Consolidation in Latin America." Paper presented at the International Congress of the Latin American Studies Association, Washington, DC, 4-6 April.

Frank, Andre Gunder. 1986 (originally 1969). "The Development of Underdevelopment." In Peter F. Klarén and Thomas J. Bossert, eds., *Promise of Development: Theories of Change in Latin America*, 111-123. Boulder, CO: Westview Press.

George, Alexander L. 1982. "Case Studies and Theory Development." Paper presented to the Second Annual Symposium on Information Processing in Organizations, Carnegie-Mellon University, October.

Gereffi, Gary. 1978. "Drug Firms and Dependency in Mexico: The Case of the Steroid Hormone Industry." *International Organization* 32: 237-86.

Gerner, Deborah J. 1992. "Foreign Policy Analysis: Exhilarating Eclecticism, Intriguing Enigmas." *International Studies Notes* 17: 4-19.

Gilpin, Robert. 1987. *The Political Economy of International Relations*. Princeton: Princeton University Press.

Golub, Stephen S. 1991. "The Political Economy of the Latin American Debt Crisis." *Latin American Research Review* 26(1): 175-21.

Griffith-Jones, Stephany, and Osvaldo Sunkel. 1986. *Debt and Development Crisis in Latin America: The End of an Illusion*. Oxford: Clarendon Press.

Grindle, Merilee S., and Francisco Thoumi. 1991. "Muddling Towards Adjustment: The Political Economy of Policy Change in Ecuador." In Anne Krueger and Robert Bates, eds., *The Political Economy of Structural Adjustment*. London: Blackwell.

Guillén R., Arturo. 1989. "Crisis, the Burden of Foreign Debt, and Structural Dependence." *Latin American Perspectives* 16(1): 31-51.

Hagan, Joe D. 1987. "Regimes, Political Oppositions, and the Comparative Analysis of Foreign Policy." In Charles F. Hermann, Charles W. Kegley, Jr., and James N. Rosenau, eds., *New Directions in the Study of Foreign Policy*, 339-65. Boston: Allen and Unwin.

————. 1989. "Domestic Political Regime Change and Third World Voting

Realignments in the United Nations, 1946–84." *International Organization* 43: 505-41.

Hermann, Charles F. 1987. "Political Opposition as Potential Agents of Foreign Policy Change: Developing a Theory." Paper presented at the annual International Studies Association Convention, Washington, DC, 14-18 April.

Hermann, Margaret G. 1978. "Effects of Personal Characteristics." In Maurice A. East, Steven A. Salmore, and Charles F. Hermann, eds., *Why Nations Act*, 49-68. Beverly Hills: Sage Publications.

———. 1980. "Explaining Foreign Policy Behavior Using the Personal Characteristics of Political Leaders." *International Studies Quarterly* 24: 7-46.

Hermann, Margaret G., and Charles F. Hermann, 1989. "Who Makes Foreign Policy Decisions and How: An Empirical Inquiry." *International Studies Quarterly* 5(33): 361-87.

Hermann, Margaret G., Charles F. Hermann and Gerald R. Hutchins. 1982. "Affect." In Patrick Callahan, Linda P. Brady, and Margaret G. Hermann, eds., *Describing Foreign Policy Behavior*, 207-22, Beverly Hills: Sage.

Herrera Arauz, Francisco. 1991. Communication at conference entitled "Perspectivas Sobre la Teoría y Práctica de la Política Exterior Ecuatoriana," held at La Facultad Latinoamericana de Ciencias Sociales, Quito, 24 June–5 July.

Hey, Jeanne, and Lynn Kuzma. 1993. "Anti-US Foreign Policy of Dependent States: Mexican and Costa Rican Participation in Central American Peace Plans." *Comparative Political Studies* 26 (1): 30-62.

Holsti, Ole. 1976. "Foreign Policy Formation Viewed Cognitively." In Robert Axelrod, ed., *Structure of Decision: The Cognitive Maps of Political Elites*, 18-54. Princeton: Princeton University Press.

Hoy. 1987a. "Congreso Sobre los Reservistas." (12 July): 1a.

———. 1987b. "Rondón: Nos Iremos si Así lo Desean." (12 July): 5a.

———. 1987c. "Marco Legal es Amplio y General." (12 July): 5a.

Hurtado, Osvaldo. 1980. *Political Power in Ecuador*. Translated by Nick D. Mills, Jr. Albuquerque: University of New Mexico Press.

———. 1990a. Personal interview with author, 25 July, Quito.

———. 1990b. *Política Democrática: Los Ultimos Veinte y Cinco Años* (Volume 1). Quito: Corporación Editora Nacional.

———. 1990c. *Política Democrática: Testimonios: 1964-1989* (Volume II). Quito: Corporación Editora Nacional.

———. 1991. Personal interview with author, 27 May, Quito.

Insulza, José Miguel. 1983. "La Política de la Administración Reagan Hacia América Latina: Un Primer Balance." *Estudios Internacionales* 16: 134-65.

Jensen, Lloyd. 1982. *Explaining Foreign Policy*. Englewood Cliffs, NJ: Prentice-Hall, Inc.

Jervis, Santiago. 1982. "Petróleo Requiere de Capital y Tecnología Extranjeros," (17 June): a2.

———. 1983. "La Conferencia Económica," *El Comercio* (15 December): a4.

Journal of Interamerican Studies and World Affairs. 1986. Vol. 27 (4).

Juez, Carlos. 1991. Personal interview with author, 29 May, Guayaquil.

Karl, T. 1989. "Hegemonistas y Empresarios Políticos: Dependencia, Democratización y Cooperación en las Américas." *Estudios Internacionales* 86: 183-223.

Kaufman, Robert R., Harry I. Chernotsky, and Daniel S. Geller. 1975. "A Preliminary Test of the Theory of Dependency." *Comparative Politics* 7: 303-30.

Kay, Cristóbal. 1989. *Latin American Theories of Development and Underdevelopment*. London and New York: Routledge.

Kegley, Charles W., Jr., and Steven W. Hook. 1991. "U.S. Foreign Aid and U.N. Voting: Did Reagan's Linkage Strategy Buy Deference or Defiance?" *International Studies Quarterly* 35: 295-312.

Kenworthy, Eldon. 1985. "Central America: Beyond the Credibility Trap." In Kenneth M. Coleman and George C. Herring, eds., *The Central American Crisis: Sources of Conflict and the Failure of U.S. Policy*, 111-35. Wilmington, VA: Scholarly Resources, Inc.

Keohane, Robert Owen. 1966. "Political Influence in the General Assembly." *International Conciliation*, no. 557.

Klarén, Peter F. 1986. "Lost Promise: Explaining Latin American Underdevelopment." In Peter F. Klarén and Thomas J. Bossert, eds., *Promise of Development: Theories of Change in Latin America*, 3-33. Boulder, CO: Westview Press.

Kuczynski, Pedro-Pablo. 1988. *Latin American Debt*. Baltimore: The Johns Hopkins University Press.

Lagos, Gustavo, and Oscar Plaza. 1985. "La Actual Política Exterior Norteamericana y su Proyección en América Latina." *Estudios Internacionales* 18: 63-80.

Larrea, Eduardo. 1983. "La Próxima Conferencia Económica de Quito." *El Comercio* (20 December): a4

Latin American Perspectives. 1989. Vol. 16 (1).

LAWR (*Latin American Weekly Report*). 1986. "Businessmen Turn against Febres." (11 April): 5.

Lecaro Bustamante, Arturo. 1988. *Política Internacional del Ecuador, 1809-1984*. 2d ed. Quito: Universidad Central, Escuela de Ciencias Internacionales.

Lernoux, Penny. 1987. "Beggaring Our Latin Neighbors." *The Nation* (12 December): 709-12.

Levy, James, and Nick D. Mills, Jr. 1983. "The Challenge to Democratic

Reformism in Ecuador." *Studies in Comparative International Development* 18(4): 3-33.

Lewis, Neil. 1987. "Reagan Sees Fatal Flaws in Central American Pact." *The New York Times* (13 September): a24.

Lijphart, Arend. 1975. "The Comparable-Cases Strategy in Comparative Research." *Comparative Political Studies* 8: 158-77.

Lincoln, Jennie K. 1981. "Introduction to Latin American Foreign Policy: Global and Regional Dimensions." In Elizabeth G. Ferris and Jennie K. Lincoln, eds., *Latin American Foreign Policies: Global and Regional Dimensions*, 3-18. Boulder, CO: Westview Press.

———. 1985. "Neutrality Costa Rican Style." *Current History* 84 (December): 118-21+.

Lincoln, Jennie K., and Elizabeth G. Ferris, eds. 1984. *The Dynamics of Latin American Foreign Policies: Challenges for the 1980s.* Boulder, CO: Westview Press.

Little, Paul. 1988. "Blazing a Trail to Nowhere." *In These Times* (13–19 January): 12-13.

Los Angeles Times. 1984a. "Latin American Debtor Nations Open Summit." (9 January): section 4, 1+.

———. 1984b. "Latin American Lenders Adopt Position on Debt." (13 January): section 4, 1+.

———. 1987. "Bush Confronts Iran Arms Questions in Ecuador." (23 March): 12.

Macías Chávez, Enrique. 1991. Personal interview with author, 31 May, Guayaquil.

Manrique Martínez, Juan. 1991. Personal interview with author, 30 May, Guayaquil.

Martz, John D. 1986. "Ecuador." In Abraham F. Lowenthal, ed., *Latin American and Caribbean Contemporary Record.* New York: Holmes and Meier.

———. 1987. *Politics and Petroleum in Ecuador.* New Brunswick, NJ: Transaction Books.

———. 1990. "The Fate of a Small State: Ecuador in Foreign Affairs." In Heraldo Muñoz and Joseph S. Tulchin, eds., *Latin American Nations in World Politics.* Boulder, CO: Westview Press.

Martz, Mary Jeanne Reid. 1975. "Ecuador." In Harold Eugene Davis and Larman C. Wilson, eds., *Latin American Foreign Policies: An Analysis*, 383-400. Baltimore: Johns Hopkins University Press.

McNeil, Frank. 1988. *War and Peace in Central America.* New York: Charles Scribner's Sons.

Menéndez Carrión, Amparo. 1988. "La Democracia en Ecuador: Desafíos, Dilemas y Perspectivas." *Pensamiento Iberoamericano* 14: 123-49.

Menkhaus, Kenneth J., and Charles W. Kegley. 1988. "The Compliant Foreign Policy of the Dependent State Revisited: Empirical Linkages and Lessons from the Case of Somalia." *Comparative Political Studies* 21: 315-46.

MICIP (Ministerio de Industrias, Comercio, Integración y Pesca). 1984. *Informe de Labors, 1979–1984.* Quito: MICIP.

Mills, Nick D. 1984. *Crisis, Conflicto y Consenso: Ecuador: 1979–1984.* Quito: Corporación Editora National.

Molineu, Harold. 1990. *U.S. Policy toward Latin America.* 2d ed. Boulder, CO: Westview Press.

Moon, Bruce. 1983. "The Foreign Policy of the Dependent State." *International Studies Quarterly* 27: 315-40.

———. 1985. "Consensus or Compliance? Foreign Policy Change and External Dependence." *International Organization* 39: 297-329.

———. 1987. "Political Economy Approaches to the Comparative Study of Foreign Policy." In Charles F. Hermann, Charles W. Kegley, Jr., and James N. Rosenau, eds., *New Directions in the Study of Foreign Policy,* 33-52. Boston: Allen and Unwin.

Moran, Theodore H. 1974. *Multinational Corporations and the Politics of Dependence: Copper in Chile.* Princeton: Princeton University Press.

Morejón Pazmiño, Diego. 1991. "Relaciones Diplomáticas del Ecuador con los Estados Unidos de América. Enfasis en las Administraciones Febres Cordero y Borja Cevallos." Paper presented at conference entitled "Perspectivas Sobre la Teoría y Práctica de la Política Exterior Ecuatoriana," held at La Facultad Latinoamericana de Ciencias Sociales, Quito, 24 June–5 July .

Moreno, Dario Vincent. 1991. "Reasserting the Hegemonic Presumption." Paper presented at the Latin American Studies Association Annual Meeting, Washington, DC, 3–6 April.

Morgenthau, Hans J., and Kenneth W. Thompson. 1985. *Politics among Nations: The Struggle for Power and Peace.* 6th ed. New York: Alfred A. Knopf.

MRE (Ministerio de Relaciones Exteriores, Republic of Ecuador). 1980. *Informe a la Nación, Agosto 1979–Julio 1980.* Quito: Dirección General de Información.

———. 1981. *Informe a la Nación,* Volume II. Quito: Dirección General de Información.

———. 1982. *Informe a la Nación.* Quito: Dirección General de Información.

———. 1983. *Informe a la Nación.* Quito: Dirección General de Información.

———. 1984. *Informe a la Nación,* Volume I. Quito: Dirección General de Información.

———. 1985. *Informe a la Nación.* Quito: Dirección General de Información.

———. 1987. *Informe a la Nación.* Quito: Dirección General de Información.

————. 1988. *Informe a la Nación*. Quito: Dirección General de Información.

Muñoz, Heraldo. 1981. "The Strategic Dependency of the Centers and the Economic Importance of the Latin American Periphery." In Heraldo Muñoz, ed., *From Dependency to Development: Strategies to Overcome Underdevelopment and Inequality*, 59-92. Boulder, CO: Westview Press.

Muñoz, Heraldo, and Joseph S. Tulchin, eds. 1984. *Latin American Nations in World Politics*. Boulder, CO: Westview Press.

Narváez, Luis. 1991. Personal interview with author, 5 June, Quito.

Nye, Joseph S. 1990. "The Changing Nature of World Power." *Political Science Quarterly* 105: 177-92.

OGJ (*Oil and Gas Journal*). 1982a. "Ecuador to Beckon Foreign Firms." Vol. 80, no.25 (21 June): 90-91.

————. 1982b. "LDCs Seek More Action to Develop Oil and Gas Resources." Vol. 80, no. 25 (21 June): 75-79.

————. 1982c. "Ecuador Parliament Okays New Oil Law." Vol. 80, no. 32 (9 August): 87.

Ontaneda, Arturo. 1990. Personal interview with author, 17 July, Quito.

Orrego Vicuña, Francisco. 1984. "The Foreign Policy Implications of the International System." In Heraldo Muñoz and Joseph S. Tulchin, eds., *Latin American Nations in World Politics*, 230-42. Boulder, CO: Westview Press.

Pachano, Aberlado. 1991. Personal interview with author, 8 July, Quito.

Palán, Zonia. 1990. Personal interview with author, 16 July, Quito.

Pallares Sevilla, Marcelo. 1991. Personal interview with author, 20 May, Quito.

Pareja Diezcanseco, Alfredo. 1990. Personal interview with author, 2 August, Quito.

Pastor, Robert A. 1988–89. "Securing a Democratic Hemisphere." *Foreign Policy* 73 (winter): 41-59.

Payer, Cheryl. 1986. "World Bank/IMF: Good Cop/Bad Cop." *Guardian* (9 April): 14.

Pérez, Hernán. 1990. Personal interview with author, 27 July, Quito.

————. 1991. Personal interview with author, 30 April, Quito.

Pion-Berlin, David. 1985. "The Fall of Military Rule in Argentina: 1976-1983." *Journal of Interamerican Studies and World Affairs* 27 (2): 55-77.

————. 1986. "The Defiant State: Chile in the Post-Coup Era." In Abraham F. Lowenthal and J. Samuel Fitch, eds., *Armies and Politics in Latin America*, 317-34. New York: Holmes and Meier.

Potter, William C. 1980. "Issue Area and Foreign Policy Analysis." *International Organization* 34: 405-28.

Primack, Phil. 1988. "Another Kind of Jungle Warfare." *Boston Globe* (31 January): 75-76.

Purcell, Susan Kaufman. 1987. "The Choice in Central America." *Foreign Affairs* 66: 109-28.

Ragin, Charles C. 1987. *The Comparative Method: Moving beyond Qualitative and Quantitative Strategies*. Berkeley: University of California Press.

Rai, Kul B. 1980. "Foreign Aid and Voting in the UN General Assembly, 1967-76." *Journal of Peace Research* 17: 269-77.

Ray, James L. 1981. "Dependence, Political Compliance, and Economic Performance: Latin America and Eastern Europe." In Charles W. Kegley and Patrick J. McGowan, eds., *The Political Economy of Foreign Policy Behavior*, 111-36. Beverly Hills: Sage Publications.

Ribadeneira, Diego. 1987. "US National Guard to Help in Ecuador." *Boston Globe* (23 March): 3.

Richardson, Neil R. 1976. "Political Compliance and U.S. Trade Dominance." *American Political Science Review* 70: 1098-109.

————. 1978. *Foreign Policy and Economic Dependence*. Austin: University of Texas Press.

————. 1981. "Economic Dependence and Foreign Policy Compliance: Bringing Measurement Closer to Conception." In Charles W. Kegley and Patrick J. McGowan, eds., *The Political Economy of Foreign Policy Behavior*, 87-110. Beverly Hills: Sage Publications.

Richardson, Neil R., and Charles W. Kegley. 1980. "Trade Dependence and Foreign Policy Compliance: A Longitudinal Analysis." *International Studies Quarterly* 24: 191-222.

Rivadeneira, Miguel. 1985. "Altibajos en Relaciones Ecuador-Nicaragua." *El Comercio* (12 October 1985): a3.

Roett, Riordan. 1989. "How the 'Haves' Manage the 'Have-Nots': Latin America and the Debt Crisis." In Barbara Stallings and Robert Kaufman, eds., *Debt and Democracy in Latin America*, 59-73. Boulder, CO: Westview Press.

Rondón, Fernando. 1991. Telephone interview with author, 2 December.

Rosenau, James N. 1990 (originally published in 1966). "Pre-Theories and Theories of Foreign Policy." In John A. Vasquez, ed., *Classics of International Relations*, 2d ed., 164-75. Englewood Cliffs, NJ: Prentice Hall.

Russett, Bruce M. 1970. "International Behavior Research: Case Studies and Cumulation." In Michael Haas and Henry S. Kariel, eds., *Approaches to the Study of Political Science*, 425-43. Scranton, PA: Chandler Publishing Company.

————. 1983. "International Interactions and Processes: The Internal vs. External Debate Revisited." In Ada Finifter, ed., *Political Science: The State of the Discipline*, 541-68. Washington, DC: APSA.

————. 1985. "The Mysterious Case of Vanishing Hegemony; or, Is Mark Twain Really Dead?" *International Organization* 39: 207-31.

SALA (*Statistical Abstract of Latin America*). 1989. James W. Wilkie and Enrique Ochoa, eds. Los Angeles: UCLA Latin American Center Publications.

Salgado, Deborah. 1991. "Relaciones Diplomáticas con los Estados Unidos." Paper presented at conference entitled "Perspectivas Sobre la Teoría y Práctica de la Política Exterior Ecuatoriana," held at La Facultad Latinoamericana de Ciencias Sociales, Quito, 24 June–5 July.

Salgado, Germánico. 1990. Personal interview with author, 25 July, Quito.

Salmon, Russell O. 1990. "Low-Intensity Conflict: The Case of Central America." Occasional paper, Center for Latin American and Caribbean Studies, Indiana University.

Salvador, Galo. 1991. Personal interview with author, 16 May, Quito.

Schmitter, Philippe C. 1989. "Idealismo, Cambio de Régimen y Cooperación Regional: Lecciones del Cono Sur de América Latina." *Estudios Internacionales* 85: 78-130.

Schodt, David. 1987a. "Ecuador." In Abraham F. Lowenthal, ed., *Latin American and Caribbean Contemporary Record*, B102-7. New York: Holmes and Meier.

———. 1987b. *Ecuador: An Andean Enigma*. Boulder, CO: Westview Press.

———. 1989. "Austerity Policies in Ecuador: Christian Democratic and Social Christian Versions of the Gospel." In Howard Handleman and Werner Baer, eds., *Paying the Costs of Austerity in Latin America*, 171-93. Boulder, CO: Westview Press.

SENDIP (Secretaría Nacional de Información Pública). 1984a. *Democracia y Crisis V: Diálogos con la Prensa*. Quito: CORDES.

———. 1984b. *Democracia y Crisis VI: La Conferencia Económica Latinoamericana*. Quito: CORDES.

———. 1987a. *Pensamiento y Obra: Gobierno Constitucional del Ingeniero León Febres-Cordero Ribadeneyra, 1984-1985*, Vol. I. Quito: SENDIP.

———. 1987b. *Pensamiento y Obra: Gobierno Constitucional del Ingeniero León Febres-Cordero Ribadeneyra, 1984-1985*, Vol. II. Quito: SENDIP.

Sibaja, Antonio. 1991. "Sindicatos los Grandes Ausentes." *Hoy* (1 May): a3.

Skidmore, Thomas E., and Peter H. Smith. 1989. *Modern Latin America*. 2d ed. New York: Oxford University Press.

Spero, Joan. 1990: *The Politics of International Economic Relations*. New York: St. Martin's Press.

Stallings, Barbara. 1987. *Banker to the Third World: U.S. Portfolio Investment in Latin America, 1900–1986*. Berkeley: University of California Press.

Stallings, Barbara, and Robert Kaufman, eds. 1989. *Debt and Democracy in Latin America*. Boulder, CO: Westview Press.

Statistical Abstract of the United States. 1990. 110th ed. Washington, DC: U.S. Department of Commerce.

Tangeman, Mike. 1988. "Safety in Numbers: Latin America Looks at Unity to Solve Debt Crisis." *In These Times* (3-9 February): 11.

Terán Terán, Edgar. 1991. Personal interview with author, 16 May, Quito.

Terry, Robert H. 1972. "Ecuadorian Foreign Policy, 1958–1968: As Reflected in the Organization of American States and the United Nations." Ph.D. diss. American University, Washington, DC.

Tokatlian, Juan Gabriel. 1990. "The Political Economy of Colombian-U.S. Narcodiplomacy: A Case Study of Colombian Foreign Policy Decision-Making, 1978-90." Ph.D. diss. Johns Hopkins University, Baltimore.

Tomlin, Brian W. 1985. "Measurement Validation: Lessons from the Use and Misuse of UN General Assembly Roll-Call Votes." *International Organization* 39: 189-206.

TSE (Tribunal Supremo Electoral). 1989. *Los Partidos Políticos: Documentos Básicos*. Quito: Corporación Editora Nacional.

Tuchman, Paula S. 1992. "Foreign Policy Change in New Democracies: The Cases of Paraguay and Pakistan." Paper presented at the annual International Studies Association Convention, Atlanta, 1–4 April.

Tussie, Diana. 1988. "The Coordination of the Latin American Debtors: Is There a Logic behind the Story?" In Stephany Griffith-Jones, ed., *Managing the World Debt*, 282-307. New York: St. Martin's Press.

El Universo. 1987. "Congreso Extra se Inicia el Miércoles." (13 July): a1.

Urrejola Dittborn, Rafael. 1991. Communication at conference entitled "Perspectivas Sobre la Teoría y Práctica de la Política Exterior Ecuatoriana." La Facultad Latinoamericana de Ciencias Sociales, Quito, 24 June–5 July.

Valencia Rodríguez, Luis. 1989a. "Política Exterior de Ecuador en 1988." In Heraldo Muñoz, ed., *A la Espera de una Nueva Etapa*, 135-49. Caracas: Nueva Sociedad.

———. 1989b. "La Presencia del Ecuador en las Naciones Unidas." In *El Ecuador y los Problemas Internacionales*, 75-121. Quito: Universidad Central del Ecuador, Escuela de Ciencias Internacionales.

Valenzuela, J. Samuel, and Arturo Valenzuela. 1981. "Modernization and Dependency: Alternative Perspectives in the Study of Latin American Underdevelopment." In Heraldo Muñoz, ed., *From Dependency to Development: Strategies to Overcome Underdevelopment and Inequality*, 15-41. Boulder, CO: Westview Press.

Van Klaveren, Alberto. 1984. "The Analysis of Latin American Foreign Policies: Theoretical Perspectives." In Heraldo Muñoz and Joseph S. Tulchin, eds., *Latin American Nations in World Politics*, 1-21. Boulder, CO: Westview Press.

———. 1990. "Las Relaciones Internacionales de América Latina en la Década de 1980: Cambio y Continuidad." *Estudios Internacionales*, no.89 (January-March): 82-118.

Veritas. 1991. *Confianza en las Instituciones*. Quito: Veritas.

Villacís, Renán. 1991. "Relaciones Hemisféricas del Ecuador en los 80: La Nicaragua Revolucionaria." Paper presented at conference entitled "Perspectivas Sobre la Teoría y Práctica de la Política Exterior Ecuatoriana," La Facultad Latinoamericana de Ciencias Sociales, Quito, 24 June–5 July.

Walker, Thomas. 1985. "Nicaragua-U.S. Friction: The First Four Years, 1979–1983." In Kenneth M. Coleman and George C. Herring, eds., *The Central American Crisis: Sources of Conflict and the Failure of U.S. Policy*, 157-89. Wilmington: Scholarly Resources, Inc.

Wall Street Journal. 1983a. "Small Latin American Nations Consider Forming a Debtors' Cartel to Gain Clout." (22 March): 37.

———. 1983b. "Debtors' Cartel Proposal Fizzles at Panama Parley." (25 March): 27.

———. 1983c. "Latin Debtor Cartel Fails to Emerge at OAS Session." (9 September): 36.

———. 1983d. "Latin American Nations Pressure Banks But Stop Short of Forming Debtor Cartel." (12 September): 36.

Walton, John, and Charles Ragin. 1989. "Austerity and Debt: Social Bases of Popular Struggle in Latin America." In William L. Canak, ed., *Lost Promises: Debt, Austerity, and Development in Latin America*, 216-32. Boulder, CO: Westview Press.

Waltz, Kenneth N. 1986a. "Anarchic Orders and Balances of Power." In Robert O. Keohane, ed., *Neorealism and Its Critics*, 98-130. New York: Columbia University Press.

———. 1986b. "Political Structures." In Robert O. Keohane, ed., *Neorealism and Its Critics*, 70-97. New York: Columbia University Press.

White, Eduardo. 1988. "The Question of Foreign Investments and the Economic Crisis in Latin America." In Richard E. Feinberg and Ricardo Ffrench-Davis, eds., *Development and External Debt in Latin America: Bases for a New Consensus*, 147-74. Notre Dame, IN: University of Notre Dame Press.

Whitehead, Laurence. 1988. "The Costa Rican Initiative in Central America." *Government and Opposition* 22: 457-64.

Wiarda, Howard J. 1987. *Latin America at the Crossroads: Debt, Development, and the Future*. Boulder, CO: Westview Press.

———. 1990. "United States Policy in Latin America." *Current History* 89 (543): 1-4+.

Wittkopf, Eugene R. 1973. "Foreign Aid and United Nations Votes: A Comparative Study." *American Political Science Review* 67: 868-88.

World Bank. 1991. *World Development Report 1991: The Challenge of Development*. Oxford: Oxford University Press.

Zuckerman, Sam. 1986. "Reagan's Man in the Andes." *The Nation* (April 5): 484-87.

Index

233–238, 240, 243, 247, 251, 253,
255–258, 262–264, 266
Cuba, 51–52, 63, 70, 73, 125, 134
Dahik, Alberto, 55, 57, 166, 206, 212–213,
215
debt, foreign, 28, 31–32, 40–41, 43–45, 52,
57, 66, 89–90, 93, 106, 116–118,
120–122, 123–124, 125–132, 134–136,
137–141, 142, 144, 146–147, 152, 211,
215–216, 227–228, 234–235, 240–241,
250, 259
Democracia Popular (DP, Christian
Democratic party), 47, 61, 69–71,
95, 163–164, 191
dependency theory, 8, 12–15, 150, 230,
268–270
development, economic, 92–93, 96, 110
domestic politics, 7, 23–25, 82, 85, 111–112,
113–114, 149–150, 174–175, 176, 196,
198–199, 201, 219, 221, 248–252, 253,
256–258, 263–264
Dominican Republic, 125, 137, 154–155
drugs, illicit, 42–43, 58, 185, 192–193
Duarte, José Napoleón, 71
earthquake, 33, 36, 177, 179, 183, 195, 197
El Salvador, 42, 70–71, 78, 153–155
Emanuel, Carlos Julio, 57, 206, 210,
213–214
Europe, 18, 34–35, 39, 133–134
exchange rates, 33
Falkland Islands (Malvinas), 4, 120, 182,
239
Febres Cordero, León, 14, 22, 24, 27,
39–40, 46–47, 49–51, 53–58, 59, 83,
94–97, 104, 137–138, 147, 149,
153–176, 178–181, 183–184, 186–192,
194–201, 203–221, 224, 230–231, 233,
235, 240–241, 243, 246–247,
248–251, 253–255, 258, 260–261, 263,
265–266
Febres Cordero administration, 5,
27, 34, 37, 41–43, 57, 67, 164,
166–167, 172, 177, 189, 193, 203,
204–206, 208–222, 224, 230,
233–234, 260
fishing rights, 29–30
Group of Eight, 138–141, 146
Group of Seven, 118, 137
Group of 77, 118
Guatemala, 42, 70
Honduras, 70, 153–154, 185, 198
Hurtado, Osvaldo, 14, 22, 24, 27–28,
39–40, 46, 47–53, 54–55, 59, 60–85,
86, 89–94, 96, 98–100, 102–105,

107–113, 115, 116–152, 205, 211,
227–231, 233–235, 240–241, 243,
245–248, 250, 253, 255–256,
259–262, 265–266
Hurtado administration, 5, 27, 34,
36–37, 41–43, 50, 54, 61, 63–64, 68,
70, 74–78, 100, 103–104, 111, 120,
124, 148, 215, 222, 251, 259
indigenous groups (Ecuador), 180, 185,
194
Inter-American Development Bank
(IDB), 37, 127, 132, 208
International Monetary Fund (IMF), 11,
41, 44–46, 123, 127–129, 132, 141, 144,
208, 235, 246
investment, foreign, 5, 32, 38–40, 45, 49,
57, 86–115, 203–210, 212, 214–216,
218–221, 243, 246, 254, 259
Izquierda Democrática (ID party),
94–96, 100, 103, 112, 164
Jamaica, 15, 16
Jarrín Ampudía, Gustavo, 87–89, 98
Kissinger, Henry, 52
labor (Ecuador), 24, 49–50, 68, 85, 96,
98, 121–122, 164, 209–210, 219
Latin American Economic System
(SELA), 62–63, 117, 119, 125
leader preferences, 5, 7, 21–23, 81–82,
83–84, 110–111, 113, 147–148, 150–151,
173–174, 197–198, 199–200, 218–219,
220, 222, 244–248, 254–258,
263–264, 266
low-intensity conflict, 185–186, 193
Manley, Michael, 15
Mexico, 28, 43, 60, 72, 77, 120–121, 125,
127, 131, 137–139, 153
military (Ecuador), 24, 29–30, 68–69, 85,
120–121, 157–158, 164, 182, 195–197
military government, 28, 40, 47,
49, 53–54, 68, 87–89, 91, 97–98, 112,
120
Ministry of Defense (Ecuador), 178, 187,
199
Ministry of Foreign Affairs (Ecuador),
51–52, 63, 69, 84, 130, 137, 141, 148,
156–162, 167, 205
Nicaragua, 5, 60–85, 181, 230–231, 234,
258–261
Ecuador breaks relations with
Nicaragua, 153–176, 240, 246–247,
260–261, 263, 265
Non-Aligned Movement, 51, 56–57, 64,
72
oil. *See* petroleum

OPEC. *See* Organization of Petroleum
Exporting Countries
Operation Blazing Trails, 177–202,
230–231, 233–234, 240–242, 244,
246, 248–251, 256, 260–261, 263,
265–267
OPIC. *See* Overseas Private Investment
Corporation
opposition, political, 105, 114, 148–149,
157, 164, 166–168, 174–175, 196, 199,
201–202, 219, 221, 230–232, 234, 249,
251, 260
Organization of American States (OAS),
63–64, 128, 131, 133, 142
Organization of Petroleum Exporting
Countries (OPEC), 56–57, 87–90,
99, 156
Ortega, Daniel, 64, 73–75, 77–79, 81–82,
156, 159–164, 167, 171–174, 230, 260
Ortega, Eduardo, 93–95, 100–101, 112
Overseas Private Investment
Corporation (OPIC), 43, 203–221,
230–231, 241–243, 246, 248
Panama, 60, 72, 127, 153, 181–182, 185
Paris Club, 139
Pérez, Carlos Andrés, 18, 53
Peru, 28, 43, 137, 153–154, 169–170, 172,
185, 198, 206, 237
Ecuador's border dispute with,
19–20, 29–30, 48, 51–52, 69, 72, 75,
157
petroleum, 35–37, 69, 100, 160, 179, 205,
259
petroleum industry, 39–40, 49,
86–115, 211, 214–215, 243, 249, 251,
262
multinational petroleum corporations, 92, 99–101, 103, 109, 180, 259
legislative reform in petroleum
investment, 86–115, 249–251,
258–259, 261, 267
principles in foreign policy (Ecuador),
29–30, 61, 63, 69, 75–76, 79, 82, 91,
93, 157, 200
Reagan, Ronald, 42, 51, 56, 58, 65, 71,
76–79, 108, 118, 134, 156, 166, 176,
203, 216–217, 231
Reagan administration, 5, 9–10,
42–44, 52–53, 58, 60, 63, 65–67, 71,
74–79, 84, 86, 106, 128, 135, 153,
155–156, 158, 164–166, 169–172, 177,
179, 181, 191, 193, 197, 203–204,
207–208, 211, 213, 215, 217, 221, 224,
228, 231, 233–237, 260

realism (realist theory), 7, 8, 12, 15, 17–
20, 80–81, 85, 109–110, 113–114, 145–
147, 150, 172–173, 175–176, 195–196,
199, 201, 218, 220–222, 238–244,
248, 253–254, 256–258, 263–265
Rodríguez Lara, Guillermo, 87–89, 98
Roldós, Jaime, 48–51, 61–62, 64, 68–69,
72–73, 75, 85, 91, 95, 100, 205, 260
Roldós administration, 51, 54, 81,
89–90, 111
Rondón, Fernando, 178, 180, 184, 186,
190–191, 193–194, 197, 199, 234
Sandinistas, 60–61, 64–68, 72–85,
153–154, 157–160, 163–171, 230–231,
246–247, 260, 262. *See also*
Nicaragua
Shultz, George, 44, 52, 58, 134
Social Christian (party), 53, 58, 94, 161,
163
Soviet Union, 63, 70, 73–74, 97, 106, 206
student groups (Ecuador), 24, 68, 75, 82,
98, 164, 209–210, 219
Swett, Francisco, 57, 206, 211
Terán, Edgar, 67, 137, 149, 154–157,
160–162, 169–170, 174, 176, 206,
212–213
trade, 32–37, 41, 44, 102, 132, 206, 212
Tribunal of Constitutional Guarantees
(TGC), 183–184, 186–188, 197, 250
UN Economic Commission on Latin
America (CEPAL), 117–119, 125
United Nations (UN), 4, 37, 64, 132–133,
153, 166, 169
UN voting data, 2–3, 9–10, 13
United States (US), 5, 8–16, 19, 27, 29–32,
34–35, 37–44, 46, 51–53, 57–58,
60–68, 70–71, 73–74, 76–77, 79–81,
83–84, 86–87, 89, 98–99, 103–104,
106–108, 114, 118, 125, 127, 129, 133,
135–136, 143, 147, 155–156, 159, 161,
165–166, 168–170, 172, 177–179,
181–187, 190–195, 197–201, 203–221,
224, 228–231, 233–236, 240,
243–244, 246–249, 251, 253–256,
260, 264, 266–269. *See also* Reagan
administration
US government, 30, 41–42, 45–46,
74, 76–77, 89, 98–99, 105–106, 108,
128–129, 142, 144, 160, 203, 213, 215,
228, 230, 232, 246
US National Guard, 185
Uruguay, 120, 137, 153–154, 167
Valencia Rodríguez, Luis, 127–128,
133–134

ABOUT THE AUTHOR

Jeanne A. K. Hey is assistant professor of political science and international studies at Miami University, Oxford, Ohio. She also teaches in the graduate program in international relations at the Facultad Latinoamericana de Ciencias Sociales (FLACSO) in Quito, Ecuador. Dr. Hey received her bachelor's degree in international relations and Spanish from Bucknell University in 1985, and her master's degree and doctorate in Political Science from the Ohio State University, in 1990 and 1992 respectively. Her research concerns foreign policy in dependent states, particularly in Latin America. She has published articles on this and other topics in *World Development, Comparative Political Studies, The Journal of Latin American Studies,* and *International Interactions.* She is also author of a case on foreign policy decision making in Ecuador, designed for classroom use and published by The Institute for the Study of Diplomacy at Georgetown University. She is co-editor of *Foreign Policy Analysis: Continuity and Change in its Second Generation* (Prentice-Hall).